Pioneer Doctor

The practice of medicine is an art, not a trade; a calling, not a business; a calling in which your heart will be exercised equally with your head.

WILLIAM OSLER

PIONEER DOCTOR

LEWIS J. MOORMAN, M. D.

UNIVERSITY OF OKLAHOMA PRESS · NORMAN

By LEWIS J. MOORMAN, M.D.

Pioneer Doctor (Norman, 1951).

"The Cystic Disease of the Lungs," in Vol. I of *The Chest and the Heart,* edited by Myers and McKinlay (Springfield, Ill., 1948).

American Sanatorium Association—A Brief Historical Sketch, Historical Series No. 3, National Tuberculosis Association (New York, 1947).

Tuberculosis and Genius (Chicago, 1940).

"Industrial and Domestic Gas Hazards Arising Through the Production, Refining, and Consumption of Petroleum and Its Products," in Vol. IV of *Oxford Loose-Leaf Medicine* (New York, 1931).

Copyright 1951 *by the University of Oklahoma Press*
Publishing Division of the University
Composed and printed at Norman, Oklahoma, U. S. A.
by the University of Oklahoma Press
First edition

To My Grandchildren
The fifth generation of my time

Foreword

IN *Pioneer Doctor,* Lewis J. Moorman has told delightfully a story of himself, of his patients, and of a changing time. It is the story of the practice of medicine of a single man as it began on the Indian Territory–Oklahoma Territory border, of country practice, of small-town practice, of sanatorium practice, and of metropolitan practice in a time when medicine itself was passing from simplicity to complexity.

No longer are there many left who have lived through such a period of American development, and very few who could have written this account as he has, for he had the pioneer spirit, the love of the patient, an innate true religion, a broad knowledge of medical lore, and an appreciation of the best in the literature of the English language. Medical men, especially those just beginning, and the lay public can learn in his story of the therapeutic value of the patient-physician relationship at its best and of the need of a return from the present-day leadership and teaching of the clinical scientist to that of the scientific clinician.

Medicine ever changes; over the years it progresses; it stagnates; alas, at times it retrogresses. As does medicine change, so does the attitude of the lay public to physicians. Man of late has grown critical of medicine, believing it has become more mechanistic and less humanistic, more mechanical and less spiritual than in the past, and unfortunately this is true.

It is such a story as this of Dr. Moorman, personally and pleasingly told, that is needed to counteract this present-day feeling about physicians. They, today, are opposing governmental control of their practice, while medical schools and hospitals are accepting governmental financing with directives concerning its use. There seems to be a decreasing interest in man as a human being as he passes through a hospital regime of technicians and tests, of apparatus and machines. Books like this one may be a balance wheel against such tendencies. Would there were more of them for the thoughtful reading public, both medical and non-medical!

HENRY A. CHRISTIAN, M.D.

Brookline, Massachusetts
   January 5, 1951

Preface

THIS is the unadorned story of a doctor who traveled to the country in Oklahoma at the turn of the last century with three questionable assets: a medical diploma, a desire to see the West, and an inferiority complex.

It is not a planned autobiography, but necessarily it includes many intimate phases of the author's life. To omit my old Kentucky home would sacrifice my first impressions of what the practice of medicine should mean to the people. To pass up Tennessee would leave untouched my first experiences as a country doctor. Not to dwell at some length on Oklahoma would mean missing perhaps the best part of a geographical experience of untold fascination to me. But the main purpose of the story is to deal chiefly with human experiences flowing from an active medical past and to bring into relief the patient-doctor relationship, which is so important in the course of civilization. Because of an unavoidable nostalgic urge, it represents an effort to escape the immediate demands of an exigent world and to recapture a sense of genuine leisure in the spacious atmosphere of other days.

The story covers equally my city practice, including adventures in internal medicine, with special emphasis on tuberculosis, its prevention and management. It considers medical education, teaching and administrative duties in the University of Oklahoma School of Medicine and University Hospitals, and services with the Oklahoma State Medical Association, as secretary-treasurer and editor of the *Journal* of the Oklahoma State Medical Association. It takes into account voluntary participation in public health, particularly twenty-five years at the Oklahoma City tuberculosis dispensary, and to some extent it shows how these various activities have helped to shape my philosophy of life, my attitude toward medicine, and my thinking with reference to the medical profession and the physician's relationship to society.

In addition, the story reveals unmistakable evidence of the socioeconomic changes and rapidly advancing scientific knowledge which have so greatly altered our approach to the problem of life, of which Alfred North Whitehead has said, "Mankind is now in one of its rare moods of shifting its outlook." It is pointed out that those who lament the fact that doctors have changed often fail to take into account the equally obvious fact that society is in a state of flux and that people have changed no less than physicians. Recently a friend asked, "What has become of the good old-fashioned family doctor?" In reply I stated, "If you will find a good old-fashioned family, I will produce the doctor."

The reader may rest assured that there are no prescriptions to be followed, no sermons to be heeded, no Atlas stunts to be endured. The writer finds it easy to escape the autobiographical concept of holding the world on his shoulders with the naïve hope of revealing its secrets. The practice of medicine is incompatible with this unfortunate affliction. It is doubtful if there is anything more chastening than the perennial witnessing of birth, the study of life in conflict with disease, and living intimately with death.

LEWIS J. MOORMAN, M.D.

Oklahoma City
    February 10, 1951

The Chapters

	Foreword, by HENRY A. CHRISTIAN, M.D.	XI
	Preface	XIII
I	The Doctor and I	3
II	In Nature's Power	8
III	A Profitable Interlude	17
IV	Big Rock	21
V	Medical School Completed	30
VI	Alabama	37
VII	Westward Ho	40
VIII	The Promised Land	48
IX	Chickasha	52
X	Jet	62
XI	O. B. on the Plains	71
XII	From the Mill Run	80
XIII	Social Amenities	92
XIV	The Profligate Plains	100
XV	My Horses	105
XVI	The Transition	112
XVII	Vienna	117
XVIII	Sparks from the Grindstone	127
XIX	A Bug Full of Tricks	142
XX	The Little Devil's Dues	155
XXI	Danger Signals and How to Meet Them	163
XXII	Prevention and Management of Tuberculosis	168
XXIII	The Psychology of the Tuberculous Patient	177
XXIV	Lights and Shadows in the Sanatorium	187

xxv	Medical Education	207
xxvi	Medicine in Retrospect and Prospect	221
xxvii	Abroad and at Home	233
	Index	243

The Pictures

After the morning rounds	*facing page*	14
Signing up for El Reno land lottery, 1901		46
Waiting for the train at Richards		54
Cheyenne Indians near Darlington		70
Noble sons of toil		78
In my office at Jet		94
Old Billy		110
The Southern Home		126
The Farm Sanatorium		158
Trudeau Sanatorium		174
Indians are eager to co-operate		206
Dr. Francis Adams		222

Pioneer Doctor

CHAPTER I

The Doctor and I

LONG before dawn on a bleak February morning in 1875, according to all available data, the old farmhouse was strangely animated. There was a sense of anxious alertness. It seemed important to be awake, yet the door to the children's room was closed and conversation subdued. The smoldering fire had been restored, the hickory backlog was glowing, and the kitchen stove was going because there was water to boil. A rider had been dispatched for the doctor who had set the date for my first birthday party. Unfortunately he could not attend because some other unborn baby was claiming priority on my natal day. Being thoroughly familiar with the ways of the stork, however, the doctor placed his wife in the receiving line. Fortunately she was not a novice at the trade. Not only had she brought other people's babies into the world, she had experienced prenatal stress in her own womb and had endured the Biblical travail. She knew better than the doctor that babies must come when they must. Serving as an experienced accoucheuse, she relieved the stork's tired wings. Knowing the pitfalls of life through the behavior of her own derelict son and being a good friend of my mother's, no doubt she blessed me with a silent prayer born of maternal sympathy.

To this day it makes no difference who launched my life, who tied my cord, who applied the oil, who washed behind my ears, who first clothed my body, or who put me to the breast. It was no concern of mine who tucked me, as number eight, in the creaky old cradle and chunked up the fire that I might be enveloped in the intriguing lights and shadows which have blended so mercifully throughout the years of my life. It matters only that the first lusty cry was not stimulated by a slap on my bottom or a dash of water on my chest, but by the doctor's absence. My first vigorous vocal performance might be considered a spontaneous protest against the community's god who had stood me up.

The period of infancy and childhood, sans immunity shots and bacterial prohibitions, was a lively adventure oblivious of danger. That I am living today suggests luck rather than survival of the fittest. Christopher Morley once said, "When a man is born, he's done for." I quote this not to refute or affirm, but to say that I have been "done" for many things since I was born. According to Andrew Lang, "Every man is born a Platonist or an Aristotelian." I knew nothing of Socratic reason, the grove of Apollo, the school of Plato, or Plato's famous pupil and rival, Aristotle. In retrospect I take sides with the lad from the womb of Phoestis who came down from Macedonia clothed in bearskins. It was the lot of this country boy ultimately to snatch the metaphysical Plato from stargazing and daydreaming and bring him down to a realistic consideration of man's earthly existence and the close analytical study of living forms. Perhaps my preference is based upon the fact that Aristotle was the son of a physician, a patron of medicine, and the progenitor of the natural sciences.

Our old family doctor, a true disciple of Aristotle, was not committed wholly to survival through luck. Long before our proposed birthday party, Edward Jenner had discovered that vaccination against smallpox not only promised an addition of three years to the span of life but assured protection against unsightly pitting which marred so many otherwise beautiful faces. So when the appointed time came, the doctor dragged me from hiding under the manger to give me all he had in the then undeveloped field of immunity. This first vaccination, with Mother and Father standing by, not lifting a hand, left me with a generous scar on my arm and an exalted opinion of the doctor's authority. A few years later, when my next older brother was dangerously ill with typhoid fever, again I came under the ferrule of this unquestioned authority. After declaring that I was suffering from walking typhoid, paradoxically the old doctor insisted that I remain absolutely in bed.

One day when this same brother, my constant bedfellow, was spitting blood, the doctor with Prince Albert coat and flowing white beard solemnly sat at the bedside with saddlebags across his knees. No doubt he was contemplating the boy's uncertain future while Mother and Father were worrying about what seemed to them a catastrophic present. I have never forgotten this bedside picture, which became more impressive as my knowledge grew. As the agile old clinician lifted the reins from over the gate post and took to his saddle, he said to my father, "If you don't watch that boy, some day he may have consumption."

I lived to see the tragic results of this drama which was so poorly comprehended at the time. Through three generations the pallid actors have taken their pathetic tuberculous course across the stage. Their lives have been punctuated by flashes of blood, bouts in bed, surgical collapse, and chronic invalidism, with all the domestic, economic, social, and psychological side effects.

But in defense of the good old doctor who failed to break the contact between the unsuspecting brothers, it may be said that he acted in the light of his time, which was little, if any, more revealing than in the days of Homer, who said, "There is a grievous consumption which separates soul and body." Fortunately a brighter day was dawning. Robert Koch was on the trail of the tubercle bacillus. Already the intrepid Trudeau was learning his lines in the Adirondacks. The founding of the National Tuberculosis Association and the American Sanatorium Association was not far away. A knowledge of the bacterial cause of disease was dawning, and medicine was approaching the end of a period in which tuberculosis was truly "the captain of the men of death." Spinoza, Descartes, Immanuel Kant, Beaumont, Balzac, Rousseau, and John Locke were among the multitudes saluting this "captain."

Molière, after playing the part of the imaginary invalid in his own comedy, coughed his life's blood into the lap of a Sister of Charity and died in less than an hour after leaving the stage. Francis Thompson, having been denied the shelter of London's public libraries because of an objectionable cough, had languished on park benches, shivering the nights away sustained only by laudanum and the exalted spirit of his poetry. After a long life of physical and psychological accomplishment with periodic bouts of fever and weakness, Voltaire had died from exhaustion following a series of pulmonary hemorrhages. Friedrich Schiller during the last ten years of his life worked frantically and sought swift recording of his creative images, knowing the Captain of Death was on his heels. Because of physical frailty, cough, and a dash of blood, Shelley had gone to Italy only to be prematurely claimed by the sea. John Keats, shockingly young, had died of advanced tuberculosis in Rome. Ralph Waldo Emerson had spent a fateful winter in the South with his cough and his pleuritic stitch only to seek further relief at sea. No wonder he blessed a suffering world with his reflections upon the compensation of calamity. Fortunately, medicine was thinking of prevention of disease rather than the compensation of calamity, and the time was passing when a doctor could sit at the bedside of a youth coughing his life's blood away with never a word about the danger of contact.

Although I was often in conflict with the doctor throughout my youth, it was his fine character, his high place in the community, his hold upon the hearts of the people, his unselfish devotion to duty, his obvious wisdom, and his unchallenged authority that influenced me to go to medical school. It was due to his interest, approval, and assistance that I decided between my junior and senior years to take the Tennessee State Board Examination for temporary license to practice medicine. It was his saddlebags filled with his favorite remedies that came down from Kentucky with my cherished saddle mare when I located in the little town of Big Rock on Dyers Creek, twenty-five miles from the nearest railroad station. Thus the good old family doctor sent his wife when I was being born and blessed the premature birth of my medical career with his own saddle-bags and his time-tried medicine.

CHAPTER II

In Nature's Power

LIKE most country boys, I was born down the lane diagonally across from the barn lots. How I escaped cowlick is a mystery. The big log house had taken on a clapboard front, but the rustic setting belied its modernity and defied description. The wide, picketed lawn, the birds and insects, and towering trees, flanked by green meadows and cultivated fields with the deep forest as a mysterious backdrop, created a picture for the reader's imagination and for the writer's eternal keeping.

Through a stile east of the house, a path led from the yard into the great apple orchard and followed its shady course to the old log barn with spacious sheds and cavernous depths. The enclosed sheds served as a haven for the sheep always exposed to the danger of predatory dogs. There was a well-chinked workshop in the orchard where harness, machinery, and tools were repaired. The most exacting of all the shop's crafts was the making of axhandles from fresh, choice cuts of white hickory wood. The old orchard is one of the most vivid and most cherished of all my childhood recollections. In retrospect, I can see the ancient trees in full bloom merging their graceful boughs in friendly intimacy, presenting a symphony of fluttering blossoms in delicate shades of shell pink. The old gray mare and her annual foal are under the great rambow trees, muzzling fallen petals in search of the first tender tufts of bluegrass. In imagination, I see them shivering the drifting petals off their shoulders.

The main barn, across the lane where the horses and mules

were housed and where the hay and corn were stored, was the center of unceasing interest and an abiding source of childish delight. In the great hayloft, through open windows, iridescent barn swallows flitted to and fro tending their young in nests securely plastered to high rafters. Naturalists say that these swallows have winged their way across North America from around Lake Baikal in Asia, but we accepted them as the product of our own little world. It was not uncommon to discover hens' nests full of eggs hidden in the hay or a bed of tight-eyed kittens temporarily deserted by the wild, mewing mother.

The endless tasks around the barn, save emergencies and routine chores, were allowed to accumulate for rainy days. On such occasions my older brothers and I worked frantically husking and shelling corn, in anticipation of the wild scramble for rats and mice as the pile dwindled. Occasionally we competed with each other in forking manure or stripping tobacco and tying it into hands ready to be bulked down to await an opportune market and a favorable season for delivery.

Only those who have never lived with tobacco and have never seen it in the bulk on the floor of the barn from month to month and year to year can chew and smoke without certain misgivings. Dogs, not often ambidextrous, seemed to favor the left-hand corner of the bulk. Occasionally horses and mules backed up to make their deposits; often chickens nested there and sometimes roosted overhead. One can never be sure what gives the juicy plug its licorice flavor, or what brings to the choice cigar its delicate aroma. Not withstanding all this, Lord Fairfax wrote to George Washington: "I would that you smoked a pipe. It confers great equanimity in times of doubt, and the Indians hold it to be helpful in council."

Coming West with this tobacco background, I found nothing more impressive than to meet a cowboy on the plains who had exhausted or lost his plug or his twist of homespun. After a friendly greeting, his first question was, "Have you got a chaw?" With marble mantels, brass fenders, and no hot coals to make the ambeer sizzle, chewing tobacco is rapidly becoming a lost art. For a genuine red-blooded plainsman, there is no such thing as soul-satisfying cogitation without a "chaw" in his cheek and a place to spit. It will be a sad day when the reflective quid entirely disappears.

Before I was large enough to do heavy work I often rode behind my father as he traveled from field to field and from farm to farm to see how the crops grew, to inspect the livestock, and to direct the work. His homemade twist of tobacco always bulged his hip pocket and disturbed my comfort. On one occasion, after riding through a deep forest, we found two young sons of a tenant farmer piling brush. Not satisfied with their work, my father dismounted to show the boys how it should be done. They dropped everything to watch the demonstration. After a while the older one said, "Mr. Moorman, you are a working old devil, ain't you?" Never had I seen my father so completely nonplused, but he recognized the truth in this frank assertion and held his peace. The ground was being prepared for tobacco, and anybody who grew tobacco in Kentucky in those days became "a working old devil."

In addition to cultivating "the weed," my father was a wholesale tobacco dealer, covering three counties. The tobacco was rehandled, prized into large hogsheads, and shipped to Louisville, where it was stored in great warehouses to face the hazards of a fluctuating market. From the time I can first remember to the time I finished college, I was a slave to tobacco. At best the tobacco crop was on the grower's hands 365 days in the year. In winter there was clearing and logrolling to make the new ground ready; in spring there were plant beds to burn and sow. Night fires illuminating wooded hills supplied ample evidence of the Kentucky tobacco growers' industry. Later came plowing and harrowing to make ready for the delicate plants grown in soil chastened by fire and protected from sun and insects by a covering of cheesecloth. There was a long season of chopping, plowing, worming, and suckering. At night our trousers would stand alone because of the gum from the tobacco and the goo from the mangled worms.

IN NATURE'S POWER

As autumn approached and frost threatened, the mature plants with their great spreading leaves took on a yellow tinge in anticipation of the knife. All hands were assembled to cut the crop, split the stalks, and string them on sticks for the scaffold. This operation required dispatch because a heavy frost might prove disastrous. After a period of curing on the scaffold, the crop was hung in the tobacco barns for further curing. Later the stripping, tying, and bulking down followed the course already described. Thus one could claim the unique experience of having been a slave to "the weed" without becoming an addict. In the over-all picture there was one redeeming feature for small children—the tobacco sticks made thoroughbred stick horses.

Feeding time at the big barn always held a lot of interest. Carrying corn into the stalls involved fascinating hazards and required experience, courage, and a certain degree of mastery. Thus boys were envious and eager to grow up to the bushel basket. No one could tell when a frightened animal might kick or whirl, pinning the man with the basket to the wall, but no farm boy past ten years of age should be denied this risk. Every winter we had from ten to twenty young mules in one large stall. Once while throwing down hay from the loft, I stepped on a loose board and landed in the center of the stall. Suddenly, twenty excited animals were cowering in fear with forty heels promptly turned toward the surprised interloper. In this emergency, the mother of invention called for mastery. Artfully employing the language of the mule skinner with a degree of authority that relaxed tense muscles and released crimped tails, I escaped unharmed.

Living on a big farm in Kentucky with its ever changing environment was synonymous with learning. Growing up involved an interesting process of progression. In fact, learning to walk and learning to work were simultaneous accomplishments. Through the channels of adventure, knowledge comes easy and work flows like fun. Having to negotiate one task after another as experience came, until the whole range of farm work was encompassed, possessed the elements of a fascinating game. Such experiences made a college education seem only supplementary to more essential ingrained knowledge.

On our farm it seemed that colts, calves, pigs, and lambs were forever being born and needing special care. Tempering the wind to the shorn lamb was among the most interesting of our childhood tasks. Nearly every day in springtime new lambs dropped down from the sky. In the daytime the sheep grazed in the meadow below the orchard, and when night approached it was a wonderful sight to see them hurrying to their fold between long rows of blossoming trees aglow with the slanting rays of the setting sun. Lambs too new to follow their mothers out of the meadow were brought in under our arms. If they were too weak to stand up and get their dinners, they were placed in a basket by the big open fireplace where they received warm milk from a bottle until they were strong enough to join the flock. Just before being driven into the sheds at night, the lambs were more playful than at any other time. In great glee they chased each other up and down the trunks of fallen trees, jumped ditches, disappeared down deep gullies, and momentarily bobbed up in unexpected places until sobered by the call to the sheds or obscured by the waning twilight. Their energy seemed to be inexhaustible.

Although life on the farm in Kentucky was full of daily duties, work was enlivened by many pleasures. In season we gathered berries, nuts, wild grapes, pawpaws, and persimmons. We hunted squirrels, quail, and wild turkey. When frost came, we indulged in hilarious sprees of possum and coon hunting. This pastime amounted to a rollicking adventure with the sons of tenant farmers, often including a few pickaninnies. The mongrel gathering of curs and hounds was equally colorful and unpredictable. On one occasion, after barking for a few minutes as if they had put the varmit up a tree, the dogs set up such a howl we imagined they were in mortal combat with a panther or a bear. When we arrived with dry throats and pounding hearts, we found old Prowler fastened in a hollow tree. He was howling bloody murder while the smaller dogs made use of this opportunity to chew him up. Anticipating a big haul, we chopped nearly all night with a dull ax. When the tree came crashing down, we expected a coon or a big possum, but nothing happened. Before giving up in despair, we searched the hollow roots of the stump and twisted out a measly half-grown possum.

On another occasion, when we were hunting in the Sunset Lick region, the dogs treed under a ledge of overhanging limestone. We were sure this should be an exciting catch, maybe a red fox or a coon. We probed the hole industriously with no luck, but determined not to give up, we built a fire to assuage the cold while we worked and waited. Long after midnight, having failed to locate the obstinate creature by digging and searching, we started throwing burning brands from the campfire back in the well-worn hole. Finally we decided to put out the fire and give up the fight. But before going, I gave the searching, forked stick one more twist. To my surprise the thrilling touch of life was transmitted through my expectant hand. Quickly I withdrew the stick and found sucpicious fur but no telltale odor. After returning to my task and executing a few swift twists I had a firm grip, and with one hard, quick jerk the varmit landed almost in my lap. The dogs closed in for a grand shake and I was enveloped in the most pungent concoction ever excreted by an expiring skunk. That night I undressed in the cowshed and for the next ten days both the cows and I lamented the act. The family turned thumbs down on me, and I learned what it means to be an outcast.

Occasionally we visited well-to-do relatives in Louisville. I was reticent and timid and troubled by city ways. Elevators took my breath, butlers spoiled my meals, and towering, close-set buildings fenced me in. The only time I ever felt at home in the big city was when I rode on the front platform of the streetcar in close proximity to the straining mules. I loved to see them belly down and strike sparks from the cobblestones as they tried to start the car on an upgrade. Always I wanted to get out and push. I longed to remove their steel shoes, to bathe their wind-galled hocks in turpentine, and to put their tired feet back on the soft soil where they belonged.

The life on the farm with its limited contacts created strong attachments, and going away to school represented a painful wrench. For a timid farm boy possessing a certain degree of subdued pride, it was indeed a sad experience. Not only was I leaving my loved ones behind and deserting my favorite haunts, but I was cutting the companionship of my faithful dog and my beloved saddle mare. There were good reasons for dreading contact with the world. My preparation for college was wholly inadequate and lessons were difficult and demanded close application. During my first semester, I often sat in silence looking out upon a beautiful moonlit campus studded with magnificent maples, presenting a maze of gaunt, interlocking branches. Though silhouetted against the sky where the mysteries of life held their rendezvous, the weaving shadows encompassed me with utter loneliness, merging my myriad moods in the merciful gift of longing.

When Christmas approached, homesickness drove me to the point of desperation. I knew that sending me to school meant certain sacrifices and that making good was nothing less than duty. My longing for home was so strong it made of me a veritable coward. I did not dare go home during the holiday season for fear I would never return to school. I explained in a letter that I was so behind with my work it seemed necessary for me to remain at school during the Christmas season. Fortunately, this course proved to be the cure for my homesickness. Often I have wondered what might have happened had I not stayed by the goods. At any rate, I was learning that a boy must grow up emotionally if he would meet the challenging world.

Work does not always keep a youth out of mischief. Several boys from the Deep South and the far Southwest remained at school during the short holiday time. Together we planned a Christmas celebration, and by pooling our spare money we assembled a generous supply of fireworks. It happened that a

After the morning rounds at the Farm Sanatorium, 1939

stray horse had frequented the campus, tramping down shrubs and destroying flower beds. Miss Fanny, our gracious matron, had mildly maligned the animal, but in our opinion she needed masculine aid to effect a good riddance. After cornering old Dobbin, we led him before the boarding hall and when nobody was looking, we strapped two twenty-shooter roman candles to his tail. Considering our designs, his friendly co-operation was touching. When the lighted candles started spewing gently, the old boy merely craned his neck this way and that to see what was going on, but when the balls of varicolored fire came roaring out and the odor of singeing hair assailed his dilating nostrils, he staged a dynamic exit, wrecking a panel of fence before plunging down the streetcar tracks like a flying flame of fire. The roman candles were shooting straight up in the air when his hind legs galloped down and whizzing by his ears when they galloped up. Our celebration had taken on unexpected animation. The whole town was agog, and we promptly concealed the remaining pyrotechnics and sought a reverential siesta far from the scene of action.

In the course of my college career, only the coiled rubber snake under McCombs plate approached this episode in catastrophic humor. This lanky country boy from the mountains of Kentucky, sitting near the meat platter, at the long boarding-hall table, could never endure the interminable grace without irreverently turning up his plate in order to help himself as soon as the blessing ended. Obviously he was in for a cure, not because of his impiety but because of his disregard of good sportsmanship. On the appointed day, in the last quarter of the prolonged grace, the plate was cautiously raised, and suddenly the snake and McComb's knees simultaneously came up with a bang, churning food, water, and china in every direction, filling laps and littering the floor. Not being able to make a get-away for our face-saving siesta, we paid our fines, McComb learned his lesson, and we relished the experience.

Although I had not decided to study medicine, the bee was in my bonnet. I was interested in botany and chemistry, and my professor of natural science had entrusted me with a key to his laboratory. In fact, I was unofficially his helper. Late one Saturday afternoon, my roommate and I secretly entered the laboratory with a can of ether and a cat under our arms. We were bent on a bit of merciful vivisection. Our pangs of conscience were soothed by the ether, and the unsuspecting puss accepted the preliminary procedures as a friendly lark. We cleared a table, and my roommate started the anesthetic. Through the exciting stage of anesthesia he suffered numerous scratches. Accepting the punishment as the scientist's lot, he held on and finally, with questionable authority, indicated that all was ready, but failed to say for what. One timid stroke of the knife set the cat on fire. With incredible energy the victim broke away, swept up the wall and through high shelves where surplus glassware had been placed for safekeeping. When she calmed down and submitted to our subdued approach, we gently gave her exit and proceeded to count the costs. She had wrecked scores of test tubes, funnels, beakers, and retorts, including a few valuable reagents. We had put up a deposit for breakage, but to our sorrow we learned that this did not cover wholesale destruction.

In comparison with farming, the business of getting an education was a serious matter. Relatively considered, even raising tobacco seemed like a picnic. Before going to college, I never awakened at night; but after embarking on my educational career, I never went to sleep, so it seemed. Though college life opened a broad new field, it played the devil with Morpheus and me. How jealous the gods are!

During my senior year, my father was financially wrecked by the advent of the American Tobacco Trust in the field of trade and by the payment of security debts. Perhaps in my mind this calamity was overrated. But while there was plenty of land, there was no ready cash, and I decided to leave school and make my own way working in a hardware and farm-implement store.

CHAPTER III

A Profitable Interlude

MY MOTHER, winsome and wise, always capable and serene, succeeded in making my sacrifice seem like a rare opportunity. The work in the store was hard, but occasionally the daily grind was broken by trips into the country to set up farm machinery and place it in operation. I welcomed the opportunity for life in the open and enjoyed rural contacts. Such trips also afforded time for contemplation of the future, which, in my mind, could not be wholly reconciled with the limitations of a lifelong clerkship in the store.

In early summer often it became my duty to help get reapers going. This was an interesting, urgent task because it helped put food in the granaries and provender in the barns. To see a knocked-down self-binder with many different parts scattered here and there at the edge of a ripening wheat field greatly augmented one's respect for old man McCormick. His ingenious mind conceived the mechanistic miracle which put the harvesting cradle on the shelf and cut and bound grain into bundles ready for the shock. But to don overalls and embark upon the task of assembling the thousand and one different gadgets, and properly fitting the myriad nuts and bolts designed to bring the scattered parts together in a workable whole, represented a genuine challenge. To see the golden grain growing more golden every minute and to realize that skilled counsel was miles away and that this, yet unassembled, invention must be made to rise up, replace manpower, and save the harvest, brought one to a sudden realization of the fact that a college education does not connote qualification for any and all jobs.

Compared to this task, the assembling and vitalization of the scattered bones in the thirty-seventh chapter of Ezekiel was simple because the Lord told the prophet what to do. Waiting for divine help at the harvest field might have lost the crop. One could not presume to prophesy upon these nuts and bolts and say unto them, "Oh, ye scattered parts, come together." Neither could he wait upon the four winds to put the breath of life into them. With hands helpless and a head full of wheels, one looked at the book of instructions and wished for his professor of trigonometry. He knew the professor could not help, but it would be good to get even with him. In the face of all this, the recruiting of poise, the exercise of common sense, the careful consideration of ultimate objectives, the patient fitting of part to part until the last nut was in its appointed place and the marvelous machine harvesting grain, constituted the most valuable experience of this entire educational interlude.

On one occasion it became necessary for me to deliver a reaper to a productive farmer in an isolated community known as Wildcat Hollow. After putting the machine in shipshape condition and satisfying the purchaser of the adequacy of its performance, I yielded to an urgent invitation to stay for supper. Obviously I was in the land of plenty. The table groaned under its bountiful load. The biscuits alone were heavy enough to break its back. Not risking one of these clammy bombs in my hungry maw, I used my handkerchief as a napkin and artfully concealed the bun while slipping it in a side pocket. This enabled me to flatter the stolid housewife by accepting a second one, which soon found its place in the opposite pocket. Finishing the meal with two biscuits to my credit, I concealed the bulge in my pockets and bowed out as promptly as possible.

Once I was on the way home, the biscuits were transferred to my raincoat to be preserved as an exhibit. As the homing instinct put the mules well on the way, the big spring seat grew harder and harder. Forgetting the biscuits, I pressed the raincoat into service. A cushion was a luxury not provided for farm wagons in those days, but there was no rule against being resourceful. Knowing how to coddle a college-bred bottom had nothing to do with book learning. To my surprise, at the end of the journey the biscuits were in good condition. They were presented to my mother intact, with the taunt that she might learn to make durable bread.

About my routine duties in the store, it is sufficient to say that they were manifold and sales ranged from tacks and nails to household furniture and threshing machines. From the cradle to the grave nothing was missing. We sold baby carriages and coffins, and occasionally we supplied gravediggers. Often my spare time was devoted to upholstering in the undertaking department. Knowing that country lanes were long and rough and that springless road wagons often served as hearse and that once the deceased is deposited in the graveyard there is no turning for comfort, I slipped in a merciful supply of padding. Although the farmers of Kentucky were known to be plenty tough, I softened the big coffins and the little ones alike. With this speculation going on in my dreams, frequently in the depths of night I was awakened by the resounding wheels of a farm wagon coming for a coffin. On such occasions I was solaced by the thought that the long, last sleep would be appropriately eased by the work of my hand and hammer.

Significant epochs in the course of life usually are marked by great emotions. Up to this time in my own life, my mother, my home, and nature had successively supplied the motivating emotions. From the dawning of my adolescence, I had been afraid of the "gracefuls." I had stood aloof, enveloped in wonder and secret yearning, never daring to touch the fringe of an animated feminine garment. But suddenly there was a new light in my soul and a rare sensation in my chest. A fair young creature had crossed my path, and for the first time I had sensed the full meaning of femininity. I had seen beautiful girls before and nothing had happened, but this one, a dainty summer visitor with taffeta gowns and winsome ways, walked right into my heart almost without knocking. Strange to say, I sought her companionship, and occasionally she came to the store to purchase some household trifle and tarried to sit on a nail keg while ostensibly I worked, realizing I was dangerously exposed to the irradiation of a female personality activated by love.

That summer a remarkable thing happened. Although the action was the result of common horse sense, it became very embarrassing. My little thoroughbred mare, Nancy Hanks, diverted from the race track to become the family hack, developed the delightful habit of turning automatically down the street that led to this charming creature's front gate. The little mare had lost one eye, but she was nowise blind to what had been going on regularly, and she was bent on intelligent co-operation. But when my mother, out for a drive with a friend or neighbor, engrossed in community gossip, came to a halt at that particular gate, it was a bit disconcerting, especially as the occurrence supplied a choice morsel for eager small-town tongues.

This story has been told only to show that a great new emotion supplied a stimulus for me to rise above the pots and pans and the nails and spikes that cluttered the counter and threatened me with the law of gravity which, unresisted, might have kept me in the store for life.

Under the influence of this new awakening, I yielded to the call of medicine, borrowed money, negotiated matriculation in the medical school, and embarked upon my studies. This act represented the final breaking of strong ties, the cutting loose from the things I loved, the giving up of much which had filtered into the very knot of my being; but I was looking forward to the study of man, the diseases which assail him, and their prevention and cure. Here was an ambition which immediately came between me and my less important pleasures. I was entering upon a long journey designed to bring the doctor and me under the same calvarium with never ending conflicts clamoring for solution. But like old cronies in their cups, we closed all controversies with interlocking arms, submerged in the power of the intoxicating blends of our dual interests.

CHAPTER IV

Big Rock

IN the summer of 1900 I went to Big Rock, Tennessee, to practice medicine between my junior and senior years in medical school. While the world for the first time in history was cutting the corners on fast-going wheels with eyes on the airways, I was turning the century on horseback, unaware of the horse and buggy days in store for me on the plains of Oklahoma. At Nashville, I took the State Board examination for temporary license to practice medicine. After spending nearly a whole day on a written examination, I was struggling with the final list of questions dealing with materia medica and therapeutics when the doctor who was conducting the examination announced that an emergency call made it necessary for him to close the office and for me to return the next day.

I have often wondered whether that emergency call meant as much to his patient as it meant to me. The doctor took the unanswered questions, promising a new list the following day. That evening while I was contemplating my plight, it occurred to me that perchance he might present the same list of questions again. I located a copy of the United States Pharmacopoeia in a near-by drugstore and fondly thumbed the book until the answers to all the questions were found. The next morning, to my delight, the identical list was awaiting me. I have never learned whether or not the good doctor was surprised at my paper on materia medica and therapeutics, but I have always had a feeling he wanted to give me a break and that the high mark in this particular subject enabled him, with the aid of a flexible conscience, to give me a passing grade.

With the coveted license in my pocket, I traveled to Clarksville, Tennessee, by rail and then twenty-five miles to Big Rock in a road wagon, sitting on my baggage. Measured by the bruises on my buttocks, we had doubled the distance. Arriving at Big Rock just before night, I had the good fortune to find the storekeeper and his wife, who became my friends, willing to take me in. I shall never forget the hospitality of that humble home where the gracious young wife was hostess, maid, and cook. With the help of these benefactors, who were both courteous and curious, my plans were well under way before we went to bed. I was to have temporary room and board in their home, and it was agreed that by adding a partition, a small lean-to adjoining the store could be converted into an office with a sleeping room in the back.

The next day we prepared the way for the carpenter by moving flour and cured meat into the store and rolling barrels of salt out on the boardwalk. Soon my father sent down the old gray mare's foal, graceful as a gazelle and black as a coal, with a white star in her forehead which gave her the name of Dot. While waiting to get settled, I was introduced to the family doctor who for years had covered that wild outlying community on horseback. One morning I accompanied him on his country calls, seeing a number of sick persons, widely separated, and learning with surprise what it really meant to take care of a country practice. Most of the people, obviously in poverty, lived in log cabins with wood fires, family albums, open Bibles, skillets and lids, hickory-bottom rockers, clay pipes, and greatgrandmothers. These gentle old grandams were made of the stuff that sights through portholes or rests the rifle on a wagon wheel. Any one of them could have told Nebuchadnezzar to go to hell and tread his own fiery furnace.

According to the doctor's diagnosis, the majority of the patients were suffering from "slow fever." Evidently this was typhoid or malaria or a combination of the two. In addition, we saw a number of children with "summer complaint." On our return, as we approached the village through a deep cut, a woman called down from a farmyard, "Oh, Doc, I want some medicine for the baby." The doctor, reining in his horse, said, "What ails the baby?" and down came this answer, "He has summer complaint." Without a moment's hesitation the old doctor, momentarily the pediatrician on horseback, said, "Give him a dose of castor oil, some dewberry–briar-root tea, and keep him out from under the plum tree." My lagging interest having been duly pricked, I then saw, overhanging the picket fence, a tree loaded with wild goose plums, just beginning to turn. Ian MacLauren's Dr. Weelum MacLure in *The Doctor of the Old School* never excelled this bit of horseback prescribing. Giving rein to our horses, soon we were in a synchronized foxtrot, silently contemplating the full measure of a good day's service. I marveled at the doctor's kind consideration of every case, his confident, forthright manner, and the trustful acquiescence of his patients.

I learned that he had had only two short courses of lectures in medicine after having been a section boss on the railroad. But in spite of meager preparation, he was rich in experience and he was a respected citizen, a conscientious medical adviser, filling a genuine need as he went from house to house among the Tennessee hills and hollows.

Late one afternoon, while I was still awaiting the arrival of my saddle mare, a Negro boy on a white mule came for a doctor. I mounted the mule, expecting the boy to ride behind me, but he backed away, saying, "No sah, dat mule don't carry double." Thus my first call was made on a white mule, bareback, with a pickaninny trotting ahead to lead the way through a dense forest. Upon my arrival at the little cabin in a ten-acre clearing, I was greeted by a rotund, middle-aged Negro mammy. After passing the time of day, she said, "Docta', dey's som-thin wrong wid dat chile o' mine. Come here, chile, come out from behine dat do' and let de docta' see what you look lak." Reluctantly, Topsy appeared and stood timidly before her mother and me—the personification of conscious guilt. Obviously, the bliss of ignorance had turned to gall, and it was no longer "folly to be wise." One or two more months would make nine, and the eternal cycle had already declared its inevitable course. Aptly, it has been said, "Through the art of being meek and submissive, the woman may inherit a child but not the earth."

Obviously the mother was not surprised. Her suspicion had been supported by her intuition and the gradual evolution of tell-tale contours. Believing her fears should be confirmed, she had called for help. Examination supported the snapshot diagnosis, and nature was permitted to take its course. Though calling for a doctor to take a look at Topsy may have been considered superfluous, it put an end to the mother's suspense. Fortunately, however, the African sex-conscience was relatively blunt in certain communities and the wounds of indiscretion correspondingly shallow.

One morning two small boys came to my office, and, after the usual greeting, the older one said, "Ma sent me down for some medicine." My attempt to ascertain why the mother thought he needed medicine was futile. Finally I decided to inquire about the simplest functions of the body. I posed the common question, "When did your bowels act?" He exhibited a puzzled expression, shifting from foot to foot; obviously he did not know the answer. In an effort to make it easier, the question was presented as follows, "When did you have a bowel movement?" After another period of embarrassing silence, he said, "I ain't had one since I come down from Kentucky." Hopefully, I said, "When did you come down from Kentucky?" and he replied, "About three months ago." Convinced that he did not understand, I said plainly, "When did you——?" With an obvious flash of comprehension, he exclaimed, "Oh yassah, yassah, I had to stop alongside the road as I come down this morning." What a profitable lesson for a prospective young doctor! I was learning that simple people respond to simple questions.

On a sultry afternoon in August a thunderstorm enveloped

the little community in darkness, which was broken only by peals of thunder and streaks of lightning. As the storm passed, a man came running down the hill in search of a doctor. We hurried back to a small house at the roadside, where we found a prostrate woman wildly tossing on her bed and screaming incessantly. I learned that she had been struck by lightning and knocked to the floor as she ran from the kitchen to the dining room. A neighbor, alarmed by the loud screaming, rushed to her rescue, placed her on the bed, and sent for the doctor. Examination revealed a scorched right cheek, a burned streak down the front part of her chest, a similar streak down the left leg, and a stellate rupture of the ball of the left foot. The sole of her shoe was torn entirely away. A great white oak tree overshadowing the house was barked by the lightning, which penetrated the roof and shattered timbers over the woman's head before passing through her body. After three days of wild delirium controlled only by heavy doses of bromides, reason returned, and an uneventful recovery ensued. In this case the old country doctor proved to be a wise counselor. Strange as it may seem, this catastrophic stroke did not interrupt the normal course of pregnancy, which was well on its way by the time I returned to medical school.

Apparently the prenatal career of this child of humble parents was much safer than that of the prospective son of Henry the IV resting in the womb of his mistress, Henriette d'Entragues, who "miscarried because of a terrible thunderstorm." Since Henriette was a slender, high-strung young creature seeking position at the Court of France, it is reasonable to believe that her anxiety became a contributing factor in the mishap. Her illicit participation in the King's love was sealed by a promise of marriage in case she produced a living son within a year. Apparently in the backwoods of Tennessee unborn babes in untroubled wombs rested more securely than those conceived in sophisticated society.

On one occasion I rode with a backwoodsman far into the forest to see a timber cutter who had stuck a sawtooth in his leg. As I looked at the wound, I was informed that the accident had occurred several days earlier and that "medicine" had been dropped in the gash at frequent intervals. The medicine was produced and the skull-and-crossbones label said "carbolic acid." No doubt the doctor who had left the medicine months before had given instructions how to use it and in what dilution. Time had erased all knowledge of its proper use, but it was medicine, and they were counting on it. Finally, because the sore got bigger and deeper with each application, they decided to call a doctor. In truth they were about to amputate the leg by the slow process of erosion.

One night I was called down on Dyers Creek to see Grandma Jones because of chills and fever. She had tried all available doctors, all patent and household remedies to no avail. Now she would try the new doctor. The challenge was stimulating, but before offering advice or giving medicine, I insisted on knowing more about the case. It was a long story and the patient was illiterately voluble, but finally she got around to her latest failure. This represented a therapeutic climax that would put to shame all the repulsive remedies of ancient times. In her own words: "Last night old Cy Thompson's widder said she hearn tell that bedbugs wuz good for chills. Before going to bed, I put two in a capsule and took 'em down, but 'twarnt morning before I had a chill." Compared to this dose, quinine in cold coffee might be considered ambrosia.

Big Rock's forward-looking residents had brought about the erection of a new school building and imported two young lady teachers. Both were very attractive, but, as time passed, the tall brunette was constantly in my eye. With the completion of my education before me and the finding of a location for the permanent practice of medicine, I was perturbed to find the sensation caused by this new experience quite satisfying and most difficult to escape, but expediency demanded that my natural response to the whispering of Cupid be curtailed. It was necessary for me to eschew the blindness of love, to throw off the biological urge and complete my medical education.

One night the teacher and I borrowed a horse and buggy to go several miles into the country to a Negro revival which was attracting much attention. After a soul-stirring sermon, the old-time singing brought the religious fervor to a white heat. On the other side of the meeting house a woman collapsed while shouting. Simultaneously, highly animated contortions broke out in our very midst. Among those warming up for the grand climax was an athletic-looking middle-aged mulatto who suddenly cut loose with this high-pitched refrain, "Oh glory hallelu, my soul's on fire, my soul's on fire, my soul's on fire!" Under the influence of this feverish enthusiasm, she lunged from bench to bench at the risk of her life until some of the good brethren took her in hand. After this physical spree was subdued, she audibly gave convulsive vent to her soul.

During the commotion we slipped away, wondering if our buggy could be identified in the dark. The strange maneuvering of youngsters dodging here and there in the wooded churchyard caused us to believe that outside under the cover of darkness the devil was holding forth in spite of the religious unction so good and plenty on the inside. Surprised to find our gig apparently in good form, we were soon on the road home. We found driving in the dark unusually difficult, and it was impossible to keep the buggy squarely in the road. Our course seemed strangely skiwaddling and precarious, giving rise to an ominous sense of insecurity, but old Dobbin, undaunted, managed to keep us on the beam. The next morning we found that the little devils in the churchyard had thrown us out of balance by switching our buggy wheels while we were at out prayers. This was a memorable occasion, affording intimate knowledge of opposing spiritual forces.

In time the short school season came to an end and the teachers were tendered a going-away party. Vaguely, I recall the beautiful brunette in the shadow of the well house, where ostensibly thirst had called us from the crowd. Romance stirred the water in the moss-covered bucket as we experienced the sweet sorrow of separation. The next morning the well house was draped in crape with a thin band ending in a bow of the same material on my office door. Although the decoration was accepted as a joke, it had a sharp sting. Obviously our trysting place had been discovered, but the crape on my heart was carefully concealed.

One night, while sound asleep in my room back of the office, I was rudely awakened by a dull ripping sound. It occurred to me that somebody might be sawing the lock out of the front door. Certainly the sound came from that direction and it seemed close at hand. For a while I lay in bed debating whether to don my trousers and negotiate an ignominious escape through the back window or whether to face the music. Finally, my courage carried me to the door, where I was surprised to find a neighborhood cow had crossed the deep gully behind the hitching rack and climbed up a steep bank to get at a barrel of the salt we had rolled out to make room for the carpenter. With her rasplike tongue, she was satisfying the universal bovine urge for sodium chloride with the precision of a well-directed saw. Swinging the door wide open, I stepped forth in my long white nightshirt. This sudden apparition precipitated a bellowing retreat down the steep embankment. After wallowing in the ditch for a few seconds, she regained her footing and made a swift exit. Cows may not believe in ghosts, but the moment I appeared in the doorway, this old sister's salt lost its savor. The next morning, knowing cows, I imagined a puzzled maid on a three-legged stool wondering why Brindle didn't give down her milk.

As I look back upon these hardy human beings living from year to year with the growing cotton crop annually mortgaged for food and clothing, I experience a sense of grateful appreciation of my sojourn among them, so interesting and so profitable. There I learned a little about medicine and a lot about human nature in the rough. This story illustrates one kind of thinking in the community. A long-time Negro credit customer of a country store came by some unexpected cash and promptly spent it with his storekeeper's competitor. When reproached because of his seeming disloyalty, he said, "Law, Mr. Bob, I didn't know you sold for cash."

When the time came to leave, my belongings were sent to Clarksville in a farm wagon, and I followed on my beloved Dot, hoping to find a favorable market for her. Although parting with her was contrary to my wishes, my father had advised this course because he had too many horses and mules to carry through the winter. After visiting all the livery stables and wagon yards without success, I was thinking that failure to find a purchaser might warrant shipping my baggage and riding through from Clarksville to Kentucky. As I indulged this happy thought, I was told that there were buyers on the edge of town purchasing small horses and mules for the sugar plantations in Cuba. The offer of a good price left me with no plausible excuse to keep the mare.

Heartbroken at the thought of turning the sensitive young mare in with the motley crowd of common mules and horses, reluctantly I removed the saddle and bridle. With her friendly muzzle in the cup of my hand, I bestowed a last pat on her graceful neck and said good-bye. Often in retrospect I have seen her gamboling in the old orchard under the shadow of the rambow tree, or swinging gracefully down Dyers Creek with perfect rhythm, and I have wondered if she found a kind master, plenty of food, and a friendly environment. If horses go to Heaven, I shall surely recover her and make amends.

CHAPTER V

Medical School Completed

HAVING had the Big Rock experience without the supervision of my teachers, I returned to medical school with a slight degree of added confidence. Yet, since I had grown up on the farm in close contact with nature, I had learned to fortify optimism with distrust. We could never be sure of comfort in winter or of crops in summer until the seasons revealed their intentions. The continued study of anatomy and physiology of the human body constituted a revealing adventure full of surprises and not without some disappointments. I was reasonably tough and I had been taught to take the bad with the good. I had learned to make the best of inescapable hardships. On occasions my nostrils had been fanned by buzzards flapping out of the cagelike chests of dead animals after they had eaten their way in. Putrid flesh and bad odors were not new to me, but practical anatomy in the dissecting room outstripped all the unpleasant experiences of my life and taught me to smoke in self-defense. A man cannot hold his nose and dissect the olfactory nerves at the same time. While a small boy I climbed on top of the schoolhouse and smoked my first cigarette behind the chimney. Soon in consummate nausea I hung on the comb for dear life. Having escaped catastrophe, I never smoked again until the stench of the dissecting room made it imperative.

To supplement our study of Gray's *Anatomy,* we kept a disarticulated skelton under the bed. The Negro janitor usually gave our room only a "lick and a promise," especially when the skull happened to crown the stack of dry bones. In order to make a more meticulous study of the head and face, we decided to disarticulate the skull. After filling it full of dry beans, plugging the hole at the base and bringing it to a boil, we set it in the window opposite a rival boardinghouse to give the beans time to swell up and spread the joints. The sight of the grinning spectacle from across the open court caused a nervous neighbor to faint. This unfortunate episode precipitated a composite complaint which nearly put us in the street. The beans didn't work, and later the same skull brought another threat of eviction.

One of the boys on our floor took pity on a timid student looking for an inexpensive room and decided to share his bed with him. This act of kindness on the part of my fellow student had hardly warmed the cockles of his heart when he revealed the dual personality of Jekyll and Hyde. In the middle of the night he feigned illness and sent the boy down the long, dimly lighted hall to get a glass of water. As he returned through a wicked collusion, my roommate with the skull on top of his head, draped in a long sheet, revealing only the hideous hollow-eyed specter, met the neophyte in a dark passage. Imagine a country boy meeting in the dark a ghost at least a head taller than the average man. We carried the boy to his room, and with a generous display of sympathy and reassurance we explained the eposide and kept him on. The average medical student learns a lot before he masters the subject of anatomy and moves on to more fragrant fields.

In those days medical school chemistry was imperfectly taught and less perfectly learned. What little histopathology we did learn left us in relative ignorance of the microscopic structure of the body. Even in that day of limited knowledge we knew enough about bacteriology and infectious diseases to arouse curiosity, to stir the imagination, and to engender a wholesome fear of germs. The study of degenerative diseases gave rise to an early realization of ultimate doom, possibly to be deferred by the inhibition of evil habits, moderation in certain genuine pleasures, and gracious acquiescence when seized by the inevitable mandates of life. Later I learned that the best way to avoid the evils of degenerative diseases is to follow the advice of Oliver Wendell Holmes and choose ancestors only after going back several generations. Or perhaps it would be more practical to discover the presence of a chronic disease in early life and live carefully ever after, as William Osler advised. In the course of a medical education in my day, the completion of pre-clinical studies and the assumption of bedside practice represented an important period in the student's life. Contact in clinics and hospitals with patients suffering from disease and poverty rapidly augments the sum of knowledge and experience, lays bare the response of human nature to sickness and pain, and exercises a chastening influence in the sphere of the student's expanding peripheries.

Early in my student days I was taught that while the doctor was studying the patient, the patient was studying the doctor. Gradually I was learning that the human organism must be considered as a composite whole, dominated by that strange intangible force we call the mind. Gradually I was learning the art as well as the science of medicine. I was trying hard to determine the relative value of these two important phases of medical practice and to find their most effective blends. After daily contact with teachers and patients over a long period of time, I was convinced that each young doctor must enter practice with his own imperfect approach to his patients' problems. I was learning that this approach could be modified and made more effective only by accumulated experience, persistent effort, and unfailing patience. Because of the patients' wide range of response to environment under the stress and strain of disease, the clinical years were never dull. The professor's individual approach to the patients' needs commanded our attention and claimed our judgment. The fascinating element of chance and the anticipation of ultimate issues stimulated interest and speculation. The alleged new concept designated as psychosomatic medicine is merely a new term for a very old practice. It may be recalled that Socrates came back from the Thracian wars stating that Thracian physicians considered the influence of the mind over the body and that he hoped Greek physicians would do likewise. His contemporary, Hippocrates, was doing just that. Plato stressed the importance of this influence, and Virgil, on his deathbed, suffering from pleurisy, harassing cough, and hemoptysis, said to Augustus Caesar's court physician, "Is there any healing at all without magic?" Throughout the ages patients have come to doctors saying, "I am sick. Can you do something for me?" Figuratively speaking, they have tossed into the doctor's lap the disarticulated, multifaceted psychic and somatic fragments of a broken body, hoping that the doctor may be able to file the rough edges, fill the worn surfaces, and fit the parts together so that they may again function harmoniously in an inharmonious world.

In every field there were clinic habitués who came to the outpatient department not only for medical and surgical care, but from force of habit or for the joy of participation in the performance. Through the practiced co-operation of professor and patient, the clinical acts often assumed dramatic aspects. I recall a family of Italian children who came regularly to the nose and throat clinic where the imperious professor had made such an impression upon them that they always entered his presence with their mouths wide open. Comically enough they knew exactly when and when not to say "ah," to gag, to cough, to spit, and when to be passive.

One morning at the old Gray Street Infirmary we had gathered for a surgical demonstration under local anesthesia. Above the operating table there was a great reflector. This made a perfect mirror in which the patient could not only see himself but every move the surgeon made. The patient, a robust Negro boy, unaccustomed to such glamour, was obviously fearful of consequences. He cast solicitous eyes upon the scene, eyes characteristically wide with a generous showing of white. Finally they were focused upon the mirror above because it revealed what was going on below. When the field of operation was ready and the scalpel flashed in the reflector, the big boy overpowered the assistants, let out a whoop and said, "I gotta left dis place." And so he did, like a streak of lightning.

In order to make up our obstetric requirements, my roommate, Barnes, and I volunteered to take care of a Negro girl who had been examined in the clinic. She lived in servants' quarters back of a brownstone front on Chestnut Street. When the call came one stormy night, the curious dental student across the hall was permitted to join us. The approach to the patient's quarters was through the alley, up narrow steps over the stable. The startled horses, unaccustomed to such unholy hours, snorted an alarm, strained at their halters, and augmented the ammoniacal odor in their stalls.

We entered a little garret room with low-pitched ceiling and found our patient well on the road to motherhood. With the cooperation of her experienced black mammy, we commandeered all available facilities. True to our teaching, we prepared to make the great event as safe as possible in the face of insanitary surroundings. When the time drew near and the pains were more acute, the child's racial instinct for spontaneous outbursts of emotion found expression. In her melodious voice came this pathetic appeal, "For God's sake, somebody fan my belly." Under the protection of the dim light of a kerosene lamp, the dental student was blushingly contemplating his escape when Barnes presented him with a palm leaf fan and said with an imperious air, "Here, fan her belly." This picture has lived in my memory as a shining example of the synergistic possibilities of the ridiculous and the sublime. We were producing a remarkable drama in black and white, representing faith, hope, and charity with a little bit of medical science thrown in for good measure.

With the mother at ease and the baby snugly tucked away above the manger, we left the scene of action just before dawn with a glowing sense of satisfaction. The intelligent horses, now less startled, munched their hay in peace. We were glad babies prefer to come in the night and that people behind brownstone fronts sleep late. Unobserved except by early delivery boys and

MEDICAL SCHOOL COMPLETED

alley cats, we returned to our boardinghouse through the back door and ate our breakfast with an air of secret superiority. Since horses tell no tales, it may have been days or weeks before the white folks in the big house knew what had transpired in the quarters.

At the turn of the century many of the Louisville medical students were from the Southwest, with a large quota from Texas. Some of them were lone rangers with long whiskers; others were trim, lithe, sinewy cowboys with colorful pasts, vociferous tongues and alcoholic leanings. Always they were ready to paint the town red. While in my own little world I was gaining knowledge of the human body and its functions, I was learning a lot about human nature and I was really beginning to believe that "cattle in Texas wear long horns." Relatively I was becoming cosmopolitan. The influence of medical schools in the winning of the West surpasses that of buffalo hunters, Indian scouts, barbed wire, and transport builders. When people are fenced in, they perish without sanitation. They must have preventive and curative medical care. In those days Louisville covered the plains with horse and buggy doctors, who indirectly turned the turf and sowed the seed to feed the world. The wheels of their buckboards crisscrossed the pioneer trails from end to end. Thus, the family doctor made it possible for early-day settlers to live in dugouts, sod houses, and prairie shacks in relative safety. The Plains Indians had found it possible to live on the prairie, but never very long in one place. Living in tipis as they did, upon the spur of the moment they could strike camp, fold their skins, assemble their lodge poles, pack the ponies, call the dogs, and move away from their accumulated filth. Early the pioneer settlers had to learn the rudiments of sanitation, and even then they could not do without the aid of medical advice.

During my senior year one of our most gifted professors devoted a full lecture period to Edward Noyes Westcott and his remarkable book, *David Harum*. He told the interesting story of the author's struggle with tuberculosis while trying to get his manuscript ready for the publishers, and of his lamented death before the full import of his work could be appreciated. This was my first knowledge of the long-suspected relationship between tuberculosis and genius, and the stimulating discourse had much to do with my subsequent studies in this interesting field. Many times I have secretly thanked the erudite professor for this intriguing interlude in the course of obstetrics and gynecology.

In 1901 I faced a doubtful June. My fear of final examinations was disconcerting and I wondered if I could ever make commencement. Fortunately the sky cleared and I received the cherished sheepskin conferring the title of M. D. But even with that distinction, I seemed to be utterly inadequate. After conferring this stamp of approval, my professors turned their attention to other students. Without further guidance, I was left in the hands of fate. Going back to the farm and letting the world go by would have been easy, but, though conscious of indecision, lack of perspective, and the uncertainty of a professional career, I knew it was necessary to embark upon the great adventure.

My decision was influenced by a growing consciousness of the significance of medicine to society. My recollection of our old family physician, my experience as a doctor on horseback, and my observation of the clinical care of the rich and the poor by my professors in medical school contrived to crystallize my conception of medicine as a service to humanity as well as a means of making a living. Through further experience I acquired the conviction, whether right or wrong, that like religion, freedom of speech, and food and shelter, medicine is fundamental and that it should strive to bring about the best possible spiritual and physical balance without making embarrassing demands. Experience has brought the realization that when adequately administered, it attends birth, it sustains life, it relieves suffering, it prevents and cures disease, it inspires confidence and dissipates fear; finally, it contends with death and if need be, it lingers to comfort those stricken and bewildered by this last great mystery of life's incomprehensible cycle.

CHAPTER VI

Alabama

THE BOY just back from war without a job is no worse off than the doctor just out of school without a location. I was equipped with a medical diploma and no place to go. Obviously I was a long way from the high hat, the Prince Albert coat, the phaeton, and the liveried footman. A modest beginning would be good enough for me. But how could this be accomplished? While brooding over the question, I discovered in the *Journal* of the American Medical Association a country practice in some forgotten place in Alabama advertised for sale. The prospects were presented in glowing terms supported by a rubber-tired buggy to go with the practice. Perhaps I was influenced by the prospect of rubber tires. I thought any country doctor who had passed from practice on horseback to such a luxury was doing well. With a little more borrowed money and a lot of optimism, I took off for Alabama. Arriving in Birmingham, I learned that the coveted location could not be reached by rail. After going as far as possible on the train, I traveled by livery team over rough roads to a primitive community lost in the hills of a thinly populated section.

The pompous old doctor, topographically conforming to the rolling terrain, took me in hand. I learned that the rubber-tired buggy was across the river and could not be reached on account of high water. In a broken down buckboard, drawn by flea-bitten horses in bedraggled harness, he took me on his country rounds. I was confused by the ever winding roads and distressed by the untidy farmhouses set in surroundings ideal for endemic diseases. After passing through a forest of pines where night lingered at midday, we came upon a little hillside shack under the shadow of typhoid fever. I waited in the buckboard while the doctor plied his pills. Out of the unkept yard great lizards came through the crumbling picket fence to strike a semi-upright position while ballooning their throats in quizzical surprise at the presence of strange bipeds in their languid world. The startled expression of these miniature dinosauria, the lonely road through forests where day never fully dawned, and one night's combat with mammoth mosquitoes in the doctor's musty home caused me to beat a quick retreat.

Back in Birmingham I learned that the industrial city of Bessemer had very few doctors. To me this prospect promised to be the end of my rainbow. Full of anticipation I climbed on the dinky little train covering the short distance between Birmingham and Bessemer. Soon I discovered that it was loaded with hilarious Negroes in full holiday regalia. When we pulled into Bessemer, the train poured its load into a veritable black sea. Evidently a Negro festival was under way. Looking across the weaving ebony crowd, I observed the orderly rows of identical cottages in regular succession where foundry workers rounded out their daily routine in drab ennui. Having witnessed the numerical predominance of the Negro race and row upon row of industrial cottages with paint and porches just alike, I decided not to leave the train. In the absence of a turntable, the little iron horse backed into Birmingham, where in a disconsolate mood I planned my return to the old Kentucky home.

Having exhausted all known professional possibilities in Alabama, I boarded the train dreading to face the home folks with the story of my failure. Thirty miles from my destination we passed through the little town of Beaver Dam where my classmate Dr. J. Henry Barnes lived. I hurried to the platform with the hope that, according to small-town custom of the day, Barnes might be at the station with other young people to see the train go through. To my delight and his great surprise, our eyes met and there was an immediate exchange of happy greetings. During the short stop he told me of his plan to go to Oklahoma and begged me to join him. It was Saturday night and he had planned to leave from Louisville on Monday morning. When the train pulled out, I had agreed to meet him in Louisville for better or for worse in the glamorous West. And as the train moved on in the darkness, the clouds of indecision vanished and the spirit of adventure possessed me. From my childhood I had been familiar with the word "destiny," and I had acquired a limited conception of its meaning, but never had I realized its overwhelming power until that eventful moment on the back of the train in Beaver Dam. I was going West without money and without plans.

I shall never forget the obvious misgivings with which my father received the news. He knew I was taking a leap in the dark, but apparently at that moment destiny loved darkness rather than light. The tender parting with mother, the long last embrace, and the fatalistic fear so apparent in her face momentarily wrenched my heart and disturbed my faith in the future, but I was in the hands of fate and the grip was firm, the home ties were broken, and we were bound for the unknown.

More than thirty years later, as president of the Southern Medical Association, I presided at its twenty-fifth anniversary meeting in Birmingham. After the meeting was over, I drove out to see the city of Bessemer. In spite of its growth, its hustle and bustle, I was glad that my lot had fallen upon the plains of Oklahoma and not among the thriving industries of Bessemer. But in retrospect I recalled the happy throng of Negroes and admired their remarkable ability to turn what many would consider privation into pleasure.

CHAPTER VII

Westward Ho

IN Louisville, I joined Barnes at the Arthur Peter Drug Company where we had arranged to buy drugs at wholesale. Acting upon the unwarranted presumption that we might not be able to purchase medical supplies in the "wild and woolly West," we laid in a good supply to be lugged about until they were stale and our patience exhausted.

In anticipation of the drawing for the last free land to be conducted in El Reno, a group of Barnes' friends from Beaver Dam were traveling with us. We were in the day coach to Memphis where we picked up the Rock Island and continued our journey with a trainload of hardy homeseekers. Literally this was a slow train through Arkansas, overflowing with high-spirited, unanchored young men going West to grow up with the country. Little did they realize that one day Horace Greeley's slogan, "Go West, young man," which they were so seriously pursuing would be changed because of the dust storms to the witticism, "Sit tight, young man, and the West will come to you." It is interesting to note that in the early nineties Richard Harding Davis reported that the citizens of Sedalia, Missouri, tried to turn the westward tide by putting up a sign "Go East, young man, go East."

Influenced by the crowd's enthusiasm about the new country, the free land, and the prospect of adventure, I decided to participate in the big land lottery, for I was conscious of my inexperience in the field of medicine, but sure of my ability to exact a living from the soil. It was good to think of the possibility of drawing a farm. I could prove up the land while trying my hand at country practice with the dugout or sod house serving as my office. Considering the eager anticipation of the restless crowd, particularly those buoyed by a touch of imbibed good cheer, this was a serious bit of daydreaming. No doubt the spirit animating this constructive speculation was influenced by the cypress swamps and the primitive forests through which we moved laboriously.

After a fitful night on the overcrowded train we came out upon the plains to greet the first rays of the morning sun. As our horizons extended, I was dreaming of buffalo and antelope and secretly lamenting our tardy trek. Although we were relatively early on the Middle Border, in my mind we were lamentably late. Washington Irving in his *Tour on the Prairies,* with its graphic descriptions of the beauty of the country and the hardships rewarded by herds of fleet-footed antelope, buffalo hunts, the viands of the chase, and an abundance of wild honey, had pictured the land as I wanted to see it. In imagination I was serving as middleman between the wild tribes of the plains and the advance of civilization. I was helping quell the Indian uprisings and the sporadic scalping parties.

This romantic rambling was interrupted by our arrival in Oklahoma City. Here twelve thousand inhabitants, gleaned from Oklahoma's advance guard of civilization, clustered about the intersection of the Rock Island and the Santa Fe railroads. We stayed here for a few days while waiting for the drawing at El Reno, thirty miles away. In spite of the physical shortcomings and the crudities of the pioneer city, we were amazed at the intellectual attainments and progressive spirit of the pioneers, who, without established precedent, were bringing order out of chaos. Though mutually unconscious of our ultimate relationships, many of these city builders were among my future friends. One of them was A. C. Scott, my long-time literary mentor and critic, who upon many occasions was to be sorely tried by my split infinitives.

He was a prenatal observer of this rousing city and chief

among the attending accoucheurs at the dramatic birth of a genuine metropolis, ten thousand strong. According to his interesting account in *The Story of Oklahoma City,* the virgin prairie clothed in the "soft new grass of spring, sprinkled with multitudinous wild flowers," scarred by the booted feet of seething settlers and the hurrying hoofs of mules and horses, was badly torn and bleeding because of the cyclonic parturition. The puerperium was short and the rollicking youngster swiftly gained self-sufficiency. Tents which had helped men to hold and to fix land titles, according to Dr. Scott, "were soon replaced by wooden structures and these in turn gave way to brick, granite, concrete, steel, and marble," and the tread of commerce had crushed the "multitudinous wild flowers" forever.

Barnes and his group found Kentucky friends in Oklahoma City. Among them was Dr. A. B. Baird, a successful practitioner standing at the top of the local profession. We were entertained in his home, and I was greatly impressed by his attainments and his position in this thriving community, but equally troubled by my mounting inferiority complex. Being in his home and receiving his advice and his blessing meant much to me.

On Saturday, July 4, 1901, President McKinley issued the proclamation for the great land drawing, designating July 10 at the date of first registration. On Sunday morning, July 5, newspapers throughout the United States carried the news, and soon thousands of land-hungry people were on the march. Again I boarded the Rock Island in order to be on hand July 10. Our coach was so crowded that we were packed tight while still standing erect. In our effort to make more room, I lifted my medicine case above my head and was exhausted before I could get it down again. But the unpleasant journey was enlivened by the proverbial drunk who kept the crowd in a continuous uproar. Among other wisecracks he repeatedly called, "All aboard for Hell-we-know. We are on the way to Hell-we-know," and finally, with a flourish of his hand and a vociferous climax, he yelled, "All out for Hell-we-know." Although he was drunk as a sailor, his remarks were as sane as if spoken by Solomon. El Reno, on that hot July day with thousands upon thousands of homeseekers ankle-deep in the burning dust, lacked only a literal devil with his pronged fork.

On our way from Oklahoma City to El Reno, we intersected the cattle arm of the old Chisholm Trail, where millions of Texas longhorns had traversed the luscious grasslands once dotted with countless buffalo. No doubt many a Texas cowboy had scanned the sky for the North Star while night herding in this area. In those days longhorns grazed on the way to market and grew fat. Now the herefords lose from 6 to 8 per cent in shipping by rail, but the time has come when they can reach their destination by air before they have time to get hungry. Recently a Hobbs trailer backed into position at the Fort Worth Municipal Airport and twenty fat whitefaces were prodded into a big DC-4. The plane nosed into the blue, crossed the old Chisholm Trail, and before sunset landed at La Guardia Field, New York, where the choice cuts were soon to be served to hungry guests who never saw the big pasture where beef steaks grow.

Long before the registration booths for the land lottery were open, El Reno's seven thousand inhabitants had exhausted their resources housing and feeding the hungry hordes. Mutual needs forced the hand of necessity, and the mother of invention drew volunteers from the milling throng. Like magic the streets were transformed into long avenues of booths and tents where, with dispatch, hamburgers, hot dogs, and flapjacks were flipped to the people as they flung coins across the crude counters. Large tents filled with cots carried signs describing accommodations and rates. Thus, in less time than it takes to say Jack Frost, a good many of the visitors had become hosts to their own good-natured crowds.

A sign over the door of a cheap boardinghouse opposite the Rock Island station which read "Lodging, Ten Cents an Hour" was indicative of the restless spirit of the milling crowds. Many of the people were too curious, too anxious, and too uncertain about the future to sleep long at one time. Lodging, food, and drink were among the serious problems. Clean sheets were out of the question, good food was scarce, and clean water was a luxury. As the magnitude of the crowd, the task of entertainment, and the problems of food and housing dawned upon local and government officials, volunteers were recruited from the multitudes to piece out the personnel of various agencies. The post office established twenty additional windows for general delivery, drawing thirty helpers from the visiting population. It is said that the Smith family alone kept one window busy. Mail booths were established in buildings yet under construction and newly employed helpers accompanied the regular mail carriers. A corps of trained clerks sent from Washington had to be reinforced by forty men picked from the street and coached for the task of filing the registrations. Every day more than one hundred notaries and assistants were kept going from nine in the morning until five in the afternoon. Even though this was not a free-for-all run at the report of a gun, suddenly the plains had come alive and the spirit of chance was in the air.

We joined the fifty thousand who came for the first week's registration. The night of our arrival we were lucky to find a loaf of bread and a cot in a tent which had been hurriedly pitched on a dusty street corner. The next day we registered at the famous old Cado Hotel which had been moved across the North Canadian River on piles and skids when the Rock Island Railroad missed the proposed Reno City north of the river and laid steel into El Reno instead. According to the prevailing story, the hotel had stood on piles in the middle of the North Canadian River all the summer without closing its doors to the town builders and the traveling public. It was necessary to await the arrival of a carload of heavy timbers to complete the crossing. We were given a bed sight unseen in the annex. It proved to be a corn-shuck mattress without springs, flat on the unswept floor. It was in a large room where many other customers were cussing their accommodations. Fortunately for the hotel clerks, those who assigned the beds were not at the desk when the irate guests returned to the office after a night's unrest.

While searching for sleep among the hills and hollows in the so-called mattress, I remembered that on the farm we never bothered to shuck the nubbins. All the next day as I held the line in the broiling hot sun to register, perspiration and dust in proper portions filled the crevices in my body and eliminated the dents made by the lumps in my bed.

I recall a patient who came to me many years later with a history of having been exposed to a bursting sack of cement. He was "absolutely sure" that the cement he inhaled had set in his lungs and that he was breathing against concrete. In spite of his seeming sincerity I always had a suspicion that the prospect of compensation had something to do with his continued complaints. In this connection it is interesting to note that in the early days it was thought by some physicians that the southwestern climate was made more favorable for pulmonary conditions by the grit and sand in the atmosphere, thereby initiating irritation, increasing circulation, and favoring healing.

Although I lived through the famous dust storms, I never saw a case of alleged dust pneumonia commonly reported from localities where the storms were most severe. I recall seeing a young man who had been in a severe dust storm in northwestern Texas and apparently because of the irritation was coughing blood and pus. Investigation revealed an abscess cavity in the upper lobe of the right lung. He gave a history of having had a lung abscess six years previously. A comparison of X-rays indicated a recurrence in the identical location of the original abscess. No doubt, exposure to dust with a point of lowered resistance was an exciting factor in his case. On the whole it is surprising how little influence the dust storms had upon physical well-being.

Having established our identity and recorded our names with the government agents, Barnes and I decided to escape the growing crowds while we patiently awaited the wheel of chance. We were assured our cards would be in the hopper when the lottery wheel was given the final whirl on July 29 and that the results would be published promptly. Rapidly it was becoming obvious that by the time registration was completed and the drawing rolled around, there would be only one chance in many for a lucky number. In spite of this discouraging revelation we decided to travel south on the Rock Island and spend the interval looking over the Kiowa-Comanche country in anticipation of good fortune. By the time this stupendous land lottery came to an end, El Reno had entertained more than 160,000 visitors and had retained enough energy and initiative to emerge from tons of debris in order to play an important part in the history of the state.

When I think of the thirteen thousand farms distributed at the time of this drawing and their subsequent development, with agricultural and livestock values running into fabulous figures, helping to fill the bread basket of the world, it is obvious that when taking my turn at the drawing I was standing in the most productive line my torso had ever shadowed.

Considering Oklahoma's productivity, it is interesting to note that in 1819, Spain, discussing the treaty of February 22 of that year, suggested that the Arkansas River be accepted as the boundary line instead of the Red River, because the land now known as Oklahoma was "characterized as worthless and unfit for cultivation." The Spanish representative wrote Mr. Adams: "It must be indifferent to them [the United States] to accept the Arkansas instead of the Red River as the boundary. This opinion is strengthened by the well-known fact that the immediate space between these two rivers is so much impregnated with nitre as scarcely to be susceptible to improvement." What would that Spanish spokesman of 130 years ago think if he could see what grows between the Arkansas and the Red today?

Among the things I remember best as I look back upon that El Reno experience in July, 1901, were the glamorous coaches drawn by four well-groomed horses meeting the trains and making the hotels. Often I saw them lined up before that early-day hostelry, the Kerfoot Hotel, built by my fellow Kentuckians,

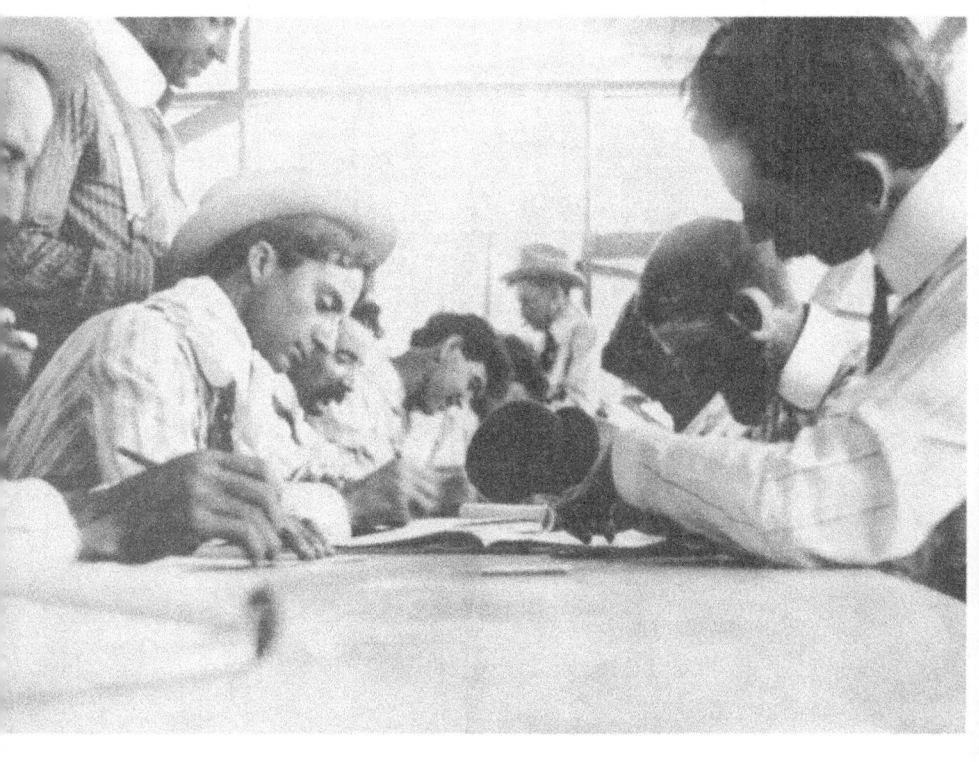

Signing up for the land lottery at El Reno, 1901

Courtesy Oklahoma Historical Society

the Kerfoot brothers, who played an important role in the development of this bountiful territory.

This unplanned retrospection represents my lingering love of the horse, my sense of loss and my lament at his passing.

He helped the white man possess the land. He brought the trapper, the scout, the prospector, the trader, the freighter, and the trooper. He carried civilization and commerce over the Santa Fé Trail before wagon wheels started the rollicking caravans rolling.

The horse became the Indian's companion, accelerated his raids, stimulated his rapacity, increased his prowess, and sharpened his resistance. He brought the prairie schooners, pushed the Indians back, turned the sod, tilled the soil, and produced the provender. He initiated community commerce and kept it going until mechanistic transportation turned him out to pasture.

It was a tough little gray mare purchased in Kansas City that carried Frederic Remington to the great Southwest, where he became the master of all those who have attempted to give the horse and his trappings a place in the sun. Remington tarried at Fort Reno to mingle with army officers, Indian agents, cattlemen, cowboys, and stagecoach travelers from the old Chisholm Trail. This setting in the midst of the fighting Cheyennes and Arapahoes was ideal for the study of cavalry mounts, cowhorses, and Indian ponies. Better than anyone else, he knew that the horse properly portrayed animated art. It was said that he knew "every strap and buckle used in cavalry equipment" and that he wanted his epitaph to read: "He knew the horse."

CHAPTER VIII

The Promised Land

GETTING out of El Reno was complicated by the ever present throngs of shifting people. We waited on the Rock Island platform while one train after another came and went before we learned how to cope with the rough and ready crowds. The cars were loaded to the guards, with passengers overflowing the platforms, pouring down the steps, and clinging to the cowcatcher. When the crowd slowed the train down, the incoming passengers were squeezed out as the departing passengers crowded aboard; before the station was reached, all seats were occupied, and those people who had not gone out to meet the train were doomed to await the next arrival. In their haste to get off, it was not uncommon to see people swinging out the car windows. Finally we took our cue and went out to meet the train. In this way we managed to get aboard.

Soon after our arrival at Fort Sill we engaged a man with a wagon and mules to show us the land. The wagon was loaded with a tent and camp supplies. In the way of equipment we had everything that Irving and Ellsworth had on the tour of the plains except bearskins. The driver took his place on the spring seat with the lines in one hand and a blacksnake whip in the other, and when he said, "Come alive, Sambo," we were off with a bang. I never learned whether both mules were named Sambo, but the simultaneous swift response to the driver's command caused me to suspect that to them "Come alive, Sambo" meant the blacksnake whip and nothing more.

Those were glorious golden days spent in the open, traveling and looking, camping and cooking, eating and sleeping, and growing whiskers to counterfeit maturity. In anticipation of the practice of medicine, we felt the need of a more dignified appearance and a genuine mark of maturity. As time passed, we learned that the mere appearance of dignity and age can never take the place of experience.

One night we camped at the foot of Mount Scott and christened the site of the well-known present-day Medicine Park. We were so intrigued by this delightful spot that we remained for several days. We followed the clear mountain streams, explored the hills and valleys, and climbed to the top of Mount Scott. On the way up the mountainside we killed rattlesnakes with a Colt revolver belonging to one of Barnes' friends. This was not a new experience for us. On the plains we had seen many prairie-dog towns where rattlesnakes, prairie dogs, and cunning little pivot-headed owls lived peaceably together. We shot the rattlesnakes, teased the prairie dogs, and winked at the eerie little owls.

While we were at this camp, our supply of coffee gave out, but we were fortunate enough to find among our belongings a one-pound package of Arbuckle's roasted in the bean, tightly sealed. All it lacked was being dated. This was the last package of this famous brand I remember seeing. It came into common use when I was a boy and replaced our fifty-pound bags of green coffee which had to be roasted in the oven of the kitchen stove and ground in the old-fashioned coffee mill. While this package was not dated, it was just as good as any of the vaunted brands of today. It is a pity that mechanistic progress has robbed us of the pleasure of roasting and pulverizing this delectable beverage. I ground this last pound in a coffee mill borrowed fron an old Indian woman at the foot of the mountain. When it was used up, we were ready to break camp.

The day before the townsite at Lawton was opened for the sale of lots by the federal government, we joined the ten thousand people awaiting this event and surveyed the prospective development with the greatest of interest. That hope springs eternal was being corroborated by this great throng of optimists. It was running high, apparently with little to sustain it, yet there were some who felt the sting of hunger and fatigue. One of my good doctor friends of a later vintage recently told me that he was there that night, holding his disconsolate mother's hand while wondering if he might be trampled underfoot. His father, stepping high, was among the optimists who stayed on to see that the town took root. Bordering the townsite on all sides there were stores and shops, banks, lumber yards, blacksmith shops, and doctors' and lawyers' offices. The proprietors of these industries and the professional men were squatting there temporarily with crude commercial signs declaring their wares and their talents, while waiting to buy lots and move in.

My young doctor friend's father bought lots and established a general store. Often the boy and his mother were left in charge while the father followed other pursuits. The mother was so afraid of the Indians that her husband armed her with a small pistol which she carried concealed in a deep pocket beneath the ample folds of her skirt. The minister, knowing how nervous she was about the Indians and learning about the gun, immediately got hold of the husband. When he warned him of the danger that his wife under the nervous strain might some day lose control and shoot, the husband said, "Never mind, I made sure the pistol wasn't loaded before I ever decided to let her carry it."

Having witnessed the sights and sensed the spirit of this unusual development in its initial effort, we pulled away to seek a suitable resting place for the night. After traveling a few miles, we pitched our tent on a beautiful wooded knoll. Our campfire was going and our coffee beginning to boil when the afterglow of the setting sun came softly through the trees to enhance the spell already cast by the thought of fried ham and the aroma of our steaming java. Just as we were contemplating a delightful repast, a dashing horseman with glamorous trappings brought his charger to a halt in front of our campfire.

While we were wondering about such a colorful visitor at this unseemingly hour, he announced that we were on the Fort Sill reservation and that we should put out the fire, knock down the tent, and move on. Then, with a less imperious mien and a more friendly inflection, he informed us that, according to our choice, we could get off the reservation without delay or come up to the fort and spend the night in an enclosure set apart for homeseekers.

We chose the latter, and presently we were in the caveyard with the conglomerate animal mass ranging from hungry hounds to *homo sapiens*. It has been said that our ancestors came down from the trees to draw up the first Declaration of Independence. On this particular occasion, running up a tree would have brought a welcome escape. All night we waited for quiet and sleep which never came. The drowsy tympanum was constantly assailed by the conglomerate chatter of man and beast. If far in the night, sweet sleep, presumptive of her prerogative, bowed a head, the shrill call, "Oh, Joe, here's your mule," brought it up again.

The enforced breaking of our beautiful camp, the loss of our brewing coffee, and the weird night in this government-controlled corral caused us to bring this otherwise delightful outing to an end. We had been fancy-free too long to come gracefully under military command. This timely decision was promptly followed by the news that we were among the unlucky thousands who stood in line at El Reno during those sweltering days to inherit only the dirt that clung to their tired bodies. For me the experience was sufficient; no doubt a farm would have been a millstone around my neck.

CHAPTER IX
Chickasha

UPON our return from the life of the gypsy to frontier society, my scientific education and my future security made it necessary for me to make contact with civilization and to apply my medical learning. After casting about for a location, Barnes and I chose the thriving town of Chickasha. It was situated on the border of the new country and served as a gateway to the fertile area soon to be developed. With the coming of agriculture and animal industry, we could imagine Chickasha as an ideal location. Having planned a partnership, with great enthusiasm we rented an office, pooled our remaining funds for office equipment and living expenses, and moved in.

After putting up our shingle, we sat waiting for patients. Day after day the waiting went on without interruption except for an occasional trip up and down the street, ostensibly for various purposes but in reality only to see how the sign looked. These sight-seeing excursions always warmed our hearts, and we wondered why sick people seemed never to see the sign which meant so much to us. After two months we looked over our books to find that we had made one call and collected two dollars. At this rate the firm of Barnes and Moorman would have an annual income of twelve dollars. Then we decided to survey the town. Our survey resulted in a disturbing revelation. The number of doctors was out of all proportion to the population. It seemed that many of them were waiting in Chickasha for new towns to develop in the three counties which had been opened for settlement.

This assessment of the local medical and socioeconomic situation brought us together with empty pockets and heavy hearts. In retrospect it may be said that no medical emergency ever presented more serious problems. Thackeray's *Vanity Fair* with its chapter "How to Live Well on Nothing a Year" had no rating in this pioneer community. Nevertheless, we decided that Chickasha was a strategic location and too good to be lightly discarded; that our future hinged upon it and that we should hold on until the surplus doctors drifted into the new territory. But to stave off starvation, we decided that one of us should go to the country and make a living while the other kept the office open. The decision was punctuated with a serious question mark. Which one should make this sacrifice, which one should hit the trail and face the weather night and day, winter and summer? During the period of speculation, I silently considered the desirability of the country while we agreed to draw straws.

Through the grace of God, I got the short straw. With the difficult question of an additional location before us, we cut our deliberations short in order to be on time at a church social. As we descended the dingy stairway, it was obvious that a foggy night and mist had dimmed the already inadequate street lamps. Up and down the unpaved thoroughfares we searched for the church social. Our minds were unsettled, our hearts were heavy, and we needed diversion.

While I was seriously contemplating the uncertainty of the immediate future and still fondling the short straw deep in my trousers pocket, I started across the plowed-up street. As I floundered in the dark, I bumped into a strange man looking for the same address. Recovering from the shock of this sudden impact more readily than I, he said, "My name is Harned." I introduced myself and audibly recalled that as a child I had heard my father speak of a Dr. Harned who lived in Brackenridge County, Kentucky. Promptly the young man said, "He is my uncle and he came West when the Cherokee Strip was opened. He now lives at Jet. He is growing old and wants to give up his practice." Involuntarily squeezing my beneficent short straw, I realized that opportunity was knocking at my door. While we walked together looking for the party, we agreed that both of us should write the doctor immediately. In a few days I received a cordial response that reflected the doctor's warm friendship for my father and urged me to make haste, for he welcomed the opportunity to turn his practice over to me. The party was a great success, but a backward glance convinces me that it was that bump in the dark that cheered my heart and ultimately put me on the road.

After hearing from Dr. Harned, Barnes and I purchased a team of ponies from a band of roving Indians then in camp on the Washita River near Chickasha. They were cunning, gentle pintos already showing the marks of age by their rounded teeth, worn cusps, and thin, lax lower lips. The Indians guaranteed that they would work together and brought them in for a trial. We bought a buggy and harness and spent nearly all afternoon punching extra holes and buckling the harness down to these miniature specimens of the equine species. Though not accustomed to glorified, silver-buckled harness, they were not unfamiliar with the feel of it, and they performed beautifully and proved to be good pals. To me as a doctor, they were not only a means to an end but an interesting study in animal psychology. Their behavior pattern had been conditioned by life on the plains, Indian psychology, and intimacy with their masters. I spent much time trying to fathom their moods and learn their needs. It soon became obvious that it was impossible to determine their endurance. They took their own sweet time and brooked no interference. I loved their naïve independence and cultivated their friendship. We became boon companions.

That night Barnes and I sat up late making plans for the new adventure and the continuation of our partnership. Early the next morning the box of drugs and all of my belongings, including my diplomas, were packed in the buggy. After repeated farewells and serious admonitions from my friend Barnes, the ponies and I took off for Jet, nearly 175 miles away.

Waiting for the train at Richards, to transfer passengers to townsite sale at Lawton, 1901

Courtesy Oklahoma Historical Society

CHICKASHA

I reached the ford of the South Canadian River at Minco in the early afternoon. The river was up and people were camping along the river bank waiting for the flood to pass. Nobody dared try to ford because of quicksand. A team of mules had been engulfed the day before. I was impatient and unhappy at the thought of waiting for the water to run down. Learning that there was a bridge at the town of Bridgeport, many miles away, I started upstream with little knowledge of the hazards ahead. After driving unmarked trails for hours, I met some hunters and inquired the way to Bridgeport. Without hesitation one of them said, "Good God, man, you can never get to Bridgeport with that team—you had better drive back to Minco." Inquiry as to whether it might be possible to find a place to spend the night without having to turn back elicited an equally unsatisfactory answer. "There is only one white woman living in twenty miles of here; she is a widow and would not think of letting you stay overnight. There are two squaw men, but they are just as apt to shoot you as to keep you." Believing that I could persuade any reasonable widow to take me in, I inquired the way to the woman's house.

Soon I came upon a well-kept cottage in an enclosure, with ample haystacks near by. The widow was busily engaged in the day's washing. I noticed that the clothes on the line were predominantly feminine, but unquestionably there were some pieces for the opposite sex. The nature and size of the garments aroused new hope. It was evident that there were both boys and girls in the home and that they ranged from infancy to adolescence. Encouraged by these observations, I put the question, but the woman was adamant. The country was "full of Sooners" and she "would not trust any of them." She could not be persuaded even to let me camp by her haystacks; emphatically I should move on! In spite of the widow's disconcerting obstinacy, she directed me to a ranch evidently owned by one of the squaw men. As she watched us turn away, I felt there was something in her keen gray eyes which the cells of her wary brain dared not reveal and thoughts in her well-turned head tempting her faltering tongue. Being the only interpreter present, I translated the partially concealed psychological sparks into the following imaginary flame, "Almost thou persaudest me." The dulcet tone of her parting words did not lessen my loneliness. In retrospect I have felt that suddenly the love for her own children caused her to realize that she was sending some mother's tenderfoot out to face the uncertainty of night on the plains.

When we reached the squaw man's little prairie shack, the sun was dipping below the horizon. The man and his woman were coming from work. The woman, with a papoose strapped to her back, climbed out of the wagon and stolidly strode around the woodpile and entered the little shack. In answer to my plea, the man said, "Yes, I guess we can let you stay if you can put up with what we have." Gladly I acquiesced and started unhitching the ponies. He followed the woman and after a few minutes returned to say, "I am sorry partner, you'll have to move on. My woman objects." While this was sad news, I figured that it was better to be cast on the plains once more than to run the risk of poison in my porridge. The man was good enough to escort me to his west line, but apparently, to my chagrin, he did so only for the purpose of locking the wire-fence gate behind me. In the waning twilight and the utter loneliness, I seemed to be an insignificant part of the uninhabited landscape.

My willing but henpecked host had told me that the other squaw man was only a few miles away. The trail already dim was soon lost in the night. To accentuate my plight, I recalled newspaper reports about the murder of a homeseeker on the plains a few days before. As the trail faded and the growing darkness added to my confusion, I observed a campfire only a short distance away. It was easy to imagine that it belonged to homeseekers who might be willing to take a fellow traveler in for the night. A clump of friendly cottonwoods with dancing leaves was illumined by the fire as I approached the camp. When the ponies came to a halt, people began to bob up in a flaming circle. The light on copper-skinned braves made it clear that we were in an Indian camp. Before coming to Oklahoma,

CHICKASHA

I had never seen Indians outside Buffalo Bill's Wild West Show. My knowledge of their ways was limited to the fireside stories of Daniel Boone and Simon Kenton and Cooper's *Leatherstocking Tales*.

Even though the Indians were no longer on the warpath, considering this background, my position was not a pleasant one. Carefully marshaling the remaining vestiges of my usual composure, I inquired the way to the second squaw man's ranch. Only characteristic grunts were elicited by this inquiry, but a lifted hand pointing in the direction I had so recently pursued was accepted as a friendly gesture. With a firm rein the ponies were turned rightabout and given the whip. Passing from the glow of the campfire into the black of night, I could almost feel my scalp slipping. Soon a small box house similar to the one I had left locked behind the wire fence loomed like a ghostly shadow in the night. The furious barking of dogs suggested that visitors were unusual, but the man came out and cheered my faltering heart with a cordial greeting and a warm welcome. The ponies were put in the straw-thatched stable, and I accompanied my new-found host to the two-room house where his wife extended her expressionless hospitality with quiet dignity.

I sat at an oilcloth-covered kitchen table near the cookstove while she prepared my supper. She placed the food before me and then stood by to stimulate my appetite. There were bluish balls of sour-dough bread, heavy slices of sowbelly with thick gravy, and stale buttermilk. The ceiling in the little lean-to was low, and every time the woman stirred, the surprised flies swarmed audibly. In their confusion, some fell in the buttermilk and others trailed through the gravy. Emerging with helpless wings, they crawled laboriously across the table leaving dull trails on the shiny oilcloth. They seemed utterly unconscious of misdemeanor and totally unconcerned about the transmission of disease. With placid countenance, the half-civilized Indian woman looked upon my animated food with irritating indifference.

Nevertheless, this service, interfering with her usual bedtime, was accepted as a hospitable gesture. Out of sheer appreciation and in order to satisfy my intense hunger, I filled my aching maw without quibbling over quality. After supper I walked out under the stars and thanked Providence for the perfect end of a hell-of-a-day. Under one of the trees near the house, two cowboys were sleeping with their heads pillowed on their saddles. My host explained that the government had ordered all cattle off the range because it was being opened for settlement and the cowboys were rounding up his own herd for market.

My bed was a pile of grass in the room adjoining the yawning lean-to, where food and flies were temporarily forgotten. When left alone, I went to the buggy and got a mackintosh to spread over the bed of grass which had long been trampled into bits. After such a strenuous day, it was good to say, "Now I lay me down to sleep" and to thank God for the mackintosh. But while I awaited the comforting arms of Morpheus, there was a brief and vague blending of fantasy with this strange reality. In imagination I saw the cottonwoods, ghostlike, faintly quivering above the Indian camp. The fire had faded, the embers were subdued by an ashen veil with a faint glow breaking through. The athletic figures were limp in slumber; peace had settled upon these unrooted denizens of the Great American Desert, and that same peace had comforted the lonely half-licked tenderfoot-cub far from home. Soon sleep came and sweet dreams supplanted my half-conscious fantasies.

Long after midnight uninvited guests awakened me. A pair of stag hounds had entered through the sagging door and condescended to share my bed. In my somnolent state, contact with their shaggy bodies was startling, perhaps because of the primitive fear of fur. But after they gave me a few friendly licks on the cheek, we became fast friends. The weary body welcomed the presence of the dogs and apparently proved insensitive to their fleas. No doubt the dogs and I shared equally in dreams of the chase. At least I was after jackrabbits and coyotes, while no doubt the doctor in me was engaged in the less exciting game of chasing phantom patients.

The next morning the woman seemed more communicative, and she had a good breakfast waiting for us before sunup. Her husband had already ridden over to the river and reported that the water had run down and a man with a team was piloting people across. While I was making ready for another day's journey, the household had gradually become more animated. The woman was waiting for me to see her papoose and two older children. In the night when awakened by the hounds, I had overheard domestic whisperings and infantile gurglings through the thin partition separating me from the family intimacies, so I was not surprised to see the children.

It was a fine morning, and even the ponies manifested a certain rejuvenation and seemed full of expendable energy, thanks to my host's hay and corn. I drove away from that humble home with a lasting impression of genuine hospitality extended in pioneer fashion with the romance of Indian and canine participation. As a physician I was interested in seeing the results of a cross between red and white. From my childhood I had been familiar with the mulatto blend resulting from the mixing of black and white, with the common result that often mulattoes had great difficulty in being accepted by either of the parent races. I was to discover that the strains of red and white were to produce something new under the sun in Oklahoma.

As the ponies turned the corner at the first section line and followed the narrow highway through sunflowers and tall prairie grass, a lone wolf loped across the road, stopped on a sand hill a few rods away, and looked back from this vantage ground with dripping chops. The well-known picture of the wolf in the moonlight on the brow of a hill silently looking down upon a sleeping barnyard always gives me a nostalgic thrill.

At the river I found two wagons waiting for the pilot and team. After seeing the first one safely across and observing the direction of the ford, the depth of the water, and the temper of the current, I decided to follow the second wagon across and save the dollar demanded by the pilot for his services. Though an exciting experience, it proved not to be disastrous. Having gained solid ground, I saluted the surprised river pilot and drove away. One more night by the roadside and we were on the last lap. The trip which required three days and two nights can now be encompassed in three hours by automobile or in thirty minutes by plane.

On the third day out, after having traveled through much interesting level land and passing through rich alluvial valleys, I saw the then small crossroads town of Coldwater in the offing. Since I had imbibed alkali water from shallow wells for days, I was intrigued by the name of Coldwater and looked forward to a good drink. But most of all, I wanted to see the wise old ponies bury their noses in clean, clear water. Entering the little town, we made for the public drinking trough. I primed the pump, glad to do a little work for the faithful pintos. Imagine my disappointment when after one unguarded swallow, they stood drooling in disgust. Making use of the common drinking cup chained to the pump, I likewise threw up the sponge and paid my respects to the man who employed the misnomer.

A can of fuzzy pie peaches and a nickel's worth of crackers supplied a sweet warm drink and a bit of sustenance. I left Coldwater hot and thirsty and under the necessity of guarding the ponies against overfatigue and the heat of a merciless sun. In spite of these handicaps we were anxiously reaching out for our destination, which was not far away. Just before sundown we entered the shadow of a cool canyon a short distance east of Jet. While I was giving the ponies a breathing spell, a weather-beaten white-haired pedestrian came up the canyon. In the friendly fashion of the Middle Border, he approached the buggy and said, "My name is Murphy. I live over there in the sod house." Learning that he was on the way to Jet, I invited him to climb in. The old man supplied the names of all the inhabitants, told where they lived, what they did, and what they thought of each other. I learned that the old doctor had his office in the back of the Jet Brothers' General Store, and that he gave all his patients, young and old, the same medicine out of the same big bottle the year round. Although I was confident this was an exaggeration, the sparkle in the old man's eye and his innocent prolixity won my admiration and resulted in a lasting friendship. To see such a grizzled old Solomon coming from that canyon was a pleasant surprise, and his continued comradeship proved to be a priceless boon. He possessed a keen sense of humor and a fine primitive perception with incredible analytical powers.

He introduced me to Mr. Warner Jet, the landowner and proprietor of the general store. Warner, one of the town builders and good friend of the old doctor, naturally was interested in his successor. He and Mrs. Jet took me into their comfortable home and gave me a double bed with mattress and springs and immaculate linens. They lived on a beautiful prairie farm a half-mile up the section line. The next morning when I awakened in the luxury of comfort and looked upon the level land I had already learned to love, I thought of the kinky-headed pickaninny, who, while surreptitiously trying out my mother's broad white bed in the big house, had said, "Gracious golly, no wonder Miss Mat lays in dis' here bed til' nine." I had occupied beds that would have made that pickaninny's eyes look like flying saucers. But in spite of that I uttered a morning prayer and scrambled out for a hot breakfast on sparkling china.

Before leaving these recollections of my Chickasha days, I should like for the reader to know that in those early years this little pioneer town had two types of doctors. One represented the quiet, modest, generous, conscientious servant of the people, always in pursuit of scientific knowledge to be used in behalf of his patients and the community welfare. The other represented the reckless, designing, dashing type in Prince Albert, high hat, and kid gloves, keeping his horses in a white lather to impress all spectators with the urgency of his calls whether genuine or spurious. It is embarrassing that such individuals could ever pursue their selfish ends under the title M. D. It is heartening to say that even in those early days, they were in the minority and that they have virtually disappeared with the progress of medical education.

CHAPTER X

Jet

WHEN I drove into Jet on a hot afternoon in 1901, the horizontal rays of the setting sun were glazing the wings of the windmill which intersected the youthful arteries of commerce then nourishing the little town and serving its outlying districts. The windmill with its watering tank served as a hub to the local settler's wheel of chance. Little did I realize that its arms piercing the sky above this pioneer mart of rural commerce were destined to become my ever present sentinel as I followed the highways and byways day and night in the care of the sick. Here was a typical midwestern crossroads village with three or four stores, a small hotel under construction, a livery stable, and a blacksmith shop. There were only one or two residences in the town proper. The storekeepers lived on their farms. After milking the cows, feeding the pigs, and arranging the day's work on the farm, they drove to town in time to open the stores for business.

As I approached this haven which temporarily settled my professional ambitions and partially quenched my roving spirit, I looked beyond the borders of the little town and saw prairie schooners capping the horizon as they rolled westward toward the Rockies. To me the vision was rich in romance. It seemed to be a realization of my dreams, an answer to my impulsive urge for the West. For the moment I was reveling in the afterglow of the life so vividly depicted by Owen Wister, Frederic

Remington, and Theodore Roosevelt. In imagination I followed the buffalo and the antelope across the glamorous horizon with a hope of recovering a vanishing period in American life. But night was falling, and it was necessary for me to be realistic. My lot was to be with the homesteaders and not with the roving cowboys, and my life was to be integrated with the hardworking men and women who had fenced the land, followed the plow, and brought permanent domestication to the trackless plains. They were the people who still live in Hamlin Garland's *A Son of the Middle Border*. According to William Dean Howells, this remarkable story of life on the prairie is so realistic "you can smell the sweat on the horses and see the chinch bugs climbing the wheat straws."

I landed in Jet owing a balance of $1,100 on my medical education. After crediting $10, which had been hidden in my hatband for safekeeping, I was still in the red. Fortunately for me the hotel proprietor's comely young daughter kicked in and helped pay my board by spraining her ankle the day after my arrival. Careful strapping of the painful part kept her on foot, and to the family's surprise she was able to "wait table" with an injury which otherwise would have put her to bed. Just forty-eight years after the ankle episode the younger sister came to my office to say that while in the city she wanted to report on the family and urge me to come for a visit and fried chicken with her and her husband on the farm southwest of Jet.

The kind old doctor who was anxious to give up his practice was doubly pleased at the thought of recommending the son of his old friend. Soon I was busy seeing patients on my own, setting up an improvised office, and making long calls in the country. The nearest railroad station was twenty miles away. The land was laid off in sections, one mile square, bounded on all sides by roads corresponding to the section lines. From the four business corners making up the town of Jet, fertile farmlands stretched far away, to be vaguely rimmed by the hazy horizon. Beyond this rim to the northwest lay the mystic salt plains and immediately to the north the unpredictable Salt Fork of the Arkansas River. Both were full of interest but not without danger for the doctor who served the outlying regions beyond their limits.

No doubt the salt plains, twelve miles long and seven miles wide, represented a marine heritage. The surface of this area was perfectly bare, all vegetation being blighted by the inexhaustible salt of a dead sea. During long dry spells, this area, seen from a distance, looked like a great field of snow because of the evaporation of moisture and the precipitation of salt on top of the sand. In wet weather it presented the appearance of a large body of water. The effect was so deceptive that in season even the migratory wild fowl came down in droves. Whether surprised or disappointed, often they remained as though fascinated by this freak of nature. They indulged their aquatic propensities in the meager currents of the Salt Fork, which abutted the northeast boundary of the salt plains. The seagulls came in great numbers, especially in springtime, and in lieu of sea food and scavenger feasts they sailed over the surrounding farmlands where often they followed the furrow and grew fat on worms turned up by the pioneers' horse-drawn plows.

In the early days, during migratory flights the plains were covered with geese and ducks and, at times while in flight, the fowl almost obscured the skies above the salt plains. It was not uncommon to see great flocks of Canadian geese feeding in the cornfields or satisfying their taste for the tender spikes of winter wheat. This was a paradise for hunters, but in those days I was constantly in the service of the sick. Later, men of leisure with a yen for sport built a hunting lodge at the junction of the salt plains and the Salt Fork River. So it happened that this strange natural phenomenon brought many of the beautiful wild fowl down to sudden death where their aquatic forebears had enjoyed relative safety.

Marquis James' *Cherokee Strip* story of tubfuls of fish enmeshed in tough, multirooted tendrils of Bermuda grass after a freshet is little, if any, more fantastic than my observation of hundreds of fish in the Salt Fork floating ashore sickened by the brine of the salt plains after a rousing rainstorm had dissolved the salt from the sand and carried it into the river.

Beyond the Salt Fork north of Jet nature spread an ever shifting pattern on the sand dunes. The wind-carved landscape was covered with sunflowers, plum brush, wild locust, and cottonwoods. Though precariously anchored, this mongrel undergrowth made a coveted haven for coyotes. The many sand mounds seemed to serve as sounding boards and sent their weird yodeling reverberating in endless echoes up and down the river. The topography of the land for several miles north of the river rivals the strange phenomenon of the salt plains. Yet its origins are more recent and more easily explained. The prevailing winds are from the south, and the unsheltered river bed is composed of a broad stretch of sand. No doubt this sand, constantly replenished by the oft repeated floods, is caught up and carried north by the prevailing winds which carve the patterns for this strange topographical phenomenon.

Practically all the land tributary to Jet south of the river was ideally adapted to wheat and alfalfa. As time passed, the settler's industry in these areas filled the horn of plenty. The land is now classified among the most productive in the state.

It is interesting to note that I was on the rim of the dust bowl thirty-five years before it was named and that I met the "deserts on the march" nearly four decades before Paul B. Sears put them in his interesting book under that title. Often I had to let the buggy top down to keep from almost going up like a balloon with the ponies dangling in the air as so much ballast. On such occasions I would put the top back, lean forward, duck my head, and take the wind as it roared across the plains loaded with sand, slivers of cornstalks, dead grass, and sometimes biting little balls of ice in lieu of snowflakes. Storms of this nature dislodged the tumbleweeds and sent them bobbing south like eerie specters against the horizon. From such journeys I would return with sandbars in the corners of my eyes and much of the wayside soil in my whiskers. In spite of this ugly picture, it may be said that I was living in a beautiful country with the people who transformed it into a land of peace and plenty long before Edna Ferber hastily seized the bizarre and unconventional in both nature and society and unjustly enveloped Oklahoma in the blinding red dust of her *Cimarron* and left us surrounded by swash-buckling desperadoes. I was on the ground approximately forty years before Steinbeck's *Grapes of Wrath* defamed a great commonwealth and threatened to make Okies of us all.

Under the influence of the plow, long before these hasty interlopers told the world about us, we saw the sod turned and the seed sown to molder in the soil and spring into life through the incredible gift of nature. Under the influence of rain and the warmth of the sky we saw the succulent vegetation grow to maturity; we saw the broad expanse of golden grain shimmering in the sun; and finally, in the midst of plenty, we saw the quivering heat waves rising between sun and sod. We witnessed the immemorial evolution from seed to seed, from kernel to kernel, a process of nature mentioned in both Corinthians and St. John to illustrate the attainment of the New Life; and often as the harvest approached, there was music in my heart which ultimately found expression in these lines:

> *Oh, mystic prairie land,*
> *Touched by labor's magic hand,*
> *Thy yield is an hundredfold,*
> *Ceres hath turned the fields to gold.*

But often this harvest song was forgotten as we traveled into broad, still untouched open spaces beyond the confines of section lines where native grasses sheltered wildlife, unafraid, and reached out to mend every break in its continuity made by wind and native traffic. If the early settlers had heeded the warning of prairie grasses, the modern dust storms could never have developed. Where the soil was unfavorable for sod, nature failed to mend bare spots, and local dust storms occurred. As early as 1846 Garrard in *Wah-To-Yah* gave a graphic account of being blinded by dust and gravel as he rode through a grass-sparse section on the Santa Fé Trail. On such occasions the spirit of the boundless plains posed the vexing questions, "Evolution or God," and made clear the harmonious fusion of the two.

Reminiscent of these experiences is the basic philosophy of Ken Hubbard expressed in the following words: "Peace is a wonderful thing, but you have to be mighty poor and mighty obscure to get much of it."

I was intrigued by the hardy, capable pioneer women. In the songs of Hesiod the three basic elements of a farmer's life were a house, an ox, and a woman. Obviously, in the winning of the West, the woman and the ox antedated the house. In fact, the wife often helped to spade the dugout or to shape the thick-walled sod house. It is fortunate that Hesoid came between the aristocratic Homer and the high-minded Pindar to champion the cause of the peasant. The place he gives to woman in his songs of the soil is comparable to that occupied by our own intrepid pioneer women. Between work in the fields and babies in the home, many farm women never had time to regain their graceful lines. Though not trained for golf and tennis tournaments, they could turn the Phoenix trick according to the exigencies of life. Their determination, their skills and capabilities are implied in the features and the stride of Bryant Baker's "Pioneer Woman" at Ponca City.

When this massive, yet graceful, tribute to all pioneer women on the plains was unveiled amid great applause, Will Rogers mounted the platform and said: "Don't bother about the dust on my clothes. I was sitting on the end of a bench when I heard a corset string give way, and I was pushed off in the dirt." By birth and at heart Will Rogers was too close to the pioneer woman and too well understood to give offense to the people of Oklahoma. On this occasion a representative of the newly established WKY broadcasting station was twitching Will Rogers' coattail trying to get him on the air, when suddenly he turned and said, "What's the big idea, I'm not selling chewing gum."

In the very early days at Jet there were no telephones, and

our calls came through messengers, who usually arrived on horseback. Often our night calls were anticipated as the clatter of rushing hoofs drew nearer and nearer. The office door conveniently opened on the main highway, and the calamitous crescendo ended with the loud rap, rap on the door and one hurried appeal, "Oh, Doc, get up quick!" My Indian ponies, accustomed to being staked at the door of the tipi, knew the ways of their master, sensed his response to the call, and stood ready to thrust their necks in the collar and to brace their backs for the harness. When winter came and northers nosed their way across the bleak plains with furious indifference to life and property, I prayed that God might answer all night calls.

Having no fire in the little bedroom, often I borrowed a buffalo robe from the hardware store and snuggled like a spinwheel under this time-tried weather screen. Responding to its encompassing warmth, I contemplated the many wintry storms it had weathered before entering the service of civilization. This experience recalls the story of the engineer who was called to the Far North to negotiate a difficult problem. After traveling as far as possible by means of ordinary transportation, he was met by an old north woodsman and tucked into a sleigh for the last lap of his journey. The cold was intense, and after driving some distance, the engineer suggested that they turn the hairy side of the buffalo robe next to their bodies. After this was accomplished and they were well on the way, he noticed the old native chuckling to himself and ventured to inquire, "Would you mind telling me what you are laughing about?" In response he said, "I was just thinking what damn fools these buffaloes have been all the time."

As the seasons passed, there was always a high average of golden days; nevertheless, there was lots of bad weather, and we learned to fight the blinding blizzards in winter, to ford the swollen streams in springtime, to endure the hot winds in July and August, but, in spite of all, we shared the settler's faith in the future. I reveled in the glorious autumn when the mauve Indian summer enveloped the land and the long silent nights were broken only by the wild geese calling overhead or the multicrooning coyotes in the sand hills.

During those early days the doctor gathered valuable experience through the haphazard practice of the time, going from dugout to sod house and from sod house to prairie shack in the service of his patients. There were times when the way seemed dark. His experience was not checked by the helpful eye of superiors nor enriched by contact with daily associates. His medicine was the child of unaided initiative born of inescapable responsibility. But remembering the advice of William Harvey, he tried to follow "the path nature walks." This professional isolation was partially compensated by the consciousness of contact with the god of medicine. His daily rounds presented many incidents which helped to keep critical curiosity alive and made close clinical observation imperative.

Fearing that this account of my early days in Oklahoma might be misleading, I hasten to say that there were many competent, hard-working farmers occupying the choice land, where the coming of babies was punctuated by periods of rest, where the farm women were feminine and comely, and where the rich new soil yielded bountiful crops of corn, wheat, and alfalfa. These last were readily marketable and the returns were converted into better homes, more spacious barns and outhouses, finer livestock, and more efficient farm machinery. As a result of this progress, there was increasing comfort and profit in the practice of medicine to offset the toil and tribulation of the pioneering period.

In spite of the early hardships and the many trying experiences, there was ample compensation in the long leisurely drives, day and night, across the far-flung prairies. It was good to see nature in the raw and man in the making, to move in vast areas of silence surrounded by fascinating horizons, beyond which imagination played with eager hopes and ambitions. In "The Song of the Open Road," Walt Whitman said: "Now I can see the secret of the making of the best persons. It is to grow in the open air and to eat and sleep with the earth."

The trails we traveled have been mercilessly scored by powerful road machines; the dainty wild flowers which hedged them and the friendly clumps of plum brush, bluestem, and horsemint which perfumed the way and shielded the furtive quail, the dynamic cardinals, and the colorful roadrunners have been destroyed. The roads have been given over to motor-powered vehicles; the horse has been retired to suburban saddle clubs where his freedom is restricted, his initiative hobbled and his intelligence insulted. Those hard, happy days are gone forever, but the memory of them is still vivid.

Cheyenne Indians near Darlington

Courtesy El Reno American

CHAPTER XI

O. B. on the Plains

THIS abbreviation O. B., which means "obstretrics," might well be "Oh Boy!" if it were not for the fact that girls come almost equally as often as boys. But even so, does not this fact justify the exclamation?

Better than anyone else the doctor knows that unfortunate episodes out of wedlock have educational value and carry warnings with sharp emphasis. It may be remembered that my first call while still a medical student was to see the foolish black child over the manger behind the brownstone front; my first call while a "premature" doctor on horseback was to see a similar victim of this susceptible race; and my first horse and buggy experience at Jet had to do with an unfortunate white girl whose family suspected that the characteristic labor pains were stomachache from cabbage she had eaten the day before. The doctor often wonders how genuine is the surprise universally expressed when he finds it necessary to tell the family what is happening. Often the emotion and tears suddenly so obvious have welled to the surface only after long-continued, hopeless suppression of the cruel truth.

Although the doctor on the plains occasionally found it necessary to trouble otherwise peaceful waters because of the indiscretions of rural lovers, in retrospect it is surprising how chaste the country girl seemed to be. When the ruthless results of indiscretion brought the doctor face to face with the truth, it was gratifying to see how wise, tolerant, and brave the victims' suffering mothers were. Perhaps having long been familiar with the unrestrained animal urge toward nativity and having been forced by her environment to meet tragedy with little outward emotion, she could bear this sorrow and humiliation with a simultaneous display of poise and mercy.

This cabbage episode was an exception resulting in great commotion. The mother of the girl was frantic; two brothers armed with guns went clattering away in search of the father. While all this was going on, the baby was put to the breast and apparently all was well. But the psychological conflicts continued in full swing. The next morning the baby was dead. It was impossible to determine the cause of death. The man hunt was unsuccessful, and gradually the family accepted the inevitable. The one genuine casualty was the innocent baby.

Jean Littlejohn, who wrote *Babies Are Fun,* rendered a valuable service to modern mothers, also to doctors who must manage both babies and mothers, but she did not know what some family doctors know. She never went through a first confinement in a dugout with no place to put the baby down. No doubt she failed to seek information from the frontier doctor on horseback or in the buckboard. Evidently she did not confer with the stork doing parcel post ahead of the pony express.

Always I have been interested in the phenomena of life, conception, the miracle of birth, growth, and development. As a boy on the farm, spontaneously I was made aware of the origin and continuity of life through the elemental forces in operation before my eyes.

After I entered upon my medical career, the privilege of sitting at the bedside in the presence of the highest function of the female organism did not wholly solve the mystery. But this opportunity for continued study and the acquisition of additional knowledge was accepted with a full understanding of the physiological implications and a keen appreciation of this sacred trust ladened with the most profound domestic secrets.

Often I considered the stork's inscrutable prescience and wondered how he makes up his mind, how he finds the way, and, in some instances, how he has the heart. His sixth sense must be that of time and direction. He knows when and where he is due, and he never fails to make connections. On occasions, in out-of-the-way places, I have scanned the sky and wondered if he would keep faith with the tired mother. I knew she was anxiously awaiting the coveted sweep of his merciful wings. At times my fears seemed warranted, because I delivered babies where previously the blood of white women had never been spilled through the act of nativity. I was helping plant the first families on the Middle Border, and yet the wise old bird found his uncharted way. Perhaps he carried papooses to the roving Indian women squatting on the plains when fate decreed an increase. For the record and the readers' edification it should be known that Frederic Remington, with his brush, once strapped a little papoose to one of his dynamic ponies. In this connection it has been said that in Custer's day at Fort Supply, Oklahoma, it was not unusual for the Indian woman on the march to drop out of line for the blessed event. It may be presumed that she strapped the newborn baby to her back, mounted her pony, and caught up in time to make dog soup for supper.

On occasions when babies were born far from civilization, it was necessary for the doctor to serve as accoucheur, nurse, charwoman, and neighbor, especially when the baby happened to be the husband's first. After all, there is nothing equal to the feeling of comprehensive competency. Since the patient was relatively immune to her own germs and far removed from the accumulated crop of bacteria resulting from long-continued human habitation, contact with the doctor who traveled from one patient to another constituted the mother's chief danger. The risk was recognized and the challenge accepted.

Occasionally I delivered babies that were so unwelcome I wondered how the stolid old stork dared take the risk. No doubt he knew that if the infant could get one chance at the mother's breast and one touch of her cheek, the barriers would be down and all doubt dispelled. The consciousness of sustenance flowing from mother to child and the delicate feel of the chaste bundle of soft flesh are irrestible. If on account of disease or for some other reason mothers must not have contact with their own offspring, it is best not to permit the slightest intimacy; even one period at the breast arouses the mother instinct and makes ultimate separation much more painful.

One night during the first winter after my arrival at Jet, the worst blizzard of the year was bearing down upon the plains. Before morning Mrs. Pat O'Leary's travail sent two husky sons for the doctor. They were driving treacherous bronchos hitched to a buckboard. This was no time for a surrey with the fringe on top. With the wind and snow whipping their flanks the boys could scarcely control the rearing mustangs while I jumped into my clothes. Old Pat had instructed them to make haste and they were almost as restless as the bronchos. I climbed in and sought a warm spot beneath the robes as we faced the wind and gave rein to unbounded energy.

When we arrived, Mrs. O'Leary's baby was well on the way. Pat was restlessly walking the floor, stroking his overgrown goatee. Since the house was already full of children with the youngest hardly out from under her feet, Mrs. O'Leary was not very happy about this unplanned addition to her family. As the time drew nearer and nearer, Pat paced the floor like a caged hyena, always better than an arm's length from the bed. Naturally, I wondered why anybody responsible for so many babies could be so nervous about one more. By and by as he came dangerously near, Mrs. O'Leary said with primitive emphasis, "Oh, I'll tell you, Pat, if I could git my hands on you I'd pull the g—d d——d whiskers out o' you." While she was thus climaxing her heroic effort, the baby was born. Later, with little Pat in her arms, she seemed to be thoroughly reconciled, and domestic peace promptly returned.

One night not long after getting settled, I was called several miles northeast of Jet. The expectant mother was past thirty and not the ideal type for childbearing. It seemed that the baby would never come. But medicine had taught the safety of patient waiting in the absence of abnormal conditions. Finally the boy was born, and in the after part of the night under the starry sky I returned with great satisfaction over the happy termination of a difficult case.

Many years later a good-looking young man with a strangely familiar name came before the Admissions Committee of the University of Oklahoma School of Medicine. At an opportune moment, I said, "By any chance were you born northeast of Jet?" He answered, "Yes, but you are thinking of my older brother." This boy made his mark in school, and I always regretted he was not the one who gave his mother such a hard time and caused me so much anxiety. Even later, thirty-nine years to be exact, the older brother came to me for his birth certificate.

In the sand hills north of the Salt Fork I attended a young mother and left her with a fine baby boy. Three days later when I called to determine progress, I learned that the baby's bowels had not moved. An examination revealed a congenital defect closing the opening to the bowel. This was an emergency and I undertook what I would not dare do today. Fortunately, my providence was working. The defect consisted of a thin diaphragm, and a simple operation was sufficient to bring about normal function. During World War II that baby, then forty-three years of age, came to my office for a birth certificate. Although there was no record, it was easy to identify this one as my very own.

One summer night a man hurriedly came for the doctor. His wife was in labor; he had left her with two small children sleeping in an adjoining room and he must "get right back." In haste we harnessed the ponies and I followed as he rode like Paul Revere. When we opened the door to the house, we heard a familiar cry and we knew that the baby had come. It was like hearing the first note of the bluebird still invisible in the spring sky. Shortly before we arrived, the baby had been born. The mother had been able to reach a sewing bag hanging on the bedpost (perhaps by design), had found scissors and thread and tied the cord, and was resting with the baby on her arm. The other children were still sleeping soundly. On the way home I heard the stars singing in unison, and occasionally to this day, when I think of that experience, I find myself dreaming of the days "when women were women."

One night I was called to attend a prospective mother in a neat little cottage on the outskirts of Jet. She was having the usual premonitory pains but was still up and about. She wanted to finish the dishes before going to bed. But the husband and I took care of the chores while she performed her last prenatal tasks. Looking in her room before she had cleared the bed for final action, I noticed two large pillows against the headboard with decorative slips bearing the following mottoes: "I slept and dreamt that life is beauty," "I waked to find that life is duty." That night the woman who had embroidered those touching words successfully negotiated one of life's most insistent and inescapable duties without time for either sleep or philosophy.

One night during a hard winter when the "wind with a wolf's head" swept the prairies, I was called to a little hut on the fringe of the salt plains to attend the wife of a man who had befriended me on many occasions. It was he who scanned the raging Salt Fork and said, "Doc, don't put them ponies in that flood." It was he who mounted me on the old "pack-of-bones," bred and born on the river, in order to make my passage safe; but it was his wife who set the stage that wintry night, and obviously it was then my time to enter the drama on the side of service and to help plant a new life in that barren region long known to the Plains Indians as the "Great Saline." It was a bitter night, and the howling wind channeled its cold breath through whispering crevices of her abode as we attended that laborious nativity. The winter woodpile had been exhausted and the coal market was far away, so at that time of patient waiting, the good pioneer, combating the blizzard, poured bushels of corn in full-blown ears through the old-fashioned drum stove. Through hard labor in the field, the father had stored heat and energy for the occasion. Ultimately the baby was born, the wind subsided, the sun came over the dusty horizon, and peace settled upon the plains as the villainous night withdrew.

Here, the doctor-patient relationship had reached full fruition, and the participants were happy in the consciousness of mutual services freely performed.

One time, after I had made a long drive to attend a confinement case, the husband came out and said, "Doc, I'm sorry but you're too late; the baby is already here." This announcement came with a finality which the farmer thought would turn me away and settle the bill. Perhaps he did not take into account the fact that I had made a long drive and was entitled to something for my time and trouble. After some quibbling on the part of the troubled father, I accepted five dollars and drove home, wondering who tied the cord, about the danger of infection, and whether or not the mother might be sacrificed on the altar of ignorance and economy.

It is astonishing, however, to recall what some of these plainswomen could do. Once after attending an easy case and adding one more to the formidable family galaxy, I returned the second morning to find the mother milking the cows.

But hardy as these women were, they could not withstand infection. One night after contending with an abnormal obstetrical problem without success, I requested consultation. A fine old doctor, now gone to his reward, came from a near-by village. It was agreed that an instrumental delivery was inevitable. The forceps were applied, and the old doctor's skillful manipulations resulted in a successful issue. Making sure that all was well with both the mother and child, I went home for an uneasy night. The patient had had a hard time, her resistance was low, the environment was not good, and antisepsis was difficult. As I had feared, infection ensued, and a few days later a chill foretold the mother's doom. Within three weeks "childbed" fever had done its deadly work, and the bereaved husband was left with a motherless baby and a helmless home.

In the winter of 1902 I was called to attend a mother who was giving birth to her third child. Crossing the Salt Fork of the Arkansas at twilight, I observed that a swift north wind was sweeping the ford and that small waves were breaking on the sandbars of the south bank, leaving a fringe of fragile ice. It was obvious that we were in for a bit of genuine weather. Not long after the river was left behind, a distant light shone dimly through the bleary atmosphere of the storm-ridden night. No doubt it was placed in the window to serve as a guide for the doctor. Progress against the blinding wind was becoming more difficult, which made the light appear as a friendly beacon to a troubled mariner. But soon the last lap of the journey was completed, my ponies were in the straw-thatched stable, and I was enjoying the warmth of a roaring fire in the big kitchen stove while making ready for the great event.

Although beyond the threshold of this humble farmhouse nature seemed to be in a state of wild confusion, according to all indications the phenomena of birth were following the conventional course, and there was little to do except await results and witness the immemorial renewal of life. After a few hours of hard work, with the merciful aid of partial anesthesia, the mother, happy in her freedom from travail, was tucked away, proud of a buxom boy. The kitchen table had been cleared, and on the shining oilcloth a great loaf of homemade bread, a dish of golden butter, a generous supply of wild honey in the comb, and a cup of steaming hot coffee warmed the cockles of my heart. On such a night with the homeward journey in anticipation, this was a "God send."

It was long after midnight when I reached the river. The ford was frozen over, and the ice was too thin for a dry-shod crossing and too thick for light ponies to successfully break their way through. I drove back for help, and the father of the newborn babe came with a draft horse to break the ice so we could get across. The wind had partially subsided and the cold was not immediately so obvious, but it was not long until my body was chilled to the bone and there was a vague consciousness of progressive numbness of fingers and toes. My ears were as fragile as candied fruit, and my gloved fingers were freezing in my pockets. While my ponies followed the frozen ruts, to stimulate circulation, I climbed out of the buggy and walked

These noble sons of toil were among my patients at Jet

the unbroken prairie, alternately skimming the frosted buffalo grass and wading through clumps of tall bluestem, tufted with fluffy snow, which sifted through every crevice in my clothing. Regardless of this rather strenuous exercise, the penetrating cold seemed to be driving the last vestige of warmth from my body.

Nearing the point of desperation, I was imagining the early-morning discovery of unattended ponies and a rigid body ready for a frosty inquest, when suddenly a light appeared in a farmhouse not far way. Fortunately it was time for country people to chunk up the fires and look after the livestock. While this humble home was not among those western abodes where Ralph Waldo Emerson found his beloved Homer on the bookshelves, for me it adorned the plains and averted tragedy. After a cordial reception with motherly attention to my frostbitten appendages and a little time before a red-hot stove, I was ready for the road. A borrowed robe, hot irons for my feet, and the promise of the rising sun made the resumption of my journey safe and filled my heart with gratitude.

Before closing this intimate chapter, I should like to pay due tribute to homemade bread, the staff of life. In the average farmhouse it was found in great white loaves with golden crust, always ready for the sustenance of the family and the delight of hungry guests. On overnight calls, when babies were being born, often I have been sustained by these self-same loaves and hot coffee brewed on great stoves serving the dual purpose of supplying hot food and warming the house. On such occasions, with bread and coffee on the inside and inclement weather on the outside, I could have welcomed a slow labor except for the safety of the unborn child, the suffering of the mother, and the ultimate need of more bread of her own making.

We take off our hats and bow our heads to the unselfish woman who lays in a bountiful store of her meager supplies for such a one-sided party. It's a hard husband who doesn't suffer in sympathy; it's a poor doctor who doesn't try to ease the pain, shorten the ordeal, and idealize the mother.

CHAPTER XII

From the Mill Run

I knew a wizened old homesteading bachelor who lived in a dugout under the high bank of a creek like a lone river rat in his hole. Once when I was called to his ramshackle abode to see about his herpes zoster (shingles), pigs ran snorting from under his bed and a squawking old hen came flapping from her nest on the shelf above his resting place. Through her motherly instinct the hen was hovering over the mystery of life while awaiting the pipping of the shells and the trilling first peep of her chicks, and the pigs were enjoying happy domicile while their owner was dreaming of fried chicken and broiled bacon. While engaged in the care of this crusty old recluse's body which, though rusty and unkept, was visible, tangible, and approachable, I was looking across the wide chasm which no one has ever spanned, reaching for a clue to the psychological phenomena in the secret recesses of his brain. Was it possible that he entertained poetic affinity for pigs and chickens, or was this sharing of shelter merely a prosaic expression of common generosity? Or, independent of his own thinking, could it have been only animal instinct on the part of chickens and pigs, taking advantage of a crack in the door which he was too lazy to mend? Be that as it may, there was never a note of embarrassment or apology. Disregarding the motive in the old man's mind, I recognized the universal need of companionship and was interested and tolerant.

In a two-room sod house on the edge of the salt plains, a mother and three small children were down with the smallpox.

The father did the cooking and nursing while they peeped out from under the covers, exhibiting crusted countenances with obvious curiosity. The disease was mild, and in due time all the victims emerged from this loathsome experience with smooth and shining faces. One day while I was on call to lift the quarantine, in a friendly spirit of gratitude, the mother requested me to join them in front of the eroded sod house for a snapshot. When I declined, she said, "Oh, please do, having you in the picture will make it more homely-like." Knowing this appeal came straight from the heart and that it represented an expression of genuine esteem, I gladly acquiesced. After all, there was much truth in what she said. At that time I was exhibiting a shaggy Vandyke to disguise my youth and my clothes were carelessly worn and had acquired the weather-beaten appearance characteristic of the busy country doctor in the horse and buggy days. My presence would have made any picture more homely.

One bright spring day, in answer to a call from across the Salt Fork, I drove to what was known as the Island, where there was a good ford only two miles from my patient's home. The stream was raging, and there was no hope of getting across with a team of small ponies. A near-by farmer, seeing my plight, suggested that his old horse, "bred and born on the river," could stem the flood if I could stick on. Though not sure of my ability, I accepted the challenge. As we bridled my rawboned confederate, the farmer exclaimed, "My God, the boys are all off with the saddles but I can tie a rope around him." Reluctantly I acquiesced in this disconcerting proposal and made ready for the adventure.

When the rope was in place and my medicine case strapped between my shoulders, the farmer gave me a hand for the high mount. If Caesar could swim the Nile and not get his "commentaries" wet, it appeared that I should be able to get across the Salt Fork and keep my cathartics dry. After reaching the water, we had solid footing for a short distance but presently we plunged into a swift current and before old rawbones could get his bearing and find his stroke, the cold water was sweeping my armpits. After alternately stumbling across shallow bars and swimming the deep currents, we gained the opposite bank. Although the muddy water, almost thick enough for topsoil, was streaming down my trousers and overflowing my shoes, we had two miles to go.

Finally arriving at my destination, I found a corpulent old woman with a gall bladder full of stones and a house full of children. Though in her sphere she had lived a full life and had almost reached the limit of her usefulness, she was suffering from gallstone colic and was sorely in need of the relief and comfort which only a doctor could give. After doing the best possible for her and receiving her blessings and enjoying the expression of satisfaction so obvious in the faces of these little denizens of the sand hills, I was ready for the return trip. But to my chagrin the news of my presence north of the river had traveled to another household, and it was necessary for me to see a sick child on the next quarter-section. This mission completed, with the river behind me, I returned to my buggy and ponies with a dampened sense of achievement.

Two years after making this call I received a small load of kafir corn for my trouble. Over and over again I had been amply paid by the memory of the mother's gratitude and the light in her children's faces.

In the summer of 1903, while the hot winds were parching the pasture lands and converting great fields of succulent young corn into ghostly shambles of blighted bounty, I was making long drives to see a mother and two little children down with typhoid fever. They lived in a wind-swept one-room box house with a dirt floor. There was a small lean-to which served as a kitchen and contained an improvised bunk where the husband slept. The nearest neighbors were half a mile away, but they carried food and shared their time, giving as much nursing care as possible without seriously neglecting their own homes.

We were facing a difficult situation. The proper care of typhoid patients required many services and environmental conditions which could not be provided. At the end of two weeks the outlook for the mother seemed grave. The husband was informed, but it was impossible to fathom his thoughts. He was uncommunicative, of little help about the house, his work on the place was haphazard, and he was without funds. In retrospect, my inability to sense his psychological conflicts and to thwart the impending catastrophe seems inexcusable. A day or two after he was told of his wife's serious condition, a neighbor called me to come in great haste. Speeding behind a fresh team in anticipation that the children might be motherless before I arrived, to my surprise I found their father stretched out on the ground near the woodpile with a bullet hole in the middle of his forehead. A .22 rifle at his side told the story. He had sought surcease through attempted suicide.

Though stupid and dazed, he was not in severe shock. We tucked him in the kitchen bunk, and a probe was introduced to see if the bullet had lodged between the layers of his thick skull, but after permitting the probe to settle gently to a depth of two or three inches in his brain without meeting resistance, it was withdrawn and an antiseptic dressing applied. The next day he was not only conscious and remorseful, but ravenous for food. In spite of this shocking experience the mother improved, and the whole family entered upon an uneventful convalescence.

After a few years these unfortunate people passed from my observation, but the bullet which found a resting place somewhere in the victim's brain seemed not to cause any serious trouble.

On a hot summer night after the construction gang had laid steel into the little town of Nash and switched bunk cars on a side track, a bunch of Negroes on the job got drunk and staged a free-for-all fight with butcher knives and razors. Two of them were found in pools of blood on the dirty floor of a bunk car. With no assistance I proceeded to repair the damage. The nearest doctor was miles away, and it seemed to me that if these men could get drunk and cut each other up without an anesthetic, they could lie still and be sewed up without the aid of medicine's greatest boon. All was well until I came to the big mulatto with a five-inch cut in his scalp and a gaping stab wound at the left border of his heart. While I made haste by the light of a kerosene lamp, my patient writhed and yelled, in spite of the fact that alcohol and loss of blood had laid him low. Repeatedly he cried out, "Oh Doc, if the money's all you want, please go 'way and let me die." To his companion holding the lamp, "Oh, John, for God's sake, come take him off! Can't you see he's killing me! For God's sake, Doc, please go 'way and let me die."

The job completed, we chucked him in the lower bunk of a double decker, and his wounds healed by first intention, with not even a stitch abscess to mar the field of operation. No doubt he was immune to the dirt of his habitat, or perhaps there was a bit of the marvelous mold of penicillin-fame or some other inhibiting factor in the footworn straw that carpeted the bunk car.

One fine morning while I was standing in front of the combination hardware and drugstore, I learned that a former patient had sold out and was moving to Nebraska. He had paid his blacksmith and all his store accounts, but had said never a word about his doctor's bill, which represented medical services rendered during the previous winter when snow and ice made country practice doubly difficult. Immediately I drove out to his place, determined to collect the hard-earned fees. I arrived just as he and his family were ready to drive off with two wagonloads of household goods. Obviously he was disturbed by my appearance on the scene and haltingly explained that he had paid as far as his money would go and that he intended to mail a check to cover the doctor's bill.

Knowing that he had received a good price for his grain and livestock and hoping he might have the cash in his pocket, I urged him to pay the bill. With some embarrassment and a display of genuine sentiment, he finally said, "Doc, I ain't got that much to spare, but if you want to take that extra horse and settle the bill, he's yourn." Then, for the first time I saw a good-looking bay horse tied behind the rear wagon. Thinking this might be my last chance, I gave him a receipt in full, transferred the halter rope to the rear of my buggy, learned that the horse's name was Billy, and followed the prairie schooner to the main highway, where we parted with a mutual sense of restrained satisfaction.

There were tears in the woman's eyes, and I could imagine a turmoil in her heart. To my knowledge, one of her babies had been born in the little home she was leaving behind, there she had bravely contended with the domestic problems of farm life, and the familiar scenes were incorporated in her soul. Now that the ties were being broken, she was giving expression to long-suppressed emotion. Under the spell of her grief there was some satisfaction in the thought that I had not succeeded in collecting money. Obviously, it would take all the cash they had and something more to recompense her heartache and make another place seem like home.

After several days and nights without sleep, I came in from a long country call haggard and hungry. I would have given my kingdom for a night's rest, but a good friend had found an old bachelor, who lived in a dugout, unconscious at the side of the road. He had carried him home, placed him in his bunk, and hurried for the doctor. In my absence he had left a note explaining the circumstances and stressing the need of attention. There was nothing for me to do except punish myself and my ponies on this urgent mission of mercy. I arrived in due time to find a grizzled old cuss recovering from a drunken stupor. He had passed completely out, perhaps on Peruna from our own drugstore. These were the days of hard and fast prohibition in the wake of Carry Nation; consequently close proximity to the Kansas line had nothing to do with his drunken garrulousness. He was in the talkative stage of the sobering process, so after making sure there was no head injury, no apoplexy, and no heart failure, I left a sedative to sand the track and keep the wheels from spinning in his head and decided to let him sweat it out. Before starting home, I brushed the sandburs away and sat on the good earth while giving the ponies a little more time to recover their wind.

One Saturday morning after a country call I stopped at a well-kept farmhouse to see an old German who had been under my care. After circling the woodpile and skirting the barnyard and the haystacks, I stopped in front of the house. His wife came to the door and in answer to my inquiry she said, "He's gone to schet." After scanning the surroundings, I again faced the fine old woman with a quizzical eye. Then comprehending my puzzled state of mind, she indignantly waved toward town and with a linguistic miracle made me understand that her old man had gone to Jet.

Ten years after I settled in Oklahoma City a young doctor now internationally known was working in my office. Since he wanted to get busy and make money to meet immediate needs I sent him to Jet. Not long afterward he appeared at my door one night and wanted to know if he might come back to work in my office. I said, "What's the matter with Jet? I had only a team of ponies and unkept trails. You have a Ford and good roads." He replied, "Well, you can't expect a man to live in that place. There's not a bathroom in the whole town." To which I replied, "When I was there, the closest one was in Wichita, Kansas." In extenuation I must admit that he was planning to get married and at the time of my residence there I was hopelessly single.

It was during my first year at Jet that a faith healer came and established what he called a class. Naturally I was interested and curious. My curiosity mounted as I learned that several of my good patrons had joined. I wondered what would happen when the tragedy of painful illness or accident struck and the need of immediate tangible aid arose. A few months later the lecturer returned to make sure the good ship was sailing on even keel.

Soon after his visit one of the members, a former patient of mine, came and said, "Doctor, I want some medicine for the itch. The children are clawing the skin off their bones."

I answered, "That's strange. What's the matter with your faith cure?"

He replied, "It's all right, Doc, but it won't stop the scratching."

Having taken care of their respiratory troubles the winter before, I knew it would require a large pot of ointment to cover the combined family surface. So I acted accordingly and about two weeks later discovered that the prescription had been refilled several times. Finding my friend in town on Saturday afternoon, I asked, "What was the matter with that ointment I gave you?" "It was fine, Doc, worked like a charm."

"Well, why did you have to get it refilled so many times?"

Then he broke down and said, "Doc I'll tell you the truth. You know while that lecturer was here he stayed in the homes of the members, slept in their beds, and gave all of them the itch. I'm the only one who had the courage to come for medicine, so I got it filled for all the rest of them."

One harvest day a great storm swept the plains and a twister caught one of my friends who had joined the faith healers. His horses ran away, and when he was found helpless, he was carried to the house, where one of the healers came to practice her art. Unfortunately, the injury to the spine had paralyzed not only the lower extremities but the bladder as well. The latter important function in suspense soon precipitated an embarrassing situation for the female healer. After a few hours the patient was in great distress from overdistention of the bladder. Also, he was learning that faith alone could not relieve that type of discomfort and dispel the eddying psychological currents disturbing his masculine peace of mind in the presence of naïve feminine faith. The thought of not being able to experience normal function when the need was so obvious could not be longer endured. His son, sensing the crisis, asked me to hurry out and take care of him. As I turned into the farmyard, the healer, following the other arm of the driveway, was ignominiously retreating. A sterile, soft rubber catheter opened the floodgates and gained the gratitude of the patient and the appreciation of the family. With the aid of a hard mattress and sandbags, the back improved, and after several weeks the necessity of periodic catheterization of the paralyzed bladder gradually passed. Even though I may have been a bit inflated by the credit received and pleased because of the comfort given, fate decided to take the wind out of my sails.

As soon as the old man could hobble on crutches, he came to town and gave his own version of the episode to the Jet *Visitor*. The story depicted a miraculous cure through faith alone. Of course it would have been indelicate to mention the obstacles encountered by the helpless female healer, the need of medical management, and the relief experienced through the use of the catheter for several weeks.

During my first winter in Jet I experienced a shocking smallpox epidemic. The disease was seldom fatal, but it was loathsome and disabling. Also, it was embarrassing, because I knew that it was a preventable disease and that its presence in epidemic form was a reflection upon the medical profession as well as the people. Since Jenner's discovery there had been plenty of time to educate the people with reference to vaccination. But they had suffered from many false doctrines. Even though doctors stood ready to offer advice and give protection, it was considered painful and troublesome to be vaccinated, and it was easy to put it off, though its relative efficiency was generally accepted. Before vaccination, approximately one person out of every ten died of smallpox, and one out of every five was badly pock-marked. I had been vaccinated in childhood, in medical school and again when the Jet epidemic appeared, but as occasionally occurs I was still susceptible to variloid—smallpox in abortive or mild form. One night while wracked with backache and a headache, I was called to go seven miles west. It was a cold, stormy night, and it was difficult to tell whether I was chilling or merely chilled.

The patient was a woman suffering from a severe attack of smallpox. There was no heat except from the kitchen stove where a smoldering fire was kept going by the frequent addition of half-cured cow chips. There was no other fuel, and after doing what could be done for the patient, I left, chilled to the bone. Before reaching home, I was genuinely ill. After getting to bed and experiencing a few hours of fitful sleep, I awakened with temperature of 103. The next day there was a single bump on my head and another behind my left ear. With a mirror it was possible for me to see the latter which made clear the nature of my illness. The bumps followed the usual pattern. Fearing I might spread the dire disease, I planned a period of self-quarantine. Mr. and Mrs. George were kind enough to go to one of their sons in the country and let me occupy their little cottage on the edge of town. My meals were sent to the doorstep by my friends at the hotel. The course of the disease was quickly run, but I remained in isolation until all danger to others had passed. The house was thoroughly fumigated before the old people came back, but to my dismay they came down with the disease. They had been exposed to other sources of infection, and we never knew whether my prophylactic technique was faulty or whether they had acquired the disease from others. Regardless of this question, they continued to be my ideal exponents of gracious generosity and unalloyed hospitality. The least I could do was to give them good care and see that they came through unscathed. This was one of my abiding satisfactions, and my life was enriched by their unfailing loyalty. A few days before the date of this writing, one of their sons called me from a small town in Texas to make an appointment for the examination of his own boy, now a prosperous ranchman. Thus I enjoyed the privilege of further service to this family, and when pressed for a bill I had the pleasure of sending it marked paid in full forty-eight years ago by worthy grandparents.

One afternoon a young woman called at my office to consult me about her little girl. After hearing her story and asking a few questions, I said, "Don't you think you had better bring the child in for an examination so I can find out just what is wrong and what can be done to help her?"

Without hesitation, she replied, "Oh, I know what's the matter with her, she has the go-backs."

Having never heard of the "go-backs" and being a novice in the practice of medicine, I determined not to reveal my ignorance and hastened to inquire, "How do you know your child has the go-backs?"

"Because I have measured her and her body is not seven times as long as her foot. You know that is a sure sign."

I decided not to take issue with her, but insisted that an examination was advisable. To my surprise, she abruptly terminated the discussion by saying, "Well, I've tied a string around the buggy wheel. If she is not better when that wears off I will bring her in." I am still longing for more information about the "go-backs," and fearing I may never know when to tie a string around the buggy wheel. Two years later, this same woman administered an overdose of coal oil to a younger child for the croup. She had continued to subject her children to the hazards of ignorance and overconfidence in her ability to determine their needs.

These stories could go on and on, but, for the sake of my reader and in some cases out of consideration for the patients, they must remain untold. A volume could be written about the "peasant's plenty" and the generous hospitality of hard-working, honest people.

These examples of the crude conditions encountered by the early-day country doctor and the intimate relationship existing between him and his pioneering patrons give a fair conception of what life meant to doctor and patient while the first homes were being established on the frontier. After all, ordinary people are the general practitioner's greatest treasure. They are rich in daily living and full of surprises. They may lack culture, but they have great strength of character. The doctor is sure of his reward; their appreciation and their unfailing loyalty is sufficient even though cash is never forthcoming.

In my second year at Jet I went to New York Polyclinic Hospital for postgraduate work. Dr. John A. Wyeth, who founded formal postgraduate teaching in America, was in his prime and actively engaged in the creative surgery of his time. Suffice it to say that his work and his personality stood as an inspiration for all who came in contact with him. Those who love a colorful life should read his delightful book, *With Saber and Scalpel*.

A few years later when the time came for me to leave Jet in order to take up graduate work at the University of Virginia, I could say with Kipling:

> *God be thanked; whate'er came after,*
> *I have lived and toiled with men.*

CHAPTER XIII

Social Amenities

LOOKING BACK upon my life at Jet, I am grateful for an easy inclination toward introversion. After the necessary friendly intercourse incident to my professional contacts, I was content to live with nature and my books. I did not purposely seek seclusion, but it always satisfied my needs. On the other hand, gradually I learned to take part in the current talk which was so good and plenty around the big stove in the combination hardware and drugstore. In winter this back-store conversation was seldom without notable participants. They came in homely garb, fresh from the soil, in cowboy boots and spurs, crisp from the land of sky and grass, and in the common habiliments of the drop-ins from the prairie schooners and freighters—all to be harried and bantered by the relatively well-informed loafers about the town. Alexander Pope frequenting London from his pastoral abode in Windsor Forest, observed "no difference between the run of town wits and the downright country fools." The members of this motley crowd made "heap big talk" as they surrounded the stove on nail kegs and empty Peruna crates. They covered all-important topics of the time and embellished them with expert profanity. Occasionally these heated talk-fests reached an intensity that put the red-hot stove to shame and became so absorbing that customers were neglected. The storekeeper could not afford to lay down the cudgel for the price of a pound of nails or a bottle of Nervine.

Rapidly I was learning the language of the Middle Border

and absorbing the independent spirit of the West. I was intrigued by the tolerance and control of brave men who could be quick on the trigger when honor was at stake.

I slept in my office, which was a fragile lean-to back of the drugstore opening into a little room where prescriptions were filled. Its insecurity was attested by the fact that one night a big hogshead, in which a stock of china had been shipped to Jet Brothers' General Store, was swept across the highway by a swift norther and knocked it off its foundation. Luckily my folding bed did not imprison me. The thought of its powerful springs and its ominous jaws often disturbed my otherwise peaceful sleep.

Every morning I renewed the smoldering fire in the big stove in the back of the store. With the exception of a small coal-oil burner this was our only source of heat. On very cold mornings I carried my clothes in by the stove in order that I might have the satisfaction of dressing by a real fire. Often after night drives in freezing weather while warming up for the cold bed, I scrambled eggs in the buttered bottom of a clipped-off paper bag. Never since then has fire been so warm or eggs so good.

One cold night a one-man show came to town in a covered wagon. The next morning while I was chunking up the fire, the owner of the show knocked for admission. He was "just about frozen" and wanted to sit by the fire. As he warmed up, I heard a strange yet familiar sound. Immediately it carried me back to the "Come alive, Sambo" days in the "promised land." In my effort to locate the ominous sound, my eyes focused on the showman, and out of his pocket came a rattlesnake's head with a flickering tongue. This was the only time I ever ordered a shivering man away from the fire. But, if he was cold-blooded enough to live intimately with snakes, he could crawl under a rock and wait for a spring thaw to limber him up rather than sneak into a place of human habitation with a snake in his pocket.

Aside from the animated arguments around the stove, there were many pleasant periods of quiet conversation with the

Careys, the Powells, the Williamsons, the Georges, the Jets, and many others who became my fast friends. Sim Randolph, the leisure-loving, easygoing real-estate agent, loafed a lot and loved the stove, especially if he could have right-of-way. Sitting in a reminiscent mood with the stove door open, he teased the hot coals with his inexhaustible supply of ambeer. Although the fretful sputtering seemed to stir his imagination, it never disturbed his aim.

One morning he came in hurriedly, mumbling through his swollen face, "Doc, my tooth ached all night. Git your forceps and pull it out." With two dental forceps to choose from I selected the one for molars and placing Sim in position and prying his mouth wide open, I found a veritable hopper where tons of tobacco had been processed. Scanning the well-worn, tobacco-stained molars, I spied his morning quid mischievously tucked in the hollow of his cheek giving the outward impression of a swollen jaw.

On another occasion Sim sat in front of the stove in solemn mien talking to me about his business. Finally, in a confidential mood, he said, "I played a trick on one of my down-east customers last week." Then hesitating as though depending upon his tobacco for inspiration, he let the secret go. "I sold him 80 acres of sand-hill land and deeded him 160." This bit of humor brought to his homely face a fascinating animation as his eyes sparkled with keen satisfaction. He was a good judge of human nature and could cut the fabric of his homespun philosophy to fit his neighbors and immediate acquaintances.

The propinquity of the pioneer and his plug is universally known. Stanley Vestal in *The Santa Fé Trail* pictures the hardened plainsman anxiously eyeing his last plug as it vanished under "the rapacious knife" of his guests. Once when on a visit in Kentucky I was loafing in my brother's drugstore when a farmer came in and said, "Mr. Bob, I want a plug of Star, a package of Bull Durham, and a clay pipe. This morning I stopped at Uncle Wid's and found him sick in bed with no flour, no meat, and no tobaccer. Not a thing in the house."

In my office at Jet

SOCIAL AMENITIES

One day a team of fine white-nosed mules from Kansas pulled into Jet with a clean-cut, well-dressed young man sitting on the driver's seat. The wagon contained a printing press and all the trappings to set up the news columns which make a small town hum. The young man and I became close friends. With his printing press, Urshel Finch turned out the Jet *Visitor* and put the little town definitely on the map. I helped arrange the news office in the back of the General Store. By keeping Urshel well and happy, I had a part in building the town and edifying the community. As well as I can remember, Warner Jet, according to his custom, took the newcomer into his home until he could get settled. Not only was this indiscriminate manifestation of good will a genuine expression of the merchant's pioneer hospitality, but at the same time it was good public relations for the Jet brothers, who were landowners, storekeepers, and town builders.

I helped carry Urshel's bed tick back across a plowed field after we had crammed it full of sweet, clean stuff from a fresh strawstack in order that he might have some place to lay his head. Later I helped him build a bedstead out of goods boxes in the back of the store. Secretly I had an eye to my own comfort and safety. In sickly seasons when worn to the nub and sorely in need of sleep, I could steal away and bury my troubles in that straw tick.

One night Urshel and I attended a party in a sod house at the border of the salt plains. This was my introduction to frontier society. We found a typical gathering of country boys and girls clothed in homespun and robust hilarity. After playing everything possible in pinched quarters, somebody suggested games in the open. The moon was shining with a soft, faint glow, ready to carry youthful fantasy far afield. But for the time being, romancing was out of the question. There would be plenty of time after the gregarious urge had spent its force and opened the way for that peculiar pleasure which reaches perfection when lovers are left alone.

After a few rounds at Drop-the-Handkerchief, it was

agreed that we should Crack-the-Whip. Through some strange coincidence I became the whip-cracker. A buxom young cowgirl, after a few skillful swirls executed with breath-taking speed, slung me in a buffalo wallow. Nonchalantly I recovered my composure and came out of the "wallow" with two broken ribs. Naturally, while I was a bit backward in society, this experience did not immediately set me forward.

Anyone who knows how to look can still find the buffalo pock marks in the unplowed short-grass country where these vanished denizens of the plains rolled the flies off and sanded the sweat from their robes before seeking shelter under the cottonwoods, where they might cool their laboring bellies and bury their expanded nostrils in coveted water holes.

That night on the way home from this party on the plains, a young couple, driving the trail immediately behind us, lost control of their bronchos and plunged their buggy tongue through the top of our vehicle, which had been let down so that we could enjoy the moon. Straightening out the wreck, we decided that they, too, had gone out for moonshine. It was of such a potency it had ladened their breath, limbered their tongues, destroyed their co-ordination, and released their inhibitions.

I loved the plain country people. Their language was simple and direct and their words often original. Their vocabulary was limited, but always adequate. They talked of everything, from religion to ridge poles, from household drudgery to animal husbandry, from the killing of hogs to the harvesting of grain, from the weaving of rugs to the canning of vegetables, from the coming of babies to the breeding of livestock. There was nothing within the scope of their comprehension that they could not discuss in plain terms without embarrassment.

Often the pioneer on the Middle Border was shockingly profane with no thought of profanity in his consciousness. The art of speech in the wide-open spaces needed emphasis and amplification. This is easily understood when we take into account the fact that it was designed not only for the purpose of conveying thought to untutored fellow beings but for the control of domesticated animals, including hard-headed mules and hungry hounds. The latter often became so insensitive to cuss words and corncobs that some good ranch wife originated the little corndodgers known as "hush puppies." She learned that a passel of these pacifiers thrown out of the back door would quiet the pack until they came again under the noisy spell of hunger. A dog not on the trail following his nose is apt to listen to his stomach. Unfortunately, the passing of ox drivers, mule skinners, and honest-to-God cowboys, and the coming of "hush puppies" have weakened frontier language.

The pioneer woman, competent and secure even with her husband away riding the fence or plowing the field, always intrigued me and stood high among my treasured contacts. I have never ceased to regret that Jo Davidson's pioneer woman was not chosen for the Marland pedestal at Ponca City. The Bryant Baker figure in a vigorous stride carrying her Bible and leading her son is both inspiring and stimulating, but the stooped, sinewy body of Jo Davidson's pioneer woman peering from under her deep sunbonnet and waving her handkerchief as though to divert the deadly swoop of a designing hawk captured my admiration and approval. How often on my country rounds had I seen her in those homely habiliments scanning the sky in the face of an approaching storm, trying to determine her barnyard strategy in behalf of her chicks and goslings. She needed no United States Weather Bureau. Out of her imagination the black and white flags went up and down according to her interpretation of the signs in the sky. Yet there was nothing imaginary about her weather sense. The barnyard fry were put up or turned out according to her incredible judgment. Upon other occasions I found her watching the distant horizon because she knew that, like a dog, the coyote followed the hunger signal and at certain seasons of the year he became the chief among the chicken thieves. At intervals during the day coyotes were apt to lie in wait for an opportune time to raid the barnyard. Her knowledge of predatory animals approached the proficiency of her weather eye. She knew how to use the shotgun and how to stretch the coveted pelt on the side of the barn. Her heart—so tender toward her own offspring and her barnyard babies—seemed never disturbed by the thought of hungry orphaned puppies in the coyote's den. As a result of her wise husbandry, her barnyard charges followed in the wake of her shadow as though envious of its close proximity to their benefactor.

Recently, while reading Christopher Morley, I was intrigued by his reference to a beautiful young woman "most remarkably coifed." Immediately I thought of my astute pioneer woman coifed in a close-fitting gingham hood, not for beauty, but for the combination of comfort and service. Beneath that coif there was a courageous spirit, confident, capable, and calculating, but always considerate.

The daily grind was hard, but these pioneering souls met it with fortitude and often with a song. Not only did they care for their own homes and help with the farm work in and out of season, but when occasion arose, they served as neighbor and nurse. When their race was run and they found it necessary to deal with death, I have been puzzled by their calm scrutinizing glance, blessed by their unfaltering courage, and inspired by their unfailing faith in the future. It was not only the doctor's duty but his privilege to steady and ease to earth the toppling temple of such souls. Young women today are made of the same physical stuff, but their souls are not seasoned by the same trials and not chastened in the same crucible. As I make rounds in Oklahoma City among silks and satins and come in contact with softened sensibilities where the sacrificial duties of womankind may be skillfully sidestepped, often I find a secret longing in my heart for the stimulating influence of the feminine pioneers with incredible courage. It was Landor who said, "We are what suns and winds and waters make us" and it was Cowley who thought, "He lives well that has lain well hidden." Chesterton wrote, "The gift of loneliness is the gift of freedom." The pioneer woman seasoned by winds and suns and waters and well hidden from the world was truly blessed with the "gift of freedom."

We cannot forget a rotund, transplanted British bachelor with John Bullish physiognomy, exhibiting rosy cheeks and round, sparkling eyes, full of interest and innate kindness. He lived in a beautiful cove under cool cottonwoods flanked by elms, redbud, and plum brush. I recall going to this delightful spot in blossom time for lamb and peas, tea and talk. This unusual man in a setting strangely foreign to his native habitat took me on long journeys across the sea with never a word to disclose his intimate past or his strange presence in this out-of-the-way haven. Under the influence of his warm heart and shining face all else was forgotten.

In time a bank was opened at Jet, and the cashier brought his wife and children and a piano. They lived across the street from me, and the attractive little girls were my constant delight. Though I was in love with the melody of the meadow and the music of the stars, those piano keys, responding to untaught fingers, were like voices from a long-lost past; a consciousness of something strangely sweet I had left behind. This chastening influence was continued when my brother came to take charge of the bank and brought his own delightful family.

CHAPTER XIV

The Profligate Plains

IN the early days the unplowed plains stretched away in limitless reaches beyond the far-flung horizons where vision failed and where imagination carried on with eager curiosity. It is difficult to think of anything more fascinating than this boundless space as the red man's one-time Happy Hunting Ground, carpeted with native grasses perennially cropped by teeming herds of buffalo, antelope, and deer. It had been only a few decades since the white man came upon the scene, usurped the land, and killed for gain.

The plains in Oklahoma, occupying a part of the most stimulating climatic belt on this hemisphere, supplied exciting variations in unparalleled degree. Climate is nothing more than weather, and regardless of locality it must cover twelve months in the year in order to be properly appraised. To live in Oklahoma and meet the weather month after month and year after year, one must be keenly alive. Emphatically the seasons declare themselves, and a certain degree of alertness and resourcefulness is necessary to make the most of them. It is easy for a vigorous young man to grow languid and die early where it requires a calendar to tell when Christmas comes. But not so in this temperamental zone.

The enchanting panorama covering the watershed of the Arkansas rises westward to the Black Mesa of Cimarron County. The streams draining this vast area are hedged with low native elms bowing to the prevailing winds and overshadowed by towering cottonwoods, silhouetting their gray branches against the cobalt blue of the sky. Hugging the banks of streams and canyons below the cottonwoods and elms are thickets of redbud, black haw, wild plum, and willows.

In spite of hawks, coyotes, and skunks the open plains served as a haven for prairie chicken and quail. In a swift staccato glide, with long stationary ears like sails on a light bark in a sharp gale, the jackrabbits skimmed the sea of waving grass, as if Poseidon ruled the plains. To see deer ducking gracefully as soon as sighted was not uncommon; a streak of antelope moving across the horizon with incredible speed was something never to be forgotten. Always it was intriguing to imagine the enigmatic intimacies of nature in the grass below the line of vision and to speculate about the harmony of life beyond the realm of audibility.

In springtime the prairie-brown of winter turned to green, and the wild flowers peeped through the spreading verdure. Seeking the sunny patches of short grass, the white and lavender anemones, half concealed, spread their delicate colors. These with the purple and cream-colored lupines were among the first to appear. Cattle on the range respectfully grazed around the latter as they stretched their fronds through the clean grass to make a floral pattern resembling the long graceful racemes of wistaria.

When the redbud, the plum brush, and the black haw unfolded their fragrant color along every swale and stream, lovers of nature could not escape spontaneous exultation. As I traversed the verdant plains in the roseate glow of early morning, in the vitalizing light of midday, or in the crimson flush of sunset with its far-flung afterglow, I was glad to be alive. At such times it was good to let the landscape soak in. I have always wished that Robert Louis Stevenson could have seen Oklahoma at certain seasons of the year. With beauty in mind he once said, "Why have Americans been so unfair to their own country?" He would have loved the profusion of wild flowers in spring and the limitless reaches of the trackless snow in winter. Hesiod, Horace, and Virgil would have prized the simple rural ways and the antique virtues of life on the plains.

In my buggy I carried a bird book and tried to identify the many different species as they came to enjoy the Oklahoma springtime and to charge the air with vernal impulses. Though I had no hope of becoming an Audubon, I learned much and developed an appreciation of my feathered friends which otherwise would have been lacking.

Occasionally when we were on the road to greet the quivering dawn and to see the first rays of the rising sun cut across the horizon, the prairie's mighty load of dewy loveliness temporarily imprisoned by acres of jeweled cobwebs was seen delicately lacing God's primeval grasses. At times when I have been driving city lanes, this picture has flashed before me with a nostalgic longing, and I have wondered if the doctor in me, so occupied with the sick, was charging any losses against the questionable city gains.

The plains in summertime, though more exacting, were no less intriguing. This was the testing time for the farmer's endurance, faith, and philosophy. All the promises of spring hinged upon drought or rain, and only God knew what the winds might ultimately bring. If the drought came and hot winds marched across the land, their blasting breath caused the succulent crops to wither. If rain came, the cornfields evolved like magic with ever increasing verdure, shading almost to black in the depths of their sunlit vitality. The vast wheat fields turned to gold, and caressed by gentle breezes, they were swayed by fascinating undulations throughout the immeasurable circle of expanding peripheries. To become a part of the interminable sweep of flowing fields ready for the harvest was to be steeped in the all-pervading sense of poetry.

Autumn slipped upon the scene like a pleasant dream gradually changing the verdant plains to varied hues of bronze and the shifting opalescence of topaz. At this time of the year with rare exception we were living in a garden of plenty. On the rolling plains Nature had reigned supreme for centuries. Yet it required the coming of the covered wagon, the people of the plow, the dugout, and the sod house, and the turning of the turf to insure provender, grain, and cotton in abundance. This transformation approached the magical, but not without sweat and blood in intimate contact with virgin soil.

It is difficult to pass this season of the year without a word about the abashless firmament with its fabulous array of inquisitive stars. On long night drives with my silent spotted ponies, often we seemed to be as solitary "as a lonely Obelisk in a desert." But the gift of imagination was so enhanced by the beauty of the night and the close proximity of the firmament that I was able to forget time and space and to accept my hardships as incidental and unimportant.

The winters brought stretches of glorious open weather for the enjoyment of frugal husbandry and the bounty of the land while making ready for spring. But occasionally rude northers bore down upon the plains apparently oblivious to the fact that only a few barbed wires were stretched between the denizens of the prairie and the furies of the North Pole. The wind, whizzing south with cruel reality, was sufficiently ethereal to pass the wire fence barbs unharmed. Life on the Middle Border was unknown when it was written "The Lord tempers the wind to the shorn lamb." Regardless of his religious beliefs, no experienced Oklahoma pioneer would have risked his lamb, shorn or unshorn, on the north line of his claim when Boreas was loosed "and the snow hurled under Arcturus." Sometimes a norther was "dry," hence only uncomfortable; but the one bringing snow was to be feared and respected.

Once when this merciless force had made the east and west highways impassible with deep snowdrifts and shunted the cattle against the south fence in search of shelter, I was trying to keep faith with the stork. Having cut across fields to avoid drifts on the highway, we were making uncertain progress over the trackless snow when suddenly the ponies plunged almost out of sight. They had fallen in a small canyon concealed by the sifting snow under the leveling influence of the wind. Hurriedly unhitching, I rescued the ponies, backed the buggy to safety, and made a new start. Winter often brought similar hazards to pioneer physicians on the plains while farmers were sitting by the fire feeling sorry for livestock on the range and lamenting the necessity of feeding and milking.

It may be said, by way of compensation, that the pioneers free from effeminate aestheticism are mentally and physically more competent because of conflict with the rigorous conditions of the frontier.

CHAPTER XV

My Horses

AMONG the horses on the farm when I was a boy the old gray mare and her annual foal in apple-blossom time stand out prominently. With the exception of a few days out for maternity, the old mare daily carried my father and me from field to field and from tenant to tenant, as the seasons and the direction of the work demanded. In that day nothing could have been more important than the transportation she supplied and the colts she produced. My faithful little mare at Big Rock on Dyers Creek, Tennessee, was among the last of her foals.

Already the reader has been introduced to this lovable creature and to my companionable Indian ponies. Although the latter were never anybody's prize winners, with intuitive sagacity they carried me from hut to hovel day and night with never a full day's leisure. But as time passed, they grew indifferent to both word and whip. Perhaps this was old age coming on rather than crass indifference. My cousin who came out from Kentucky to spend the summer noticed their devastating indifference, and being accustomed to swift equine response, he determined to wake them up. One day while I made ready for a country call, he volunteered to hitch up the ponies. Soon I heard a great commotion and looked out to find buggy and team whizzing around the corner in a cloud of dust. My cousin Percy, sitting erect, was triumphantly prodding the ponies with a sharp nail in the end of a broomstick. For a long time I carried this goad under the buggy seat and occasionally used it when the exigencies of practice demanded speed. But never did I resort to this questionable expedient until I had made sure nobody was looking. Those who think this prodding was cruel should know how Indian ponies were brought up. Early they became innured to the spurs they could not flee, and the heavy loads they could not escape. Relatively speaking, they became pachydermous. I loved the languid little devils, and as they grew more decrepit, they were left in their stalls or turned out to pasture for long periods of rest. Livery teams took their place, and finally Old Billy balkingly came on duty. Although these lazy pintos were sometimes backward about going forward, they never lacked courage when emergency demanded or when danger threatened. Certainly they belong with Weelum MacLure's faithful Jess, Stonewall Jackson's Little Sorrel, and Robert E. Lee's immortal Traveler.

One night I took a team of treacherous grays from the livery stable and went on a long drive. I had been warned and urged to watch these spirited roughnecks, but that night on the way home inadvertently I fell asleep. Awakened by the unusual velocity of the careening vehicle, I found the reins had slipped from my hands and disappeared over the dashboard. The ponies in pandemonium were speeding down a long hill as though powered by a turbine. While I was wondering what to do, one of the mares kicked out of the traces, hung one leg over the buggy tongue, and fell in the middle of the road. Her fall brought a momentary halt and gave me a chance to jump for life and grab the bits before the wild brutes could regain their hazardous momentum. This episode taught me a lesson, but in time my shattered confidence in common horseflesh was retored by a rare bit of equine equanimity and devotion. I learned much about the value of patience and kindness from an unpedigreed, unwanted animal with an unusual store of common sense.

As I have related, Old Billy came to me in payment of a bad debt. When I brought him into the livery stable, Uncle Joe, who took care of my ponies and knew something about every "critter" in the community, knocked my mounting pride into a cocked hat by saying, "Where did you get that balky horse?"

MY HORSES

I replied, "On a bad debt," and silently reflected, "A balky horse in hand is better than a fleeing debtor." But Uncle Joe's stinging remark possessed the ring of authenticity and explained why the owner had been so ready to part with a good-looking horse in payment of a relatively small obligation.

One day when nobody was looking, I hitched the balking bay to a single buggy and cautiously drove away. Having grown up with horses on a farm in Kentucky, I felt that it was embarrassing to be beaten in a trade, even when gambling on a bad debt. But there was some comfort in the thought that nobody could be expected to spot a balky horse loosely tied behind a wagonload of household goods. Now that I had Old Billy in harness, I would soon know the truth. My well-grounded fear caused me to drive east, where for a long distance a smooth, slightly descending road made it unnecessary to stretch a trace. Knowing that of all undisciplined animals a balky horse is the best showman, I was trying to get out of town without creating a scene.

Everything was lovely until we started up a sandy hill. As soon as the tugs lost their slack and the collar settled snugly against Old Billy's reluctant shoulders, his ears assumed an ominous backward turn and he skillfully executed a familiar weaving movement, accurately synchronized with his tossing head. Immediately I recognized his actions as the work of an artist. My first impulse was to use the whip, but I knew whipping would fail. Likewise, my experience had taught me that building a fire under him would never quench his balking spirit and that it might move him forward only enough to burn the buggy. Conscious of the futility of whipping, cursing, and burning, I decided to surprise him by leaving the whip in its socket and cooly withholding profanity. Having definitely adopted this policy, I casually crawled out of the buggy to talk things over with him face to face, as man to man. After I patted him on the neck and gently stroked his nose and whispered kind words in his ear, he became quiet and nuzzled the palm of my hand. Believing we had reached an understanding, I climbed back in the buggy and Old Billy went up the hill. After that we traveled together night and day for four years, with never a rift. There seemed to be a mutual understanding and a sincere regard for each other's welfare.

As time passed, I was convinced that Old Billy was always looking out for me. He had an unusual store of good sense which enabled him to negotiate difficult roads successfully, to anticipate approaching traffic, and to avoid undue hazards. As mutual confidence grew, I counted on him for night driving, and after all my calls were made, I would go to sleep, trusting him to take me home. Often I would be awakened by his coming to a halt at the water trough in the town square or at the stable door. When sick calls kept me going day and night to the point of physical exhaustion, this confidence in Old Billy, combined with an innate faith in Providence, gave added sleep and helped to keep me on the road.

On one occasion I was awakened by a sudden halt and was surprised to find we were standing, not at the public watering trough or the stable door, but at the side of a country road. While I was rubbing my sleepy eyes and trying to make up my mind what to do about this doubtful action on the part of my faithful pal, a farm wagon emerged from a narrow cut where passing was impossible, and Billy, with an obvious air of self-esteem, turned in behind the wagon and resumed his usual gait.

One night after heavy rains, we were on an infrequently traveled cross-country road when a sudden stop wrenched me from a deep slumber into a state of startled alertness. Peering through the darkness, I found that we were in open, level country, and there seemed to be no reason for such an abrupt halt; but Billy refused to move forward and when threatened with the whip reluctantly tried to turn out of the road to the right. Further investigation revealed a bad washout around a small culvert. On the right there was a poorly marked, rather hazardous detour, which apparently he preferred not to try without my inspection and approval.

In the spring of 1905, during a heavy sleet which turned

to snow, I was on a long night call, and in spite of unusual hazards along the way and the necessity of crossing a newly constructed jerkwater railroad track, I had succumbed to fatigue and was sound asleep, when a sudden, severe wrench, followed by a sense of speedy flight and a rushing noise, rudely awakened me. Old Billy had dashed precipitately down an embankment, barely saving me from destruction by the night train, which came out of the weather-ridden darkness without a warning light or the sound of a crossing signal. Later, I learned that sagging, sleet-laden telephone wires had wrecked the train's antiquated headlight, and the engineer, in an effort to keep his schedule, was deliberately flirting with fate.

One night, after bringing a sand-hill baby into the world, I had to cross the Salt Fork of the Arkansas at an unfamiliar ford before I could get well on the way home. While the young mother was in the throes of her reproductive crisis, the elements were on a stampede. Wind and rain were penetrating every crack and cranny in the crude little shack, and on the outside we could hear the fragile branches of the cottonwoods crashing in the storm.

On the way out I had noticed the wide, sandy bed of the Salt Fork stretching away like a miniature Sahara with a narrow ribbon of water hugging a forty-foot bluff on the south bank. On the north, a low sandy bottom, shaded by friendly cottonwoods and native elms hedged the river bed. As I drove away from the house, I hoped that the thirsty sand had swallowed up all the rain; but when I reached the ford, the river was bank full. Although the night obscured the racing flood, there was audible evidence of the treacherous caldron. I recalled a team of mules swallowed up by the quicksand of the South Canadian, and as I sat in the inky blackness, contemplating the similarity of the two river beds, wondering whether we could escape the hazards of the flood and find the one possible landing on the south side which would enable us to negotiate the otherwise impassable bluff, I experienced a feeling of utter dependence upon Old Billy. He was willing to try, so I gave him the bit.

After what seemed to be an interminable period of floundering across rapidly shifting sandbars beneath the seething flood of deep currents which had driven me to a perch on the back of the buggy seat, Old Billy came to a halt, and by peering through the darkness over his head, I saw the dim outline of the ominous bluff and experienced a sinking sense of failure. But the rushing water was dynamic; there was no time for contemplation. Obviously Old Billy wanted to go downstream. It was up to me to marshal my wits and consider the consequences. Was he exhibiting good horse sense, following his primitive instinct, or was he blindly yielding to the current and accepting the line of least resistance? Because of my resignment to fate and my abiding faith in his intuitive sagacity, I acquiesced and offered no further guidance.

While I was still stunned by the exigencies of the situation, my despair was turned to joy when Old Billy suddenly swung to the left and lunged for the deep cut in the bluff which carried us up to the low plateau. Having once reached the top, we were greeted by a luscious carpet of buffalo grass, the plainsman's constant friend, come flood or famine. As we traveled on with a mutual sense of gratifying accomplishment, there was a rift in the clouds and the stars seemed strangely near, as though with hushed approval they were coming down to acknowledge our success and express their pleasure.

If space would permit, many other examples of Old Billy's intelligence and perseverance might be cited, but what has been said is sufficient to show that his reaction to environment was almost human and always helpful. Only those who know horses and have spent much time with them in silent places can appreciate the inherent possibilities of mutual understanding and companionship. When I gave up country practice and permitted the automobile to replace Old Billy, I suffered a distinct loss. He was placed with a good farmer on a pension which provided pasture in summer and feed and shelter in winter. But I always feared that he missed me and that his life might be monotonous without the opportunity to do my bidding.

Old Billy always took me where I wanted to go

Fording the North Fork of the Canadian

In retrospect, it is easy for me to imagine him standing ready for service, amenable to any reasonable request and responsive to the slightest touch of the rein. Often I think of him as he appeared after a brisk thunder shower, with hair plastered to his skin, accentuating the sculptured lines so cleanly chisled by the slanting rays of the returning sun. This striking picture recalled the story of Michelangelo, who, when engaged to design a pedestal for the equestrian statue of Marcus Aurelius, was so impressed with the Emperor's magnificent mount, he slapped him in the flank and said, *"cammina"* (Gee-up).

If, perchance, some day I should encounter the shade of this long-lost friend, I would expect to hear the familiar whinny, which, on our nightly rounds, always greeted me as I emerged from the lonely farmhouse. Even though he was restless from having waited at the hitching post, this greeting never lost the sympathetic note of genuine friendship and affection.

CHAPTER XVI

The Transition

AFTER six years on the plains with only three months away for postgraduate studies, I was in need of a brain dusting and the refurbishment of my intellectual furniture and the addition of new experiences. With vague ambitions tugging at my heart, the lonely drives on starlit nights helped to bring a crystallization of plans for travel and opportunities to catch up with scientific progress. Finally the desire for a broader foundation for my professional pursuits embraced a plan for two years at the University of Virginia followed by two years abroad. With this program in view, I gave up country practice, and with a sense of uncertainty, said good-bye to the plain people I had learned to love and respect.

Unfortunately my studies at the University of Virginia, where I had planned to lay a good foundation for my work abroad, were interrupted by the serious illness of my mother. Her long-continued invalidism wrecked my ambitious plans, and after spending many weeks at her bedside, I located in Louisville, Kentucky, only seventy miles away from our home, so that I could observe the course of her slow convalescence and be available when needed.

Here I was favored with the friendship and guidance of my former professor, Dr. Philip F. Barbour, a skilled pediatrician with a rare store of diagnostic intuition and a fine sense of the patient-doctor relationship. Working with him in practice and at the medical school was stimulating, but the autumn was

THE TRANSITION

passing and the weather depressing. Ultimately my mother's improvement made it unnecessary for me to be near her, and Louisville on the verge of a long winter was enveloped in soot and fog. This narrowed my perspective, depressed my spirit, and accentuated the need of prairie sunshine.

I had suffered an attack of influenza and remained physically substandard and mentally unsettled. Having lived too long on the clean level of the plains beneath a clear sky to be happy in this murky spot on the Ohio, again I yielded to that call of the West which had brought me to Oklahoma City six years before. Looking back upon this second decision in favor of Oklahoma, I realize that even then I was beginning to believe in my own special providence which has been so obvious throughout my life. Since there is no reason for me to claim any special dispensation from above, perhaps I should say my own good luck. Often I have wondered what would have happened if my plans for study abroad had not been interrupted. Certainly life would have been different, but I have never indulged any regrets because my life has been rich and full of treasured experiences. Any gains I might have achieved necessarily would have been accompanied by distinct losses. After all, this was not choice but destiny.

My office in Oklahoma City was on Main Street, up a relatively easy stairway over a candy store. While I waited for patients, the mechanical piano in the store below played the same tune day after day. While I was once delighted by the ivory, it seemed that the monotony of this tune constantly in my ears would undermine the sensitive cells in a cortex attuned to the harmonious notes of nature and send me to the madhouse. It may be added that after having been busy in the country, I found it difficult to sit with folded hands. Yet, experience with the inevitable on the plains, plus my belief in Providence, supplied sufficient fortitude to keep hope alive. Nevertheless, sitting in a dark office across the hall from busy doctors for months, with seldom a professional call, was exasperating. Patients overflowed their reception room and peeped furtively at me as though wondering if it would be safe to make use of a strange, idle doctor rather than lose time waiting for a tired, busy one, but they remained true to their family physicians.

After each long day of waiting at the office my salvation came through contact with the kindred clan at the Southern Home, where in the twilight of just another day, hope and courage were renewed. A number of cultured young men and women who had cut loose from family ties and spurned ancestral traditions to get on with life in this new land of promise, gathered there regularly for ham, hominy, and hot biscuit, and often a bit of after-dinner harmony. No doubt it is good that such lowly things must soothe and support the intellectual pursuits of life. I was fortunate enough to have a room and a cordial welcome in the home of fellow Kentuckians not far away from this rendezvous. These friends generally employed their influence to broaden my acquaintance and forward my interests. The husband was superintendent of the city schools, and his wife was endowed with intellectual charm and rare good judgment. Although they moved away from Oklahoma City long ago, recently it was my good fortune to be able to serve them professionally.

Approximately one year was required to overcome professional handicaps because of lack of contacts and city experience. My books showed that my total income for the first year was pitifully small. As contacts grew and practice increased, I became more hopeful and more prosperous, but still the way seemed very dubious, and often I pined for my ponies, my beloved prairies, and the people who believed in me and followed my instructions with a steadfast faith, unknown to physicians who have never practiced among country people. I was fortunate in that I had known the love and loyalty of log-cabin folk as well as prairie pioneers in sod houses and dugouts. It was my lot to await professional recognition patiently and to hope for the esteem so freely bestowed by my plain friends with hearts of gold. Although many years have passed and unmerited advantages have come to me, I am still missing the blessings of

THE TRANSITION

country practice. In my atempt to combat the pungent nostalgia during the long, lonely wait, I read John Burroughs, John Muir, Hamlin Garland, Francis Parkman, Robert Louis Stevenson, and David Grayson. Thus the chastening experience did not pass without compensation.

In time I joined the Pickwick Club and was subjected to its disciplinary rules. This club served as a friendly haven, and it provided a premium for professional or business success and social position, at the same time fixing cruel penalties for matrimony. On the wall of the living room there was a large placard known as the graveyard, with lines cutting it into approximate squares or burying plots for each member, with room for cruel epitaphs in case he decided to surrender his bachelor's degree. When my time came, I was given a rough burial below a crude tombstone, and I can speak with feeling about the funerals for the living.

I was placed on the staff of Saint Anthony's Hospital and given a minor teaching position on the faculty of the struggling young medical school. Having had some special training in diseases of children and a short service at the New York Infant Asylum, I aspired to enter the rising specialty of pediatrics, but to my surprise I found a fellow Kentuckian, who was to become one of my best friends, already on the ground. Although Oklahoma City now has more than twenty pediatricians, then I thought one would be enough for a lifetime. I lived to treasure this pioneer pediatrician as with rare skills and perspicuity he cared for the community's children, including my own and ultimately some of my grandchildren.

I decided upon general practice, but after a short time, Drs. Blesh and Reed, already well known in the field of surgery, moved to Oklahoma City. I had referred work to them from Jet, and gladly I shared offices with them when the prospect of greater opportunities brought them from Guthrie to Oklahoma City. This association placed new obligations upon me and led to a decision to give attention to internal medicine with special emphasis on lungs and heart.

As time passed, cases of tuberculosis in young adults frequently presented grave problems. Having discarded the longtime belief that the person afflicted with tuberculosis should get across a state line under the unwarranted hope of a quick climatic cure, I was facing new duties in my chosen field. I could not conscientiously wash my hands of responsibility and say, "Go West." The majority of my patients were single young men and women far away from home and in need of much more than mere medicine in the literal sense. They wanted friendship and psychological support, and occasionally they needed financial aid. The physician is not fulfilling his mission until he understands the patient and his environment as well as his disease. I became intensely interested in these unfortunate people, and whenever possible, I placed them under home management approximating sanatorium care. They were put to bed on sleeping porches or in improvised bunks outside bedroom windows or wherever even crude facilities could be provided. The difficulties of securing good food, reconciling friends and other contacts who were justifiably concerned about exposure to the disease, and overcoming the patient's fears pointed to the need of local sanatorium care which would provide a more favorable environment and a more wholesome psychological outlook.

In a rented house with a nurse in charge of ten beds, these ends were accomplished. The institution provided approved management for the patient, helped to educate the people of Oklahoma about the disease and its dangers, and slowed down the costly, often hopeless, trek across state lines in search of climate where the patients had to face the loneliness common in a strange, far-away country. Gradually, the sanatorium was enlarged to meet increasing demands.

Thus, through the slow evolution of what might be termed manifest destiny, I was practicing internal medicine with a special interest in diseases of the chest. This meant that I was gradually acquiring a working familiarity with what was known in my chosen field, and I was learning more and more about the mysteries of medicine in general.

CHAPTER XVII

Vienna

IN 1909 I entered the University of Vienna for graduate study. At this time Vienna was the world's focus for postgraduate medical students. This school had placed in operation the first clinic on German soil. Starting with twelve beds in the middle of the eighteenth century, it had progressed through ups and downs to its position of world-wide renown. Its original stimulus came from Hermann Boerhaave and the Leyden school, through Gerald Van Swieten and Anton de Haen. After a period of success followed by a decline, it was rejuvenated in the first half of the nineteenth century by the clinico-pathological and diagnostic advances made in the Parisian school.

Working in contact with mature students from all parts of the world and coming with them under some of the greatest teachers of the time, I was gaining a medical perspective not within the compass of prairie practice. Though it was not clearly evident to me at the time, it was a realization of what I had vaguely dreamed of as I followed my ponies on the plains.

Not only was I coming under the spell of my teachers, but unconsciously I was absorbing the school's traditions and profiting by the work of Skoda, Maximilian Stoll, Auenbrugger, and, indirectly Bichat, Bayle, Louis, and Laënnec of the French school, as well as many others.

It was an exciting time for the student of medicine. The recently acquired science of bacteriology was initiating unprecedented progress, disclosing the cause of many diseases with the possibility of more scientific management and always the probability of specific therapy.

It was gratifying to note that physicians refused to let material progress obscure their sympathetic concern for human welfare. With all the scientific advances and mechanical aids to diagnosis and treatment and the promise of ever greater revelations, they were always on the alert, and the graduate students greeted each new day with a spirit of eager curiosity and hopeful anticipation.

In the last decade of the nineteenth century the American Medical Association of Vienna was organized by Dr. James W. Ellis of Richmond, Virginia. Dr. Ellis found that many American doctors could not speak German and as a result much time was lost in getting them properly oriented. He believed that through organized effort much good could be accomplished; and, indeed, the success of this movement was phenomenal. We found this association most helpful. Through its headquarters, its registration system, its library and subpost office, many American doctors received valuable services and were spared much confusion.

Most of the American doctors who sought postgraduate studies in Vienna had long since established their philosophy regarding "all work and no play." Consequently, this same resourcefulness led them to the beer gardens and coffeehouses where harmless conviviality gave rise to unrestrained communications. These sessions often resulted in the exchange of valuable ideas and the growth of lasting friendships.

After some experience in the wards, I was surprised to see how hospital patients were managed by some of my professors. Often it seemed that even the best among the clinicians were more interested in the diagnosis than they were in the welfare of the patient. While they were proud of therapeutic success, they looked forward to autopsies with eager anticipation, especially in obscure cases. It was said that every patient gaining admission to the hospital signed an authorization for postmortem examination in case of death.

VIENNA

Considering this provision and the fact that at that time Vienna was the world's rendezvous for postgraduate medical students, perhaps this attitude toward the ultimate diagnosis, whether at the bedside or in the dead room, should be looked upon with an added degree of tolerance. From an educational standpoint the practice was profitable.

My time was spent chiefly in the wards and in the dead room. For the first time I was given a chance to correlate symptoms with pathology, to study disease in the light of its damage to tissues and organs. I was intrigued by the ability manifested by some of my teachers as they discovered, observed, and interpreted symptoms and signs, diagnosed disease, and predicted pathological changes. Often their powers and their skills proved to be incredibly keen. In the dead room where we saw several autopsies nearly every day we had a chance to appraise accurately the diagnostic acumen of our teachers.

While pathologists are exceptionally honest, it may be said that they are equally ruthless. Often they seem to take delight in the exhibition of the diagnostician's mistakes. But this is a natural consequence of their task. They are dealing with the lifeless body, the cold, impersonal flesh after all the defensive mechanisms have departed. Upon the authority of the victim's relatives or the court the pathologist can explore every crevice and cranny without objection or resistance. without the least vital response. How dull his life would be if he could not elicit some response from the attending physician. After all, there is a question as to which one is missing the most. Occasionally through a wrong interpretation of symptoms and signs the physician may miss the true diagnosis while the pathologist must always miss the spark of life. The physician finds many things for which the pathologist may search in vain, no matter how accurate his autopsy findings may be, namely courage and hope or depression and despair. There are no such satisfactions or disappointments in the dead room after life and personality have departed. But only through the frank and friendly controversies of the clinician and the pathologist over the ante-mortem and post-mortem findings can medicine arrive at serviceable concepts of disease.

My most highly valued clinical teacher was Professor Hermann Schlesinger. He was followed in the wards with the greatest enthusiasm because of his quiet, sympathetic approach to the patient and his comprehension of the human body's response to disease. He was richly endowed with what Oliver Wendell Holmes called "intuitive sagacity," yet he was not dependent upon such uncanny skills. His comprehensive knowledge of the ills which assail the flesh was so obvious and so impressive, his analytical powers so keen, and his presentations so clear that he invariably gained the admiration of both his humble pupils and his hopeful patients.

The famous anatomist Professor Tandler, who had succeeded Zuckerkandl in his field, seemed to be endowed with similar knowledge and skill. In his classes on regional anatomy, standing confidently before the cadever, he could tell in the most minute detail not only what a few strokes of the knife would reveal, but with a few scraps of colored chalk he could draw swiftly an accurate picture of what he would find if it was "as nature intended." Upon one occasion he indicated that he seldom attempted to show the normal lung because from the very beginning of extra-uterine life, the lung is exposed to the varied insults of environment and soon exhibits the resulting scars. In this connection he impressed us with the fact that we begin to die as soon as we are born and that even with minor injuries and infections certain cells pass forever and, if it were not for abundant reserves and marvelous restorative powers, the span of life would be much shorter than it is.

Under Carl Von Noorden and Wilhelm Falta, I learned something of the mysteries of metabolic disturbances, and never have I emerged from the enigmatic spell they cast upon me.

In the pathological department where Anton Ghon and Oskar Stoerk adroitly searched for the secrets of disease and revealed their devious ways, I learned much. Ghon was completing his work on the primary lung focus or what we now call the first infection phase of tuberculosis, chiefly conducted at St. Anne's Children's Hospital in Vienna and later published under the title *The Primary Lung Focus in Children*. His findings constituted an important advance in our knowledge of tuberculosis.

Rapidly I was learning how completely wrecked the body may be before the long-suffering soul takes flight. I could better understand how Keats and Francis Thompson could live virtually without lungs and yet be poetically sound. Also I was learning that in certain cases death may ensue when there is little or no pathology to be found. Yet the lamp of life was seldom extinguished by the natural process of growing old and coming to the end because of a gradual decline. While it is most interesting to make careful inspections of the gross changes in the organs of the body and, if need be, follow them to the microscope for more meticulous examination, I prefer to see people alive. Considering all the ills that assail the human flesh and the continuous snuffing of the candle by accidents on the highways, along the airways, and in industry, and perhaps we should add war, when we do find a body grown old in a state of fair preservation, we can agree, "Strange that a harp of a thousand strings should keep in tune so long." With increasing longevity and the growing interest in geriatrics, soon we should know more about the mechanism of growing old. It requires more than old age pensions to keep the harp in tune.

Under the guidance of such authorities as Ghon and Stoerk, it was most interesting to check clinical and dead-room findings and to prove or disprove the accuracy of bedside conclusions. Here I learned never to be satisfied with the discovery of a single pathological condition in the living patient. The diagnostic search must be directed toward every organ of the body with the understanding that the finding of multiple pathological conditions in one individual is quite common. Seeing the demonstration of sixteen distinct diseased conditions at the autopsy of an obese middle-aged woman was sufficient to place me on guard for a lifetime.

Pirquet and Hamburger were pursuing the tuberculin test with exciting revelations. One morning we were given an impressive object lesson. A small child who had been admitted to the hospital a few weeks previously with a negative tuberculin test had shown a positive reaction to a subsequent test. She was admitted to the hospital because of an acute minor respiratory infection. There was no history of tuberculosis in her family and no evidence of previous contact, but when convalescent she had been permitted to play on the floor of the ward where an open case of pulmonary tuberculosis had been discovered. Obviously she had become infected because of this contact after her admission to the hospital. I knew of the long-time belief of the infectious nature of tuberculosis and had accepted the proof as demonstrated by Robert Koch's discovery of the tubercle bacillus in 1882. I had observed its evolution in tuberculous families, but never before had its dire significance been impressed upon me so vividly. I came away from Vienna with a much better understanding of tuberculosis and its dangers, especially where innocent children are exposed.

Professor Adolf Lorenz, whose fame had spread throughout America, was attracting much attention, and his clinics were eagerly attended by students from the United States because of his "bloodless operation" for congenital hip disease as well as other orthopedic accomplishments. He had received much publicity through his operation on the Armour child in Chicago, and students from all quarters were eager to see his work. Constantly we were going from one clinic to another in search of knowledge, and seldom was the quest disappointing.

During the fall of 1909 there seemed to be an epidemic of suicides in Vienna. Often the victims were brought into the hospital to die and to the pathological department for autopsy. Always it was interesting to try to discover the motive, the method, and the results. Extreme frustration from minor causes seemed to motivate the act in the majority of cases. Suicide among young female misfits was quite common. I recall one girl, disappointed in love, who had soaked a box of matches in a large tumbler of water in order to drink her death. Another had swallowed carbolic acid, and another who had quarreled with her mistress saturated her clothing with alcohol, touched a match to the hem of her garment, and went out in a veritable holocaust. As I look back upon these experiences I am reminded of what Robert Burton in *The Anatomy of Melancholy*, said about Democritus who was found ". . . busy at his study with a book on his knees. . . . The subject of the book was Melancholy and Madness; about him lay the carcasses of many beasts, newly by him cut up and anatomized; not that he did condemn God's creatures, as he told Hippocrates, but to find out the seat of this *Atra Bilis*, or Melancholy, whence it proceeds, and how it was engendered in men's bodies to the intent that he might better cure it in himself and by his writings and observations teach others how to prevent and avoid it."

What a worthy but hopeless ambition. The psychiatrists of today are overworked because Democritus did not find the answer. Though ultimately he destroyed his own eyesight, "the better to contemplate," he left the world without knowing why people are given to "Melancholy and Madness."

Soon after I came to Oklahoma City in 1907, I joined some friends in the purchase of a big undeveloped ranch in Grayson County, Texas. The sum was small, but it represented a good part of my savings which had been hard-earned on the plains. In making the investment, I might have been influenced by the fact that I was born in Grayson County, Kentucky. It was Grayson County that, absent-mindedly, I always scribbled on my notebooks after I went away to college. To this day while off guard my pencil may turn this trick. At any rate, I was upholding the immemorial reputation of doctors—I was gullible. I trusted new-found friends to invest my money with no guarantee of returns. I learned that the ranch deal, which was virtually consummated before I left home with the assurance that my principal would be doubled, had fallen through. I was told that the negotiations in the hands of the group's representative in Chicago had gone on the rocks because just at the wrong time he went on a prolonged spree and was incapable of attending to business when the mortgage came due, and we lost the case and our equity through foreclosure. Not only had I lost my anticipated profit which would have helped keep me in Europe for two years, but I was sans principal as well. In fact, I was in Vienna on a shoestring, and with my young wife I was facing a situation which convinced me that two cannot live as cheaply as one. But I had hope and credit, and there we remained blissfully spending against the uncertain future.

Before time for us to leave Vienna, Dr. Reed and I attended the International Congress of Surgeons in Budapest. We were happy to find our own country well represented and our own tongue probing the polyglot assembly. Looking back upon this occasion, I recall that our famous Chicago surgeon John B. Murphy and my erudite professor Lewis S. McMurtry, who had aroused my interest in tuberculosis and genius by a discussion of *David Harum,* were on the program. Both were outstanding in performance and to us they were pride-stirring figures. Dr. Murphy's exceptional presentation with spectacular demonstrations enthralled the audience, and when the presiding officer called the time according to the accepted rules, there was a universal clamor for more, even though the majority could not understand the language employed.

While Mrs. Moorman and I were still contemplating two years abroad with study in Berlin, London, and Edinburgh, the consciousness of a new life dawned upon us. We had consulted a carefully chosen obstetrician and all was going well. Daily we discussed the advisability of a natal day in Vienna or a return for birth in our native land. Finally we decided to give up the two-year plan and return to America. But the physician we had engaged refused to give his consent on the grounds that we had waited too long. Not content with this decision I secured an appointment with the famous Dr. Schauta. Apprised of the situation, he put a friendly arm around my shoulders and said, "Young man, secure passage on the largest boat available, take your wife, and go on home." The next day I was fortunate enough to secure reservations on the *Mauretania* and soon we were on the high seas. It was an unusually rough trip, but by keeping the prospective mother in bed, we were whole and hearty when the Statue of Liberty appeared as our godmother. After we landed, I breathed a prayer for America and entrained for Oklahoma City where we waited not only for the anticipated time but for a month longer than the Vienna obstetrician had predicted.

In view of what has happened to Vienna since the beginning of World War II, I believe that these paragraphs from an old professor of mine, written after World War I, are of sufficient interest to warrant their inclusion in this chapter. The old teacher's philosophical remarks emphasize the penalties of war and the resulting decline of a world-renowned center for medical education.

"Dr. Reed has perhaps informed you how I have fared since you left Vienna. One seldom reaches the biblical age unpunished.

"The disease of our time, Bolshevism, has also caught hold in Vienna. Everywhere the germs have been scattered, into England (coal miners' strike), into Central America, into China and Australia. Here in Austria it has found an especially fertile soil and is constantly spreading and gaining strength. Everyone runs to the red apostles of the new religion of Lenin's, and especially the women number among the most inspired followers for the new theorem. Even the grand-daughter of the Kaiser, Arch-Duchess Elizabeth, Princess of Windischgratz, has become revolutionist-socialist, has renounced all titles, and has stuck the red rose in her lapel. There is no communistic assembly from which she is absent. Vienna is not prospering under the blue star of Bolshevism. Industry is constantly going backwards and the number of unemployed at the same time going forward. The mental workers are especially bad off, and to give *one* example, here in Vienna among the practicing physicians, *one thousand* are unable to buy enough bread for themselves, wives and children out of their professional earnings, and must therefore seek side earnings. One fears that many university professors will leave Vienna and go where richer laboratories and other teaching facilities are offered. So has our famous Professor of Medicine Physiology, Dr. ———, made the resolution to emigrate to the Berlin University because here they *will not* or *cannot* provide the necessary means for the execution of his research work."

In the light of what has happened, we wonder what this old philosopher would think today.

The Southern Home
I am at the extreme left on the porch

CHAPTER XVIII

Sparks from the Grindstone

I returned to Oklahoma City from Vienna with renewed confidence and a strong desire to put to work my newly acquired knowledge in the prevention, discovery and treatment of disease. As the years passed, experience accumulated and responsibilities grew, but I discovered over and over again that the daily grind of a doctor's life is colored by recurring humor and pathos and that the relationship between patient and physician is not without rich rewards. In order that the reader may share this interesting part of a doctor's life, I have chosen a few episodes to relate here.

One afternoon I was called to come quickly to a little cottage on the east side of town where a young woman was having a hemorrhage from the lungs. To be prepared for any contingency, I carried my pneumothorax machine with which to introduce air for collapse of the lung if necessary. When I arrived, two men in worn Prince Albert coats bowed out of the scene. At the bedside on a chair there was a washpan containing blood. The pillowcase was spotted, and the floor was spattered. Apparently there was no immediate danger of death, and I seemed to sense a tense, if not belligerent, attitude on the part of the patient, who evidently had committed her welfare to the faith healers who had left the house as I entered. While pondering her psychology, I made a physical examination, careful not to arouse nervous strain or to permit physical effort for fear of a recurrence of the hemorrhage which temporarily was under control.

Having made up my mind about what was going on in her head as well as in her chest and what should be done about it, I expressed sympathy and offered reassurance with the hope of full co-operation. I explained the danger of a severe hemorrhage which might prove fatal and suggested the introduction of air for collapse of the lung in order to control the bleeding. Then her troubled response revealed the state of mind that I had suspected: "I have decided to let God take care of me." Respecting her sincerity, recognizing the turmoil in her soul, and realizing our mutual predicament, I pointed out that according to the Bible there is only one God and that necessarily her God must be my God, too. I urged her to credit my interest in her welfare and to accept my belief that God might have sent me to serve as an instrument in His hands. Furthermore, I said, "If you do not accept my advice, you may have another hemorrhage and lose your life before I could reach you, even though I were available at the moment. Wouldn't you like to have all the security I can offer in the name of your God?" With a complete change of expression she looked into my face and said, "If you feel that way about it, I will do what you want me to do." The lung was collapsed, and when it was considered safe, she was transported to the state sanatorium. I had invested a good deal of time and trouble in a case regularly falling into the charity group, but the satisfaction derived was worth more than money.

Patients presenting problems such as this are legion, and they need physicians who will search the secret recesses of their souls, resolve their psychological conflicts, and take care of their physical needs. Under our present system of medical care the responsibility is a personal one. The patient's welfare is at stake, and the physician's conscience must be served.

In 1919 I saw an old gentleman who had a persistent cough with expectoration. He was in good physical condition, and his psychological response was unusual for a man of eighty-four. I learned that he had come West at twenty years of age because of tuberculosis, which had developed while he was clerking in a store in New England, and had taken up blacksmithing in

Kansas. Apparently he had fully recovered and had moved to Texas where he had been quite successful, having held an important federal appointment under President Taft. At the time of my examination he was living in Oklahoma City. The history of his case indicated that he had not been able to recover his strength after an attack of influenza in 1918. Examination revealed advanced tuberculosis, which progressed from bad to worse in spite of everything that could be done. He died of tuberculosis sixty-four years after having apparently achieved a cure. Tuberculosis is quite common in elderly individuals, and now that so many people are living longer, the disease assumes an unwonted significance.

A young woman from up in the state came to my office with her eighteenth-months-old baby in an ominous state of somnolence. Apparently the child was resting peacefully, and the mother displayed only moderate anxiety, not realizing that this semi-stupor was the forerunner of eternal sleep. The child was suffering from tuberculous meningitis, and the mother, though a former sanatorium patient, seemed strangely unaware of the sad reality.

This was before the days of streptomycin, and even the faint hope of a magic new drug could not be proffered. It was difficult for the doctor to know what to say, especially in this case because the mother would know from her own experience that in all probability she was responsible for the child's condition. Consonant with this sad possibility it was discovered that the mother had suffered an unobtrusive spread of the disease in her own lungs with a positive sputum. Always there is the danger that physician and patient may not be sufficiently vigilant after a known bout with tuberculosis. It is reported that a great physician once said, "If I could have only one prayer answered, I would pray that tuberculosis might hurt as soon as it develops."

One Sunday morning when I had planned to go to church with my family, a woman with a pleasing voice and compelling appeal called to say she had been referred to me and that while she regretted troubling me on Sunday, she traveled with her husband, and they would be on the road early the next morning. I agreed to meet them at my office. To make the story short, she was pregnant and did not welcome the condition because she wanted to be with her husband, whose territory covered five states. It was easy for her to believe she was too sick and too nervous to have a baby. My examination failed to reveal any good reason why she should not make the best of the bed she had made. Patiently I pointed out the true significance of what she wanted me to do and explained that for good ethical reasons no self-respecting doctor could conscientiously comply with her wishes. Not only did I explain the dangers connected with the interruption of pregnancy, but I went into the moral question of conception, life, and death and her responsibility as well as my own. Instead of going to church, I preached, but when we parted, I was not sure of a convert. I had admitted that she might find an unscrupulous doctor or a professional abortionist who would perform at a price, but warned her of the danger and the legal aspects of participation in such an act. She was gracious enough to thank me, but not good enough to assure me that she would keep the faith.

About twenty-two years later a handsome young man who had waited without an appointment was shown to my private office. He said, "Dr. Moorman, I am not sick, but my mother, who lives in another state, wanted me to come by and tell you that I am the result of the text and the sermon you preached that Sunday morning when my future was at stake and you were bent upon my salvation. She thought you would be proud of your evangelical powers."

A friend and one-time patient who had made a great deal of money in oil called me from an adjoining state to say that his brother living in a small Oklahoma town was very ill with pneumonia, and that he had arranged with Rock Island officials to have a special train made up at the division point in El Reno to take me to his brother as soon as possible. He had arranged for clearance all the way, so I could count on a nonstop race with death. In an empty, poorly padded passenger coach I was precariously pummeled back and forth over a distance of seventy-five miles as we clung to the curves without slackening speed. Unfortunately there was no penicillin, aureomycin, chloromycetin, or sulfa drugs in those days, and as I had anticipated, the patient was in a hopeless condition when I arrived. Too often when people become frantic about sickness, it is too late. Miracles, even in this ultrascientific day, are relatively rare.

Approximately thirty years ago when a prominent figure in national political circles, allegedly slated for a Cabinet position, was shot through the liver in a near-by city, Dr. Horace Reed and I were called in consultation. We were told to stand by for a plane which would pick us up within the hour.

In those days planes were somewhat backward about taking to the air and often equally reluctant about remaining aloft. Before we could get off for the designated landing place, another call informed us that the plane had refused to leave the ground, and we were requested to catch the first train out. When we arrived, the patient was already moribund from shock and loss of blood. He died, frantically fighting the inevitable end. Political and financial prominence made no difference in the presence of death.

Tucked away in the newspaper files, there is an exciting mystery story with jealousy and homicide staged by living characters and followed by colorful court proceedings.

An old woman living south of the Oklahoma City oil field fell ill while the wild oil well Mary Sudik was out of control. She could smell the fumes from the oil field, and she found it easy to believe that her malady was due to this "miasma." As the weeks went by, she gradually became weaker and shorter of breath, but being loath to give up, she purchased her annual batch of spring chicks. A few days after they were safely installed, a touch of blackberry winter chilled the air, and the old lady closed up the chicken house, built a coal fire in the old-fashioned monkey stove, and set the damper for a smoldering fire which she thought would radiate uniform heat throughout the night. This it did, but with the heat, ominous, odorless, death-dealing carbon monoxide was generated and diffused throughout the chicken house. In the morning three hundred of the six hundred chicks were dead. Then the woman knew her failing health was due to the gas from the oil field. If it could kill her chicks, it could make her sick. She brought suit against the oil companies for a large sum.

The case was to come before the federal court, and I was asked to examine the woman and appear as a witness. By appointment she came to my office and gave a straightforward, well-connected history, conscientiously associating her ill health with the development of the Oklahoma City oil field. She alleged that she had become so sensitive to the fumes of oil and gasoline that she seldom came to town because she thought the emanations from gasoline stations added to those from the field accentuated her trouble. My examination revealed arteriosclerosis (hardening of the arteries) with evidence of changes in the heart to account for her symptoms, and I concluded that the opening of the oil field and the spouting of the Mary Sudik had nothing to do with the illness which happened to be coincidental.

My office was equipped with gas-steam radiators supplied by natural gas just the same as that escaping from the oil wells. While she was on my examining table I put out all the lights to make sure there was no danger of accident, ignition, and explosion. Then I turned the gas on without lighting it. We were in the room together where the gas was flowing with ever increasing saturation of the atmosphere, and she made no complaint. Finally, without letting her know what was going on, I opened the windows and turned off the gas. I knew that a dose of natural gas would do no harm as long as the degree of saturation was not sufficient to cut the oxygen in the air below the level of safety. After completing my examination, I dismissed her with a mingled feeling of sadness and satisfaction. No doubt she was honest in her belief that the fumes had caused her symptoms, which were normally attributable to the coming on of old age and the associated arteriosclerosis. It appeared that this might be my one chance in a lifetime to qualify as a genuine expert witness, but fortunately for the old lady, the oil companies compromised, and the case was dismissed.

One summer about thirty years ago I was troubled because my patients were receiving disconcerting literature from an off-brand doctor who claimed that he could make a diagnosis from a drop of blood and guarantee a cure by treatment with the Abrams machine, which for a time was the quack's bonanza. I secured a piece of this proselyting literature and planned my strategy. Dr. Sherrill Caughron, then a dental student, was in my office doing routine laboratory work. Having been assured of his co-operation, I called the quack, and without revealing my identity engaged his interest in an imaginary young woman who allegedly was too ill to come to his office. He would be glad to supply a needle and blotting paper for a drop of blood, and a blank to be filled out, all on the receipt of ten dollars. The dental student, dressed in old clothes to heighten the effect of authenticity, delivered a ten-dollar bill and received the articles with instructions. Then, in accordance with our plans, he went to St. Anthony's Hospital for a drop of blood drawn daily from the old ram, known as "Kaiser Bill," in the service of the laboratory for years. However, my confederate in crime called in great distress and announced that the Kaiser's blood had already been citrated. I replied, "If it's still red enough to stain the blotting paper, it will be good enough." The specimen was delivered, and in three or four days we received a report which indicated that the old ram had syphilis, tuberculosis, and cancer. It would require so many ohms of this and that to effect a cure, and the cost would be three hundred dollars. Only this sum stood between Kaiser Bill and the Abrams machine. Often I have regretted we did not put up the three hundred and give the Kaiser a seat in the imposter's reception room and a look at the machine that had defamed his character.

Later, one of my good patients on Bonton Street said to me one morning while I was in her home on sick call, "Dr. Moorman, I feel that I should make a confession. I have done something you would not approve of." Surprised but curious, I urged her to tell the full story. She said, "I went to see Dr. —— about a diagnosis and treatment with his Abrams machine." To her surprise I said, "I can tell you just what he found; you have syphilis, tuberculosis, and cancer." With obvious chagrin she asked, "How did you know?" I replied, "Knowing what I do about the methods employed, naturally I expected a machine-made diagnosis to place the lovely lady in the same category with the battered old ram." Not only was she embarrassed by the implications of the diagnosis, but she was furious because the machine did not differentiate species and sex.

One night an oil producer requested me to go to see one of his oil-field workers who was down with pneumonia at Erick, Oklahoma. I caught the Rock Island west and was due at Erick about 2:00 A.M. My train had to pass through Clinton and Sayre before reaching Erick. At Clinton I told the porter that I was going to take a nap and charged him with the responsibility of putting me off at Erick. I must have gone sound asleep because it seemed no time until I was rudely shaken. By the time I had gotten my eyes open and recovered my bearing, the porter was way down the aisle, and it seemed that everybody was getting off. Without asking questions, I made my way to the platform, climbed into a hotel bus, and was put afoot in front of a cheap-looking hotel. Still asking no questions, I registered and went to my room expecting to call the doctor early in the morning. At 6:00 A.M. while I was eating my hot cakes and coffee at the lunch counter, it seemed necessary to ask a question. I said to the man who was doing the cooking and also serving what he cooked, "Can you tell me how I can get in touch with Dr. B——?"

"I guess you could get him over long distance. He lives in Erick."

"What place is this?"

"Oh this is Sayre. You know, there's been a wreck between here and Erick, and last night's passenger train couldn't go through." Considerably nonplused because of my unsuspected plight, I found rapid strategy imperative.

A snowstorm had blown up during the night, and the roads were slick, but I found a man with a Ford and chains who agreed to take me on to Erick. After meeting the doctor and seeing the patient, I had just time to get the afternoon train back to Oklahoma City.

A few years ago after a serious illness, I promised Mrs. Moorman that I would not make any more night calls, but on one occasion while she was sound asleep in an adjoining room, the telephone rang, and forgetting my promise, I agreed to make a call. The woman on the telephone explained that her sister, who was in the city on a visit, was having a hemorrhage and she had been referred to me by a good friend Dr. Leroy S. Peters of Albuquerque, New Mexico. To refuse would have been difficult. I slipped out and was clipping along on the designated street, enjoying my stolen freedom when suddenly I saw a light on a front porch. I looked for the number, and there it was. When I walked in and sat down at the bedside, the very nice patient said, "Dr. Moorman, I heard that you have been very sick. Why didn't you send somebody else?" Immediately I thought, Why didn't your sister tell me that? But under the discipline of training and experience I refrained from saying what I was thinking. Instead I said, "You must remember I started with a team of Indian ponies twenty miles from a railroad; consequently it's easy for me to get in a closed car with headlights, back out on a lighted, paved street, and make a night call. I feel sorry for the young fellows. They have never had to hitch up a team and hit an unmarked trail with the promise that somebody would be waving a lantern on Jones' Hill. Not having been seasoned by hardships and not having the advantage of experience to aid judgment by comparison, they think city practice is hard and that night calls are something to be avoided. It was Molière who said, 'We want ups and downs in life; the difficulties arouse our energies and augment our pleasures.' "

My young Greek-American friend went to St. Anthony's Hospital many years ago because of a lung abscess. The course of the disease was devastating and finally resulted in empyema (pus in the pleural space), making surgical drainage necessary for recovery. Nick, who knew more Greek than English, found it difficult to understand the need of an operation and even more difficult to accept it.

Nevertheless, one of my surgical friends was called in, and Nick was slated for a rib-resection and a drainage tube. As a matter of safety it was decided that the operation should be performed under local anesthesia. This method of procedure was not easy for the sensitive foreigner. The next morning when I walked into the ward and spoke to Nick, he said, "Oh Doc, I go to the graveyard today. That surgeon, he is a butcher. I go to the graveyard today."

He made an uneventful recovery and after a few years slipped from my ken. Exactly thirty years from the time of the operation Nick called and wanted me to see his brother who was desperately ill with pneumonia. Although I had sicked the "butcher" on Nick, he thought I might be able to help his brother. Unfortunately the sick man's pneumonia was only coincidental or terminal. A recent arrival in America, he had been wrecked by the war in Greece and was shockingly emaciated from malaria and long-continued hunger. This lasting loyalty of patients to their physicians stands among the abiding satisfactions of a medical career.

An elderly gentleman referred to me by his family doctor was placed in the hospital for diagnosis and treatment. He wanted to go into the ward for the sake of economy. Sixty years of age, tall, square-shouldered, graceful, and distinguished in bearing and appearance, he was endowed with unbounded optimism and humor. It was a pleasure to visit him and to note the animation of the whole ward as his speech and personality expanded under the slightest provocation. After he returned home, he invited me to come for a quail hunt. There were no prohibitions except on three coveys in the orchard which his wife had been feeding with the chickens.

The old man had traveled west from Kentucky and had settled on a farm in western Oklahoma. His Kentucky background, his name, and his unusual qualities intrigued me. Upon inquiry I learned that he was a direct descendant of the world-famous Dr. Ephraim McDowell of Danville, Kentucky, who had performed the first operation for cystic ovary, without benefit of anesthesia, when the little college town was one of the outposts of civilization. Mrs. Crawford, the patient, who had ridden miles on horseback to see the doctor, sang through the operation to keep up her courage and lived to be seventy-eight years old. It is interesting to note the patient's astounding faith in contrast to the temper of a group of the townsmen, who waited outside with a rope, determined to swing the doctor from a tree in case the operation was not a success. The home of Dr. McDowell has become a medical shrine of sufficient importance to have brought the American Association of the History of Medicine to Danville for one.session of its 1949 meeting at Lexington, Kentucky.

Years after I had attended McDowell, it was reported that a dentist belonging to the McDowell family and living in northern Oklahoma had a genuine portrait of his famous medical forebear. As secretary of the Oklahoma State Medical Association I tried to locate the portrait but never succeeded. At the meeting in Lexington, Dr. Edward Skinner of Kansas City appeared with a portrait, which, according to all available evidence, seemed to be the original Davenport painting that had long been missing. Somewhat chagrined, I learned that he had borrowed it for the occasion from his neighbor in Kansas City and that it had previously been in the possession of the Oklahoma McDowell relatives. This disclosure put an end to my quest, and the state association's ambition for the Davenport McDowell.

Another Kentucky friend came to me for examination chiefly because of advancing age. He was seventy-seven years old, and in addition to cardiovascular degeneration (heart and blood vessel disease) he was suffering from dilated bronchial tubes on the right side which caused an aggravating cough and purulent expectoration. The history of his case indicated that he had sucked a piece of hickory nutshell down his windpipe when he was seven years of age. When he was eight, he coughed it up, but he continued to have a distressing cough with about four ounces of sputum daily. He had maintained reasonably good health throughout the period of seventy years following aspiration of the nutshell. The most remarkable thing about his case is the fact that at the rate of four ounces daily, he had expectorated approximately fifty times his body weight. Several years after my examination I saw him attending the funeral of a mutual friend.

From the time my nephew, Dr. Floyd Moorman, came to St. Anthony's Hospital thirty years ago for intern service, I have been known as "old Dr. Moorman." Following his intern service, we were associated in practice for a number of years. After he established his own office, I continued to be "old Dr. Moorman." While the situation often led to humorous episodes, it also had its more serious aspects. One morning after I had examined a young man from Long Beach, California, he said, "Dr. Moorman, I'm glad to see you looking so well." After thanking him, I inquired how he happened to make such a remark, considering the fact he had never seen me before. He said, "My doctor in California, a former student of yours, told me to see "old Dr. Moorman" if he is still living, and if not, to see "young Dr. Moorman."

On one occasion I was called in consultation to one of the local hospitals to see an elderly woman suffering from pneumonia. A few days later her son-in-law inquired if I had presented my bill. Receiving a negative answer, he said, "Doctor, when you do couldn't you add enough to cover what I owe you for the care of my children? You know I work hard, and my mother-in-law comes from down in the state and lives off me, and this is the only way I have to get even with her." I explained that I could not do so, but that I would be glad to wait until he was able to pay his own bill. While he may have been suffering from an exaggerated mother-in-law complex, I was sympathetic because he was finding it hard to support his family and pay doctor bills, too.

In Webster's International Dictionary, "good-afternoon"

is given as short for "God give you a good afternoon." In a period of hard picking during the last national depression, while at lunch one Saturday, I remarked to Mrs. Moorman, "I have worked months without profit. Do you think I could afford to stay home this afternoon regardless of any appointments I have at the office?"

Just then the telephone rang, and with a sympathetic gesture she passed the receiver across the table. To my chagrin, this message came clarion clear, "Doctor, the office is full of people. Can you come over early?" Obviously, my receptionist was not at fault. Neither could the patients be blamed for seeking medical advice. Driven by a sense of duty and spurred by professional pride, I hurried to the office, praying for a good afternoon. On the way I derived a certain satisfaction from the thought that at least somebody wanted my services, and I determined that neither the nurse nor the patients should know what had been going on in my mind.

When I entered the office, I found the wife of a former colleague who had died of tuberculosis. She was breaking up her home and moving back East to live with her people. She could not leave without having her two sons thoroughly checked, and, as a doctor's wife, knowing the danger from her close contact with her husband, she thought it advisable to have her own chest examined, too. Three new examinations with the accustomed attention to every detail constituted a fair afternoon's work, but they were handled with dispatch. Since doctors, their wives, and their dependent children are never charged for such services, there was no fee.

The next patient was a registered nurse seeking medical advice. She received similar consideration and proper management was prescribed. There was no charge because of the courtesy existing between related professions engaged in a common cause.

The third appointment was with a well-dressed, prosperous-looking woman bringing her precocious young American. Her family physician wanted the boy carefully examined because he was having a little afternoon fever. In the course of our conversation she said, "I am sorry my husband couldn't come down, but he is tied up with a board meeting." I wondered whether her husband was presiding over a board of bank directors or of an oil corporation. Ultimately it was revealed that he was a Baptist minister, occupied with a special meeting of his board of deacons. Knowing that preachers are poorly paid, I had made it a lifelong practice to say, "There is no charge; please consider this a contribution to the cause you represent."

Under the impression that I had completed a good afternoon I was discarding my white coat when lagging footsteps were heard in the hall, and my nurse said, "There is a bedraggled-looking woman who has waited in the reception room all afternoon without an appointment. She says she must see you. When she appeared, I was struck by her shifting eyes, her physical frailty, and her sallow complexion. A casual inspection caused me to believe she was in need of medical care. With some hesitation she said, "Doctor, once you had my brother at your sanatorium, and you did so much for him, I thought you might be willing to help me. I have a monthly pension of fifty dollars, and my brother-in-law will help. Would you please let me come to your sanatorium for a rest? I need your help."

Too weary of well-doing to follow my established rule, I omitted the usual diagnostic study and accepted the hazard. I agreed to admit her on the following Monday. Preparing to go, she hesitated at the door and then turning her pallid face toward me she said, "If you cannot admit me tonight, I will have to go back to my brother-in-law. Can you let me have fifty cents to pay my interurban carfare?" Producing the coin, I cleared my desk and called it a day.

Soon after this patient's admission to the sanatorium it was discovered that she was a morphine addict and that her sickly appearance and her sallow complexion were in all probability due to long, continued use of the drug in excessive dosage. Without it she became a raving maniac, requiring physical restraint. It was necessary for us to keep her for two weeks while arranging admission to one of the state institutions where psychiatric cases and drug addicts are expertly managed. She had no pension, and as far as I could ascertain, no brother-in-law. Thus to my free services on that good afternoon I had the privilege of adding the cost of two weeks' care in the sanatorium. Though not particularly disturbed by the financial phase of this afternoon's work, I was very tired, and wondered if I might dare dream of a comfortable resting place just inside the pearly gates with a soft cushion on an alabaster couch, or a long siesta in a plush rocker.

As I look back upon this experience and contemplate the strenuous life the average physician leads today, I long for a return to the time when a doctor could leave his office with this sign on the door: "If anybody wants Doc Syphers, he's down by the bridge fishing."

There is no end to the interesting episodes in the family physician's life. Some are funny, some are tragic, some are extremely shocking, some are sacred, and many are never to be told. Purposely I have related a few bizarre experiences and left out the physician's routine services that are well known to everyone, and have avoided the more shocking experiences such as incurable diseases, suicides, murders, horrible deaths by accident, orphaned children, homes wrecked by war, divorce, and other disasters resulting from errant impulses. All these occasionally flash across the physician's consciousness in the stillness of the night, at the cocktail hour, or perhaps on Sunday morning at church, without a rift in his well-disciplined countenance to suggest such reminiscences. Occasionally they serve as a welcome refuge, especially if the sermon is poor.

CHAPTER XIX

A Bug Full of Tricks

FREQUENTLY my friends have urged me to shed whatever light a man may, who has lived long enough to see the light, upon the problems which beset both patient and physician when they come face to face with active tuberculosis. This has always seemed to me an invitation to be garrulous, but I must confess that this commendable curiosity has gradually shattered my resistance. So, having calculated the risk, I will attempt, largely by expository means, to present in this and the immediately succeeding chapters some of the facts about the malady which has claimed most of my professional career.

I shall attempt a discussion of its behavior, its socioeconomic and epidemiological implications, which are important not only to the patient and the doctor but to every living individual. Although the casual reader may consider it a recondite subject, it should be known that we have had many thousand years in which to learn about this, the most ruthless and devastating of all diseases. Is it not time to give it some attention; do we not owe it to our children and those who follow them, to get on with our knowledge of the greatest killer in the prime of life? Without applied knowledge we cannot hope for prevention and control. Already knowledge is ample, needing only acquisition, dissemination, and application.

What we now know about tuberculosis is intimately connected with the despicable little parasite known as the tubercle

A BUG FULL OF TRICKS

bacillus, which may well be called a bug full of tricks. This microscopic wax-covered bit of protein and sugar was plaguing humanity long before the days of recorded history. In subtle, evasive, insinuating fashion, this ancient enemy of mankind pursued its nefarious trade. It boldly registered its own ravages as revealed in exhumed prehistoric skeltons and Egyptian mummies. The record consists of angular spines (the hunchback) and distorted joints resulting from healed tuberculosis. These stimulating question marks, while partially revealing the secrets of a deadly disease, accentuate its mysteries.

Passing on to the serious study of recorded history, we find that the code of Hammurabi, written more than two thousand years B.C., indicates a knowledge of tuberculosis. In the fifth century B.C., Hippocrates and other Greek writers recognized the essential clinical features of the disease and described them well. They observed its shocking effects upon body weight and energy and appropriately called it "phythisis" (wasting of the body), a term later replaced by the word which for us is more descriptive—"consumption." Aretaeus, in the second century A.D., gave an accurate clinical description of tuberculosis and suggested routine treatment similar to that employed today. His contemporary, Galen, accepted the teachings of Hippocrates and recorded his own observations concerning the disease, expressing the belief that it might be transmitted from one person to another.

In spite of their keen powers of observation and their illuminating clinical descriptions, it is obvious that Hippocrates, Aretaeus, and Galen were groping for light while hopelessly submerged in the occult phenomena caused by this baffling bacillus. For more than two thousand years, successive generations have suffered and died in the dim light supplied by these renowned Greek physicians. During this long period there was much confusion about the pathological and clinical manifestations of the disease. Bizarre beliefs and practices befogged the issue, and finally the many absurd therapeutic measures were climaxed by the royal touch for scrofula (glandular tuberculosis), and only occasionally a flickering light appeared on the dim horizon to encourage further investigation.

In 1546, Girolamo-Fracastorius suggested the modern conception of contagion through micro-organisms and expressed the belief that phthisis is due to invisible germs. In 1567, Paracelsus wrote about miner's consumption and boldly broke away from Galenic teachings, becoming one of the first advocates of chemistry in medicine. This is particularly noteworthy in the light of our present interest in chemotherapy. In 1590, the compound microscope was introduced by Hans and Zacharias Janssen. In 1650, Franciscus Sylvius declared that tubercles (small masses or nodules) are the cause of phthisis (tuberculosis) and sensed the connection between scrofula and phthisis. About this time the British physician Christopher Bennet published his work on *The Nature and Cure of Consumption*. He was a victim of the disease, and his practical ideas about treatment in the midst of uncertainty and confusion may have resulted from personal experience. Bennet's contemporary Thomas Willis made valuable contributions to our knowledge of the anatomy and physiology of the lungs. He wrote interestingly about "consumption arising through a fault of the lung," and ingeniously he said, "In the lungs rather than in the heart or the brain the threads of life are spun, and there are oftenest broken." It was during this period in Great Britain that the famous Thomas Sydenham advocated fresh air and horseback riding for the cure of tuberculosis. In 1683 Anton van Leeuwenhoek described micro-organisms and initiated the study of bacteria; in 1689, Richard Morton published a voluminous treatise on consumption, entitled "Phthisiologia." He stressed the teaching of Sylvius that tubercles are connected with phthisis. In 1700, Manget gave the first post-mortem report of miliary tuberculosis (tubercles the size of millet seeds, scattered through the organs of the body). About this time the great pathologist Giovanni Battista Morgagni was laying the foundation for the study of gross pathology, but refused to perform autopsies on the known victims of phthisis because of his fear of contagion.

About the middle of the eighteenth century, the tuberculosis death rate reached a high point. No doubt it was this fact that prompted Richard Morton to say, "I cannot sufficiently admire that anyone, at least after he comes to the flower of his youth, can die without a touch of consumption." This peak of mortality in the midst of universal confusion about the cause and manifestations of the disease was coincident with rapidly increasing facilities for the acquisition of knowledge and may have inspired the dawning urge for more specific investigations.

In 1761, Leopold Aurenbrugger, though unheeded at the time, made an epochal contribution through his *Inventum Novum* (New Invention), which described immediate percussion (tapping the body for variations in sound). In 1765, William Stark, fresh from the University of Edinburgh, came to London to study pathology. He devoted his energy almost entirely to the study of tuberculosis at the autopsy table. Contemporaneous with Stark, Robert Whytt described tuberculous meningitis, and Percival Pott first described tuberculosis of the spine, which justly took his name (Pott's disease) but remained to be proven of tuberculous origin by Jacques Mathieu Delpech in 1816. Soon thereafter, Marc-Antone Petit described tuberculosis of the larynx and Antoine Portal suggested a definite connection between engorgement of lymphatics (lymph vessels and glands) and pulmonary consumption. William Stark, at the early age of twenty-nine, presumably died of miliary tuberculosis as the result of an infection which he acquired at the autopsy table.

Matthew Baillie, having recently graduated in medicine, received an appointment to St. George's Hospital to work in the autopsy room, possibly where Stark had received the fatal infection. No doubt Baillie was inspired by the work of young Stark and sought the opportunity of pursuing the latter's pathological researches. For eighteen years, Baillie dilligently followed his post-mortem studies of diseases of the chest and made valuable contributions to our knowledge of tuberculosis. He also received an infection of the hand while performing an autopsy but lived to die of advanced pulmonary tuberculosis at the age of sixty-two. His work on *Morbid Anatomy* was published in 1795, and his investigations clarified our knowledge and led to a better understanding of the disease.

After much painstaking research in pathology, Gaspard-Laurent Bayle described tuberculosis as a constitutional disease caused by tubercles. Flick says: "Bayle's life and work might be termed a melancholy romance of science. Born in 1774, he died of tuberculosis in 1816 at the age of forty-two; probably contracted at the autopsy table."

In a volume on *Pulmonary Phthisis*, Bayle carefully presents results of his clinical observations, checked by autopsies on more than nine hundred individuals dying of consumption. His exhaustive studies at the bedside and in the dead room enabled him to have a better understanding than any of his predecessors of tuberculosis in all its stages and various pathological phases.

Early in the nineteenth century Lucient Covisart, Napoleon's physician, translated Auenbrugger's *Inventum Novum* and popularized percussion, which, in spite of a previous French translation, had never achieved general recognition. Strange to say, Covisart first learned of percussion not through the French translation of 1770, but through the influence of Maximilian Stoll, who had succeeded Anton de Haen as director of the clinic in the Allgemeines Krankenhaus (General Hospital) at the University of Vienna. In addition to his wide influence in the field of clinical investigation, Stoll manifested a special interest in tuberculosis, perhaps because of its ravages in his own body, to which he succumbed at the early age of forty-six in 1776.

Covisart's greatness is attested by the following quotation from his brief preface to the translation of Auenbrugger's pamphlet: "I know well how little reputation nearly all translators and most commentators earn, and hence I might have secured for myself an authorship if I had published a work on percussion based upon a recasting of the writings of Auenbrugger. I then would have sacrificed the name of Auenbrugger to my own vanity. That I did not wish to do. I wanted to snatch him and his beautiful, regularly made discovery which he, with entire propriety, called a new invention from forgetfulness." Covisart's recognized ability and his position as Napoleon's physician brought his translation into immediate vogue.

We now come to the significant awakening with reference to clinical and pathological investigations with Antoine Portal, William Stark, Matthew Baillie, Marie François Bichat, Gaspard-Laurent Bayle, and Lucient Covisart supplying a stimulating background for the important work of Laënnec and Louis in the first quarter of the nineteenth century. René T. H. Laënnec promptly grasped the significance of the clinico-pathological (bedside and dead-room observations) implications, and with an avid genius he appropriated all previous scientific advances as he entered upon his monumental career. In spite of the handicap of progressive tuberculosis in his own person, he worked with remarkable industry and conspicuous determination. Before he was twenty-two years of age, he had drawn up a minute history of nearly four hundred patients, which served as a foundation for his future researches and discoveries. When Laënnec came upon the scene, the diagnosis of diseases of the lungs and heart was still more difficult than that of other internal organs. In a short time he had made the most exacting diagnostic tasks relatively easy. In half the time now allotted for a medical education, virtually without chart or compass, he observed, recorded, tabulated, and communicated practically all that is now taught with reference to the physical diagnosis of diseases of the chest. His remarkable work of nearly eight hundred pages on auscultation and diseases of the chest was published in 1819 and translated into English by Forbes in 1821.

Allowing full credit for Covisart's revival of Auenbrugger's neglected invention, it is doubtful whether the remarkable advances of the nineteenth century would have followed each other so rapidly without the stimulus of the stethoscope. Korns, in a recent article, confirms this statement: "The great merit of Laënnec's invention [the stethoscope] lay not so much in the instrument itself, as in the fact that it served to focus the attention of the entire medical world on the auscultatory method. Rolleston, in his Harveian oration [1928], expresses this idea as follows: 'Though the stethoscope had some obvious advantages over the naked ear, the enormous advances that followed its introduction were not so much due to the stethoscope as a mechanical instrument, as to the psychological effect that this new method exerted on Laënnec, who otherwise would not have so ardently pursued auscultation as a means of diagnosis.' "

At the age of forty-five, after a brilliant career, Laënnec died of advanced pulmonary tuberculosis.

The great clinician Pierre Charles Alexander Louis who was contemporary with Laënnec and survived him by many years, also suffered from tuberculosis, but lived to be eighty-five years of age. Louis made use of the facts Bayle and Laënnec had brought to light and gave them added significance through his own observations, his writings, and his wonderful influence as a teacher. He carefully correlated the symptoms and the pathology of tuberculosis; he amplified the study of clinical manifestations in the light of autopsy findings. Finally, when thirty-four years of age, he gave up general practice in order to pursue more satisfactorily his scientific investigations. Louis established the numerical or statistical method of investigation in medicine. Through his teachings and his pupils, he was largely responsible for the establishment of clinical medicine on a sound basis throughout the world. The results of his studies were published in a volume of six hundred pages under the title, *Louis' Researches on Phthisis*.

In the University of Vienna the eccentric, impetuous Josef Skoda (1805–81), taking his cue from the French school, enthusiastically pursued the study of percussion and auscultation, with emphasis upon the investigation of tonal or sonorous phenomena elicited by these methods of examination. Skoda's skill in diagnosis so inspired Turkheim, the minister of medical education, that he established a special department on chest diseases with this great clinician in charge. Skoda's appointment as professor of medicine in 1846 and his skill in physical diagnosis attracted students from all parts of the world. However, the magnetic attraction of the University of Vienna for students of clinical medicine in this period was shared by an illustrious contemporary of Skoda. The rapid rise of this school to the highest rank was largely due to Rokitansky (1804–78), perhaps the world's greatest clinical pathologist. Skoda's work was brilliantly complemented by the latter's illuminating demonstrations in the dead room. Rokitansky performed fifteen to eighteen hundred autopsies annually. It is said that he conducted over thirty thousand post-mortem examinations during his lifetime.

By the middle of the nineteenth century the stage was set for a great scientific awakening. In 1865, Jean-Antoine Villemin demonstrated the specific nature of tuberculosis through animal inoculation. Five years later, A. C. Gerlach proved that milk from tuberculous cows conveyed the disease, and, in 1873, Edwin Klebs, through feeding experiments, produced bovine tuberculosis. Medicine was moving into a new era. The consolidated methods of clinical, anatomical, and pathological studies were soon to be supplemented by modern laboratory methods.

It seems worthy of note that much of the general progress in physical diagnosis and pathology has been evolved through a sustained desire to solve the mysteries of tuberculosis. It is equally interesting to note that a large percentage of the most zealous investigators have suffered from tuberculosis, some apparently experiencing an excitation of genius which spurred them on to greater accomplishments, thus partially compensating for an early surrender to the enemy they ardently pursued. It seems that the tubercle bacillus in its attack upon these men of science, in spite of its magical powers of deception and evasion, was preparing the way for its ultimate discovery and the gradual surrender of many of its secrets.

The English physician Dr. George Bodington was the first to follow sanatorium methods in the management of tuberculosis. In 1840 he wrote a book based upon his experience in the treatment of tuberculosis. It was entitled *The Treatment and Cure of Pulmonary Consumption*. In this volume he outlines his methods, and Professor S. Lile Cummins, quoting him, reports this attractive therapeutic regime: "Fresh morning air to make the patient breathe; good wine to bring down his pulse, a good dinner to make him fat and an opium pill to make him sleep." Bodington's claims, far in advance of his time, aroused the critical wrath of his contemporaries in the medical profession, and he suffered the fate of many who have had the courage to follow a vision. Today his methods, amplified and supplemented by new discoveries, are gradually bringing tuberculosis under control.

In 1856, Rudolf Virchow, in the city of Berlin, established the first pathological laboratory. It served as a model for nearly all laboratories in Germany and in other countries. The first hygienic laboratory was opened by Pettenkofer in 1878. Robert Koch, stimulated by the discoveries of Pasteur, had already begun his special researches.

The story of Koch's step-by-step discovery of the tubercle bacillus and proof of its specificity is so well known it is not necessary to repeat it here. It is important to note that the snags encountered were due to the fact that the tubercle bacillus is a nonconformist, and only a Robert Koch could have successfully accomplished the task. Quoting Krause: "Given the same circumstances, the same pioneer quest, the same limited knowledge of possibilities, the same imperfection of initial media—and the view is almost compelling that only the rarest of investigators would have maintained the prolonged and heartbreaking vigil for the earliest showing through of minutest particles that belonged, as yet, only to the shadowy realm of a 'working Hypothesis.' "

This perfect performance, which marked the zenith of Koch's career, and its presentation in irrefutable terms did much to clear up the existing confusion and to bring about a better understanding of tuberculosis in its varied manifestations.

Even Virchow, ever ready for controversy, quick of mind and body, remained speechless and immobile, thus accentuating the profound silence that followed Koch's dramatic presentation of the world's most perfect bit of research. Something new to mortal ken had sounded the death knell to some of Virchow's convictions, and for this war horse of pathology it was like the passing of a cherished child. Although, on this occasion, he left the Berlin Physiological Society without a word of response, it is worthy of note that in the language of Krause, "When, full of years and every honor that a man of medicine can accumulate, he passed on to eternal peace, he could not reconcile himself to the idea of the all-embracing and unified cause of that appalling diversity of effect that tuberculosis comprehends."

The discovery of the tubercle bacillus in 1882 did not satisfy Robert Koch. Having once seen the tubercle bacillus and having proved its specific role in connection with the disease, his dauntless spirit was soon busily engaged in search of a cure for tuberculosis. In 1890 his announcement of tuberculin caused great excitement throughout the medical world.

Koch having discovered the cause of tuberculosis and, as he first thought, having found a cure in tuberculin, it then seemed reasonable to anticipate the surrender of the tubercle bacillus and the end of humanity's greatest scourge. Unfortunately, we were doomed to descend from this hopeful height, but even so, we were left far above the level attained by Laënnec and Louis and legions of others who had spent their lives in search of a cure. Koch's discoveries led to many valuable epidemiological, diagnostic, therapeutic, and preventive principles, and initiated a sustained search for additional knowledge.

Though disappointing as a cure, tuberculin proved to be a valuable diagnostic agent and helped to stress the high incidence of infection and the ubiquitous nature of the tubercle bacillus. Through Wilhelm Konrad Roentgen's discovery of the X-ray, properly called Roentgen ray, the value of ordinary inspection was immeasurably increased. The Roentgen ray amplified vision and supplied knowledge not previously imagined. Later the bronchoscope and the thoracoscope (for the purpose of looking inside the chest) extended our means of exploration, enabling the human eye to see normal and pathological phenomena never seen before and revealing manifestations of tuberculosis and other diseases of the chest not previously suspected. In spite of all these diagnostic advances, the tubercle bacillus was undaunted. Space will not permit a detailed discussion of therapy, but a brief reference to its development is sufficient to emphasize further the baffling problems of the tubercle bacillus and its protean manifestations.

While tuberculin as a therapeutic agent was a great disappointment to Robert Koch, the equally bold conception of Albert Calmette and C. Guérin in 1924 launched B.C.G. (vaccination against tuberculosis) on its tardy course, which is now receiving much attention in the field of prevention. Although tuberculin proved not to be a cure, as a diagnostic agent it speeded discovery and favored control. If B.C.G. prevents the development of tuberculosis, even in an appreciable number of persons, ultimately the percentage of cases in need of treatment may be greatly reduced. Today B.C.G. is widely employed in some countries, but in the United States it is recommended only in certain segments of population where exposure is continuous or frequently encountered. Among these, medical students and nurses serve as examples. Although routine management supplemented by collapse therapy and all the new drugs has to some extent mitigated the evil effects of this bug full of tricks, it has never yet been irretrievably trapped; and even now we must remember its devious ways and its surprising strategies and tincture our optimism with eternal vigilance.

Immediately prior to Koch's epochal discoveries, George Bodington, Hermann Brehmer, Peter Dettweiler, and Edward Livingston Trudeau pioneered in sanatorium management, which has been so successfully pursued with untold benefit to both the patients and the public. Through this method of management has come a wealth of accumulated clinical, pathological, preventive, and therapeutic knowledge, in addition to statistical data, the value of which is difficult to estimate. In my history of the American Sanitorium Association, the role played by Trudeau and others in the sanatorium management of tuberculosis in America is fully discussed and our indebtedness to these pioneers gratefully acknowledged.

In spite of all that has been accomplished, the unsolved problems in the field of tuberculosis are infinite, and in the words of David Riesman, "No matter what we take away from infinity, infinity remains."

Briefly, I have tried to state a few of the principal facts bearing upon the problems now in the scope of our consciousness, to say nothing of those not yet conceived. Merely to enumerate the research projects now devoted to these problems would fill a great volume. More than seven million dollars were spent in this field in 1949. The bibliography of the tubercle bacillus and the disease tuberculosis, as reflected in the quarterly *Index Medicus*, now occupies many times the space devoted to such subjects thirty years ago. The voluminous literature on tuberculosis indicates that constantly we are making new observations of age-old conditions in this difficult field which still intrigues all investigative minds.

Even though our command over the course of natural phenomena has speeded up immeasurably, we are unable to find our way to a full understanding of the tubercle bacillus. With all our studies of immunity and infection, the chemical fractional analysis of the tubercle bacillus, the cultural mutations with their varied morphological forms, our genetic studies, and our modern advances in diagnosis and therapy, tuberculosis has dotted the world with innumerable graves and killed more people in civilized lands than the combined wars of all ages; and still it goes where we go, it lodges where we lodge, and it remains the arch enemy of physical competency and the greatest killed during the most useful period in the cycle of human life.

With these intriguing problems in mind, the impact of ever increasing knowledge and the open field for pioneer work in Oklahoma, I could not resist the challenge to participate in the clinical study of the disease. It has been engrossing to follow the wary bacillus with the hope of calling its tricks as knowledge has increased and the therapeutic ways and means have developed, but far above this game of outwitting the bacillus comes the satisfaction of following the patient with all available aids, including compassionate hope, which often helped to replace the blight of disease with the bloom of health. Undaunted by this rather discouraging picture, physicians in general practice, in the specialties, in clinics, in sanatoria, and in laboratories throughout the world are face to face with this ancient foe of mankind—striving for more effective means of control.

In other chapters on compensatory reactions, routine treatment, psychology of the patient, and sanatorium management, I have recorded some of the lights and shadows which are common in the life of every doctor who enters this intriguing field of practice.

CHAPTER XX

The Little Devil's Dues

HAVING devoted the previous chapter to the evil ways of this bug, I am committed to a discussion of its intellectual, spiritual and creative values. This discussion follows the line of my work on tuberculosis and genius,[1] which dealt primarily with those who devoted their lives to poetry and literature. Daily the disease snatches important people from all walks of life and puts them down with time for contemplation, reorientation, and often reconsecration. It may completely change the course of life, and often the change is profitable, especially for the more intellectual. In the crucible of calamity there is a chastening influence sometimes resulting in a new birth. Only those who live with the disease fully appreciate this fact, consequently the story may be worth telling. If space were available, I could cite many instances where conflict with tuberculosis has molded human destiny and changed the course of world events. Here is a rich field calling for further cultivation. We are inclined to fear the implications and to avoid the paradoxical position they pose—yet a few examples will intrigue the curious and launch the investigative mind on a fascinating quest.

As previously mentioned, Emerson's "Essay on Compensation," with its wonderful balance and remarkable antithesis, serves as one of the most striking examples. No doubt it was written, at least in part, because of the chastening influence of

[1] Lewis J. Moorman, *Tuberculosis and Genius* (Chicago, University of Chicago Press, 1940).

his own experiences with tuberculosis, for we find sympathetic reference to the compensation of calamity.

Homer, evidently influenced by the presence of the disease among his contemporaries, said, "A grievous consumption separates soul and body." In Deuteronomy, seventh century B.C., we find "a consumption, a fever, and an inflammation."

A little later, the Elder Pliny wrote that the journey to Egypt was not for climate alone, but for the long sea voyage. It is recorded that Pliny sent his own favorite servant to Libya for rest because of hemoptysis (spitting of blood).

We may be justified in saying that the sands of North Africa were spotted by the blood-letting lance of the wary tubercle bacillus long before the veins of contending races were opened by the implements of modern warfare on this ancient battlefield. Rest assured that no one could spend one to three years in the silence of the desert without being changed morally and intellectually. Certainly, it may be said that the famous old Greeks of the marvelous fifth century B.C. philosophized, sang, and chiseled more gloriously because of tuberculosis.

Cicero was suffering from a bronchopulmonary condition presumably because of too much declaiming in the open forum, and after a consultation his physicians sent him away for three years' rest and change of climate. Apparently he traveled and studied under a tutor for a period of approximately two years. No doubt he returned to wield a greater influence because of the conditioning effects of his disease, which gave time for travel, study, and the acquisition of knowledge not within the scope of his daily activities at Rome. Since his fame rests largely upon his letters, possibly we may assume that he perfected the art of letter writing during his absence from home and routine duties. No doubt our Latin lessons have been more interesting because tuberculosis interrupted for a time the demands of the Forum.

The venerable Seneca spent much time on his country estate because of "trouble in his breast." According to his own statement, there were times when it seemed that each breath would be his last gasp and that "living was like practicing how to die." There is no way to prove that Seneca had tuberculosis. Even though he suffered only from asthma, it may be said that his moral epistles are more interesting and perhaps more moral because of the chastening influence of his pulmonary affliction.

Galen, the last of the Greek physicians, living in Rome during the second century A.D., apparently suffered from tuberculosis. It is recorded that on two occasions during his student days it was necessary for him to drop out of school because of physical frailty and that later, while in the practice of medicine in Rome, he bled himself from the vein between the right thumb and forefinger because of pain between the liver and diaphragm. If Galen suffered from tuberculosis in his early life, it is reasonable to believe that this pain may have been caused by a tuberculous pleurisy, especially as there is no history of subsequent trouble with gall bladder or liver.

No doubt Galen should have credit for establishing the first institution for the treatment of tuberculosis. The records show that he sent his patients to Stabia on the most beautiful beach in the world. Here they rested in the balmy atmosphere of Mount Vesuvius, with the beautiful Isle of Capri in the offing. Contented cows conveyed warm milk to the patients after grazing upon the foothills of Milk Mountain. Here, according to Galen, was to be found the most suitable herbage in the world for the production of therapeutic milk. No doubt the lives of many prominent Roman personages were influenced by this therapeutic regime. It is interesting to note that Galen's decision about therapeutic milk was not based upon arbitrary conclusions, but arrived at after exhaustive investigations including a study of the milk of the cow, the goat, the ass, the mare, the hyena and the wolf.

Because of his remarkable career, Galen attracted the attention of Marcus Aurelius, the best of Roman emperors, who in all probability suffered from tuberculosis. It is recorded that throughout his life periodically he suffered from cough, fever, and hemoptysis. No doubt because he feared his son Comodus might suffer the same fate, he placed him under the care of Galen while he went away to pursue the war with "barbaric" Germany. Perhaps Galen's own tuberculous condition influenced his acceptance of this commission. It is known that he spent approximately six years at the Emperor's country place at Lorium, where, while guarding the health of the Emperor's young son, he found time to pursue his physiological and anatomical studies in his own inprovised laboratories.

Through his untiring industry, Galen, utilizing the time provided by Marcus Aurelius' fear of tuberculosis, gathered all the Hippocratic writings and added his own voluminous works in preparation, unwittingly of course, for their survival of the Dark Ages. This remarkable feat proved to be of the greatest importance in the intellectual and scientific progress of the world. Some authorities have thought that Galen should be considered the first experimental physiologist.

While he was conducting a public demonstration of the intercostal muscles by a dissection on the chest of a live pig, his knife went a bit too deep, and suddenly the pig ceased squealing. Galen followed the cue and discovered the recurrent laryngeal nerve. He proved that this nerve motivates the vocal cords and moderates the voice. Modern meat packers have bragged about utilizing everything except the squeal of the pig. Approximately eighteen hundred years ago Galen utilized the squeal of the pig for the benefit of humanity. He made other important contributions to our knowledge of the central nervous system and its functions.

If space would permit, we might show how the development of our knowledge of tuberculosis since the Renaissance has come largely through the work of doctors suffering from tuberculosis and stimulated by its conditioning effects. Many doctors, enriched by unusual acquisition of knowledge and experience, found time to record the same for the benefit of posterity only when tuberculosis made it necessary for them to retire from active work and rest over appreciable periods of time. Merely to stress the significance of this influence among men of medicine the following examples are given: The famous

The Farm Sanatorium in 1920, before pavilions were added. This building was the original Oklahoma City Country Club

Dr. John Hunter of London had a hemorrhage from the lungs while confined by the incessant pursuit of his pathological studies. Not knowing about the virtues of rest but being impressed with the need of a change, he joined the British army and on an island campaign with a surgical assignment he acquired the experience and knowledge which gave to the world his famous monograph on gunshot wounds. If John Hunter had not been seized with an attack of blood-spitting in the pathological room, he never would have known so much about this subject, and succeeding generations of surgeons would have waited long for the important facts accurately recorded through the influence of the then undiscovered tubercle bacillus.

William Withering never found time to assemble and record for publication his remarkable knowledge of foxglove (digitalis) until he had a similar attack of blood-spitting while a busy doctor in Birmingham, England. The data representing his remarkable observations and research as a country doctor at Stafford had remained in his files for ten years. How fortunate it is that tuberculosis brought time for the task before a coronary occlusion or some other calamity snuffed the light which only his mind could focus on the subject at that time. In the profession of medicine there are many examples among the dead and the living, but let these suffice.

Tuberculosis has influenced our knowledge of medicine, in general, through the fact that it has been prevalent throughout the history of the world and has presented varied symptoms and signs, referable chiefly to the chest, but at times to other organs and structures of the body. Thus the varied and widespread manifestations of tuberculosis have supplied abundant material for clinical teaching, particularly of physical diagnosis as applied to the chest. Tuberculosis may present virtually all the physical signs found in other diseases affecting the bronchial tubes, the lungs, and the pleura. In addition, the disease has had a peculiar moral, social, and economic appeal, which has stimulated universal interest in its recognition and control, not only among physicians but on the part of the lay people as well.

What has been said about the development of our knowledge of tuberculosis through this conditioning influence among literary men and doctors is equally applicable to persons in other fields of endeavor.

It is well for us to remember that genius may appear on Main Street as well as in the more secluded places where creative effort finds expression through arts and sciences. It is found in business and industrial pursuits and may be similarly influenced by tuberculosis. The same statement may be made with reference to politics and statesmanship. To offer examples: Cecil Rhodes, son of a clergyman, suffering a physical decline and spitting of blood while a student at Oxford University, traveled to South Africa in search of health and discovered diamonds. As a result he became a great financier and statesman. Through his influence the course of empire was materially altered, and through his accumulated wealth and broad comprehension, the United States Rhodes scholarships at Oxford were developed. Throughout this country we have college professors, editors, scientists, and other leaders in the fields of business, social, and intellectual development who got their training because Cecil Rhodes' life was conditioned by tuberculosis. Again, many other examples could be cited.

Turning to the realm of statesmanship, James Madison, because of his unusual erudition in the realm of government, was George Washington's right-hand man in bringing about a lasting union of our colonies. It has been said that on account of frail health, Madison had eschewed social and public contacts, dedicating himself to intellectual pursuits, including the study of government, particularly democracies from the time of Pericles. In connection with his researches in this field, he lamented the imperfect reporting of the formation of various governments; consequently, when the Constitutional Convention was in session in Philadelphia, he sat at a desk and recorded the proceedings, thus doing one of the most outstanding pieces of reporting extant in the United States today. It is not possible to assert confidently that James Madison had tuberculosis, but the history of his health and behavior is at least suggestive. At any rate he had profited by the relative isolation of a solitary life conditioned by his health. Here again we see the compensation of calamity.

After the Revolutionary War the Constitution was in jeopardy because we were surrounded by hostile British outposts on the north and on the west, with unfriendly Spain and France beyond the Mississippi. George Washington, conscious of these hazards, sent John Jay to London for the purpose of dealing with England in such a way as to improve our position. The Jay Treaty, while not considered satisfactory in every respect, was designed to remove these threatening conditions and to permit national expansion westward, naturally within our manifest destiny. When in 1796 the Jay Treaty was apparently doomed to defeat in the House of Representatives, it was the persuasive eloquence of Fisher Ames and the pathos of his wasted body that brought about the appropriation necessary for its ratification and compliance with its provisions. In William Roscoe Thayer's life of Washington Ames is described as "a young lawyer, feeble in health but burning, after the manner of some consumptives, with intellectual and moral fire which strangely belied his slender thread of physical life." The climax came when this impulsive champion of our freedom closed with these telling words: "When I come to the moment of deciding the vote I start back with dread from the edge of the pit into which we are plunging. In my views even the minutes I have spent in expostulation have their value, because they protract the crisis and the short period in which alone we may resolve to accept it. Yet I have perhaps as little personal interest in the event as anyone here. There is, I believe, no member who will not think his chance to be a witness of the consequences greater than mine. If, however the vote should pass to reject and a spirit should rise, as it will, with the public disorders to make confusion worse confounded, even I, slender and almost broken as my hold on life is, may outlive the government and Constitution of my country."

It was reported that "Vice-President John Adams sat in the gallery, the tears running down his cheeks, and that he said to the friends beside him, 'My God, how great he is.' " If it were not for this eloquent appeal of Fisher Ames, conditioned as he was by advanced tuberculosis, the military posts might not have been removed, and I might not be able to live in Oklahoma today and call it my own.

Apparently fear of tuberculosis sent Theodore Roosevelt and Frederic Remington west and drew them together in a history-making friendship resulting in lasting pictures of the pioneer days on the plains, done with pen and brush, culminating in the immortal "Charge up San Juan Hill," graphically portrayed by Remington, who had followed the Rough Riders.

This account could go on indefinitely without exhausting the known examples of achievement under the influence of tuberculosis. It is significant that at least two-thirds of the doctors who organized the National Tuberculosis Association were suffering from active or arrested tuberculosis, and this movement was equally inspired by the presence of the disease in their own bodies and the appeal of those suffering from the disease and the disaster they had witnessed in the wake of its ravages.

Fortunately the law of compensation is always with us. If we conquer tuberculosis, no doubt something else will arise to spur us on.

CHAPTER XXI

Danger Signals and How to Meet Them

IT is not easy to penetrate the veil of mystery which accompanies the invasion of the tubercle bacillus and which may unobtrusively attend its subtle operations in the human body throughout a lifetime, or until the veil is torn asunder by some manifest pathological change. This usually takes place in the lung and is accompanied by cough and expectoration, pulmonary hemorrhage, or possibly pleurisy and effusion. Such declarations from the housetop are easily understood, even by many laymen. While the usual symptoms may be obvious from the beginning, grave pathological changes may masquerade in nondescript symptomatic garb requiring the most discriminating methods of examination before a definite diagnosis can be made.

Few physicians can justly lay claim to what has been termed diagnostic instinct, but all are endowed with special senses which, if properly trained, may become incredibly keen in their search for diagnostic guidance. To go on the trail of disease with such weapons, is like playing a most interesting game.

What the average person should know is the fact that it is not necessary to have the physician's keen diagnostic sense in order to suspect tuberculosis when the common symptoms appear. In this brief discussion the leading symptoms are listed in the order of their importance and in sufficiently plain language that anyone with average intelligence should be able to detect their presence. They are as follows: fatigue, loss of weight, cough, nervous instability, fever, indigestion, spitting of blood, chest pains, pleurisy, sputum, frequent colds, tickling in the larynx, and flushing of the face. Less obvious to the patient are fever, increased pulse rate and secondary anemia.

Any one of these symptoms or signs or any combination of two or more of them, not promptly subsiding, suggests the advisability of a careful examination including an X-ray of the chest. If upon examination nothing is found and if the symptoms persist, further investigation is indicated. If the family physician cannot make a diagnosis, a specialist in diseases of the chest should be called in consultation. If one examination by the consultant does not reveal the cause of symptoms and if they persist, the search should be continued with periodic X-rays of the chest.

It should be remembered that these symptoms may be caused by other conditions, and even the patient may be able to employ a certain degree of wise discrimination. It is well to know that an ordinary cold should disappear in twelve or fourteen days even though it may be accompanied by a mild bronchitis. It is equally important to know that while bronchitis may be caused by a number of different conditions, only a thorough examination can eliminate tuberculosis. While this subject is under consideration, attention should be called to the fact that often elderly people are allowed to toss off a chronic cough as an old bronchitis or asthma. Tuberculosis in old people is not uncommon, and elderly authority should be overruled in favor of a medical examination and a definite diagnosis. Discovery of the disease in the aged becomes more important as longevity increases and the old-age group continues to grow. Its urgency is augmented by the fact that increasing age is accompanied by greater intimacy in the home and increased danger from continued contact.

As indicated in the first paragraph of this chapter, tuberculosis may be active and progressive without obvious symptoms. This fact emphasizes the importance of periodic health examinations including an X-ray of the chest. Likewise, it supports the wisdom of mass X-ray surveys and tuberculin testing when advised by the doctor or public health agency.

Since tuberculosis is a preventable disease and is communicated from one person to another through contact, full employment of all facilities for its discovery should have the hearty support of all the people. Through popular education and case-finding programs and increasing diagnostic alertness on the part of all physicians the mortality rate has been reduced from 200 per 100,000 population at the turn of the century to less than 30 per 100,000 at the present time. Higher standards of living and a better understanding of food values have helped reduce the death rate.

Everyone should know that the earlier the diagnosis the easier the cure. Those who slam the door on diagnostic opportunities may be shutting out their best chance for recovery in case active disease is present. A positive X-ray finding or a positive tuberculin test is not comparable to a death sentence. Certainly it should be known that a positive tuberculin test, in the great majority of cases, does not indicate the presence of active tuberculosis, but rather that the body harbors tubercle bacilli which may be carried a lifetime without causing active or manifest disease. Yet a positive test does call for a careful search for activity, conservative living, and periodic examinations, even though there is no manifest disease. A positive tuberculin test has other implications. Infection with the tubercle bacillus means contact with the tubercle bacillus. Usually this means contact with someone suffering from tuberculosis. Naturally someone in the home must be considered the most probable source of infection. Search for the contact should not cease until all members of the household have been examined and X-rayed. Yet there are many possible sources of infection. The baby on the floor may acquire hand-to-mouth infection from germs carried in from the street, or the child playing jacks on the sidewalk may make contact with bacilli deposited there by some victim of the disease who may never pass that way again. Because of imperfect and inadequate application of the knowledge at hand and because of ignorance and human depravity, infection goes on, and we must keep up the fight.

Parents should know that infants in intimate contact with people suffering from tuberculosis may develop acute forms of the disease; tuberculous meningitis, general miliary tuberculosis, or tuberculous pneumonia. Thus the removal of the infant from contact immediately upon the discovery of disease is imperative.

In contrast to this sad picture, it should be remembered that few children from five to twelve years of age develop active disease, even though exposed; there is greater danger of activity after puberty. Safety from this age on depends upon watchful attention to health, with annual X-rays and medical examination, and additional X-rays in case symptoms appear.

Space will not permit a detailed discussion of all the symptoms and signs mentioned above. But some of the more important symptoms deserve definition and amplification. Fatigue, the most common and often the first symptom to appear, is often so insidious and so constant it may be overlooked or accepted as a natural phase of daily existence. Usually it becomes more obvious as the disease advances. Its persistence and its cumulative character should help to distinguish it from the normal fatigue following sustained physical effort. Fatigue that becomes more noticeable from day to day under the regular routine of life should have serious consideration.

Fever from tuberculosis usually swings a daily rise in the afternoon or evening. It is necessary to have a temperature reading with an interval of not more than three or four hours throughout the day, covering a period of two weeks in order to properly appraise this symptom. This is particularly true in early tuberculosis where a very slight daily rise may be significant. An occasional slight rise of temperature above normal may not be important, but if it recurs daily over a period of ten days or two weeks, it calls for investigation. Apparently few people realize that the normal temperature fluctuates from one to one and a half degrees in the course of a day. It may be normal for a given individual to register 97 in the morning and 98.6 in the afternoon. Sputum should be recognized as a sign of irritation or destruction of tissue. When present, it should be examined for tubercle bacilli. If other symptoms are present and the sputum is reported negative, it should be examined repeatedly until the attending physician is satisfied. This is important not only from the standpoint of diagnosis in behalf of the patient but because of the question of contact and the danger to others.

Other symptoms might have detailed consideration, but they are not so apt to be misunderstood and misinterpreted, and yet they are more likely to send the patient precipitately to the doctor. This is particularly true of blood-spitting, cough, and pain in the chest.

No one who was not observing professionally the sanitary, hygienic, dietary, and recreational standards of fifty years ago can fully appreciate the profound changes which have occurred in those departments of human welfare during half a century. We now accept as common knowledge what few people knew, and millions little suspected, when Theodore Roosevelt assumed the presidency. How much American medicine has influenced this profound transition only those connected intimately with the problems of health can know. And how much these changes have contributed toward the control of tuberculosis can never be accurately determined.

CHAPTER XXII

Prevention and Management of Tuberculosis

IN half a century of popular publicity the people of our country have learned much about tuberculosis. This wide dissemination of knowledge about the disease has come about largely through the untiring efforts of the National Tuberculosis Association, a voluntary agency established in 1904. Recognizing the socioeconomic as well as the medical importance of tuberculosis, it endeavored to engage the interest of laymen as well as the medical and allied professions. Always its main objective has been the education of the public. Almost unconsciously we have generously supported this organization by the purchase of Christmas seals.

Shortly before the organization of the National Tuberculosis Association, Edward Livingston Trudeau pioneered in the treatment of tuberculosis through his newly founded Adirondack Cottage Sanatorium. Because of his remarkable influence, similar institutions had sprung up throughout the country. With this stimulus and Trudeau's example, including his struggle with the disease in his own body, many physicians became interested in the sanatorium management, which inevitably accentuated the importance of the social, economic, and environmental factors in connection with the prevention and cure of tuberculosis and the rehabilitation of the patient.

The nature of tuberculosis, its long, hazardous course, its pathetic appeal, the necessary contacts in the pursuit of its cure, and its heavy toll in the prime of life gradually carried the light to forward-looking laymen and prepared the way for organized effort in its control.

While the increasing knowledge of tuberculosis was broadening the humanitarian spirit innate in medicine, the growth of mechanistic ingenuity was augmenting the speed of the machine age.

Although the march of medicine easily matched the progress of industry, its spiritual values were not disturbed. Remaining true to their traditional Hippocratic principles, doctors refused to let materialistic progress obscure their sympathetic concern for human welfare. Having been disappointed in Koch's attempt to develop a special cure for tuberculosis, the members of the profession, fully conscious of the difficult task ahead, pooled their knowledge, their convictions, their skills, and their influence in a concerted movement toward the study and control of this stubborn disease. Relatively aloof from the materialistic urge, doctors interested in the control of tuberculosis were anxious to activate science with a bit of common sense and sentiment for the sake of humanity.

It was largely through this influence that the National Tuberculosis Association was organized. Fortunately, the first meeting in January, 1904, following the eventful Tuberculosis Exposition in Baltimore, was presided over by Dr. William H. Welch of Johns Hopkins who had the foresight to appoint a representative committee, headed by Dr. William Osler, with power to pass upon all pending plans and with authority to lay the foundation for a permanent organization.

Thirty-seven of the thirty-eight representatives at this meeting were physicians. The list reads like the honor roll of American medicine for that period. The same may be said with reference to the second meeting at the staid old College of Physicians in Philadelphia, called by Dr. Osler in March, and the organization meeting in Atlantic City, June 6, 1904. Of the 197 founders gathered in the Public School Building at Atlantic City, 193 were physicians. At the second meeting in Philadelphia, it was resolved "that we here assembled do now organize ourselves into a United States society for the study of tuberculosis." It was decided that "The objects of the Association shall be: (a) the study of tuberculosis in all of its forms and relations; (b) the dissemination of knowledge concerning the causes, treatment, and prevention of tuberculosis; (c) the encouragement of the prevention and scientific treatment of tuberculosis."

Since from the beginning the ambitions of the National Tuberculosis Association were primarily the dissemination and utilization of medical knowledge through popular education, it is significant that the three meetings leading to the final organization were successively convened at Johns Hopkins University, the College of Physicians in Philadelphia, and the Public School Building in Atlantic City. In further confirmation of the purposes of that original group meeting in Baltimore, Dr. Welch's address at the Founders' Dinner during the twenty-fifth anniversary meeting in Atlantic City is pertinent. Speaking of the National Tuberculosis Association, he said, "Its conception, if you like, was in Baltimore, its birth was in Philadelphia, but it was hardly viable until the meeting here in Atlantic City, when the organization was completed." Again quoting Dr. Welch: "It has been said of the Founders of the Association that 'They builded better than they knew.' That is undoubtedly true. Nevertheless, I think we did realize at the inception of this organization that we were creating something which met a really urgent national need."

As further evidence of the medical profession's interest in the movement, Dr. Hermann M. Biggs, at an early meeting of the board of directors, moved that each of the thirty physicians on the board should extend a personal invitation to one hundred prominent members of the medical profession in his locality to become members. It was decided that publicity should be sought through both medical and lay journals. In this connection Dr. Biggs suggested that the sanitary officers throughout the country be induced to become interested in the Association, and that members of the American Public Health Association should be approached with the same view. With "great foresight" he observed that the appeals for funds sent out on letterheads showing the board of directors made up of physicians would cause people to think this was strictly a medical organization and to wonder why they should give money for its support. It was then that he wisely suggested that the Association needed a council of laymen in order for it successfully to obtain subscriptions for its work.

The development of the American Sanatorium Association, now the American Trudeau Society, and the National Conference of Tuberculosis Secretaries, the latter representing state and local organizations, followed, and their interdependence was promptly recognized. Through the harmonious interlocking of these three groups, the fight against tuberculosis has been heroically pursued. While all available knowledge is being broadly applied, the research committee of the National Tuberculosis Association is constantly looking for unexplored sources, promising the possibility of additional scientific discoveries. Always there are fact-finding, planning, and work committees exercising unusual initiative and originality in the execution of the Association's plans.

It would be impossible to estimate the mounting assets of this organization. The sum total of health and happiness and the prolongation of life which have resulted from its comprehensive program in behalf of humanity are far beyond our power of comprehension. The National Tuberculosis Association was among the first to realize that technology was running far ahead of sociology; in other words, medical science was awaiting general recognition and application of available knowledge. Through education and practical demonstration, people in health and in disease have learned the value of rest, fresh air, adequate nutrition, proper housing, personal and household hygiene, and finally graceful acquiescence in the limitations placed by their environment. They have learned the dangers inherent in their neglect of these principles. Also, they have learned the value of the tuberculin test and the symptoms of tuberculosis and have been forewarned by the same. Now they are learning the importance of routine X-ray of the chest, which promises a great advance in the control of tuberculosis. The influence of the National Tuberculosis Association on the development of general public health measures and health education cannot be estimated. The same may be said of the position of tuberculosis in medical education and the devlopment of special skills in the diagnosis, prevention, and cure of the disease, thus bringing incalculable reductions in infection, morbidity, and mortality.

Finally, in return for the relatively few millions spent by the National Tuberculosis Association and its affiliated units throughout the country, the yield in dollars and cents is literally a hundredfold. Whether we base our figures on the estimated value of a human life or the earning capacity of those who have been treated and have been partially or wholly rehabilitated, a conservative approximation of values runs into tens of billions. But of greater satisfaction is the fact that justly we may say that all who have wrought faithfully in this field have helped to dramatize the story of the Good Samaritan, and that those who have died in the harness have left a priceless heritage.

It is interesting to note that many of the participating physicians, particularly in the early history of this organization, suffered from tuberculosis and worked valiantly with keen minds and tired bodies. This history-making undercurrent is well known to those who have grown up with the National Tuberculosis Association, and it is revealed by a study of available correspondence, official and unofficial. In personal notes, unobtrusive sidelights, and brief postscripts, the pathetic truth sheds its shroud and shines forth as a living reality, and the historic worth of these "bouts in bed" becomes strikingly obvious.

As I have already pointed out, often the conditioning factors connected with disease help to unlock the mystery of history. This is the age-old influence Allen K. Krause referred to when he said, "Some day a man will write a new kind of history. Its keynote will be the shaping of human destiny by disease." In such a history tuberculosis would necessarily occupy a prominent place. Leaving out of consideration the possible psychic stimulation of tuberculosis, we know that calamity has its compensations and that even temporary physical suspense may send the creative mind on important missions. On such occasions there is time for contemplation; vital problems may be analyzed, expanding peripheries explored, and far-reaching plans and purposes spring into being. Obviously there is no way to estimate accurately the influence of enforced rest upon the minds of these tuberculous doctors and on the course of the American Sanatorium Association, but it is reasonable to believe that the impact upon policies and procedures, both spiritual and physical, is too great to pass unnoticed. No doubt much of the soil was turned and many of the seeds from which the harvest sprang were silently sown in "the land of the counterpane." The historian who sifts the data and weighs the evidence finds that the influence is very important and that it lives in the Association's traditions and accomplishments and will go into the mold that shapes the future of the American Trudeau Society.

In view of the mounting interest in tuberculosis, particularly on the part of the medical profession, armed with much new diagnostic and therapeutic knowledge, it was deemed wise to reorganize the American Sanatorium Association, which had its origin as early as 1905. This plan was consummated in 1939 and resulted in the American Trudeau Society, which officially is the Medical Section of the National Tuberculosis Association.

While the Sanatorium Association had a membership of approximately 350 physicians, the American Trudeau Society now has more than 4,000.

This long story leads us to the subject of treatment, more properly termed management because of the multifaceted problems involved, not the least of them being the psychological and socioeconomic aspects.

This is not the place for a detailed discussion of management, but everyone should realize the fundamental principles which must be met through the co-operation of the attending physician, his professional staff, and the patient.

The first duty of the physician is to appraise the patient's psychology, determine his response to the plan of treatment, assess his psychotherapeutic needs, and see that they have intelligent and sympathetic attention. Since the psychology of the patient is carefully considered in another chapter, other important factors will be considered here.

Whether management is being pursued in the home or in a sanatorium, the well-known principles of rest, adequate nutrition, personal and household hygiene must be faithfully followed according to the doctor's orders. This brief statement opens the way for a discussion of the education of the patient. I have always taught that the program designed to convey sufficient fundamental knowledge to help the patient get well and keep well should be under the direction of the attending physician. He should know better than anyone else what his individual patients need to know and how best the necessary lessons may be learned. This is very important, and patients should enter into the program as though they were preparing for a university degree. What they learn may lead to an added decree of life.

In addition to rest, good food, and fresh air, perhaps the greatest boon that has come to the tuberculous patient is collapse therapy. This method of treatment was first successfully employed in 1892 by Carlo Forlanini, an Italian physician. Forlanini collapsed the diseased lung by introducing gas or air into the pleural space, that is, between the lung and the chest wall. This brings about a certain degree of collapse, and if periodically repeated, the desired degree of collapse may be secured and maintained. This procedure is known as artificial pneumothorax. Its chief virtue lies in the fact that the lung is put to rest on a cushion of air, that cavities are closed by the resulting compression and the diseased areas placed in a more favorable condition for healing.

This method may be impossible or ineffective because of adhesions between the pleura and the chest wall. When pneumothorax is possible but unsatisfactory because of adhesions and the adhesions are string or bandlike, they may be severed

Trudeau Sanatorium, Trudeau, New York

Photograph by W. F. Kollecker

by means of a cautery under indirect vision through an instrument introduced between the ribs and known as a thoracoscope. If this can be successfully accomplished, artificial pneumothorax may be satisfactorily pursued.

If cauterization of the adhesions cannot be accomplished, other methods of surgical approach may be indicated. Of course, the simpler procedures are first employed as indicated by the existing pathology, and when these fail, other even more radical procedures may be employed. The choice becomes ever more difficult, and the successive surgical measures may require more technical skills. Suffice it to say that rib operations may become necessary, or perhaps the removal of a part of one or both lungs or the whole of one lung.

Obviously decisions concerning major surgery and their proper execution require teamwork. The knowledge and skills of the attending physician, the consulting surgeon, the laboratory worker, and the anesthetist must be integrated and carefully weighed with the patient's welfare ever in mind. While this discussion merely scratches the surface of the standard methods of treatment, the reader may be able to see how difficult it is and how heavy the responsibility.

This leaves us with some of the newer methods, particularly the administration of certain drugs, including the much-publicized antibiotics such as streptomycin and many others now being employed experimentally. These have been given singly and in various combinations, with varying reports of their effectiveness. As always, in tuberculosis, we have a long time to wait before adequate appraisal can be expected. At the present time it appears that streptomycin in combination with para-aminosalicylic acid is the most promising of all the drugs on trial.

Although the exact place of streptomycin alone or in combination with other drugs has not been fixed, it is possible to say that never before has the tubercle bacillus been forced to fold up and make a rapid retreat because of a given therapeutic agent. Unfortunately, the annulling action is not germicidal, but inhibitory or retarding in character, and we are faced with the dual problem of streptomycin-sensitive and streptomycin-resistant tubercle bacilli and the possibility that many of the bacilli, while on the run, may acquire sufficient resistance to turn victory into defeat. Also we now know enough about the cunning proclivities of this wary foe to fear that in the future tuberculosis in man, tubercle bacilli having already acquired streptomycin resistance, may not so readily respond to treatment. But now there is hope of inhibiting the development of streptomycin resistance by the use of other drugs or by their combination with streptomycin. So the fight goes on while the future of the disease remains uncertain.

The investigation carried on by various agencies, committees, and laboratories in connection with these new agencies has been stupendous. Chief among these are the research committee of the National Tuberculosis Association and the Tuberculosis Division of the Medical Department of the Veterans Administration. Anxiously and hopefully we await the results. But conservative physicians who know a lot about tuberculosis realize that patience and perseverance are perhaps the most important ingredients in any research program having to do with this disease.

CHAPTER XXIII

The Psychology of the Tuberculous Patient

IN previous chapters briefly I have discussed the origin of my private sanatorium and to some extent development of our knowledge of tuberculosis. For many years the sanatorium served as a workshop for me and a friendly haven for patients. The patients came suffering not only from the disease itself, but from its psychological and financial effects as well. From a practical standpoint the sanatorium was organized primarily for the patient. Early I took the position that the treatment of tuberculosis would be relatively easy if it were not for the patient. Many of those who find it necessary to chase the cure in an institution are admitted with *The Plague and I* concept. It is my belief that few institutions are guilty of the cold, impersonal reception the author of this interesting book describes. Certainly private sanatoria cannot be accused of such an unsympathetic response to the patient's psychological and physical needs.

Immediately upon admission the patient's psychological condition should be studied and all frustrations resolved as far as possible. Hippocrates warned that it is important to know what kind of a patient has the disease, and wise old Seneca said, "The wish to be cured is of itself an advance to health."

It has been said that "Socrates, returning from the Thracian campaign, praised the wisdom of the physicians of Thrace in their understanding and application of the principle that the body could not be relieved of symptoms without first curing the mind. He adjured the physicians of Greece to do likewise." Already his contemporary, Hippocrates, was giving careful attention to the influence of the mind over the body as he went about the cure of disease. Broch reports that Virgil, on his death bed, frustrated by cough, hemoptysis, pleurisy, and depression, had the good sense to embarrass Augustus Caesar's court physician with this question: "Is there any healing at all without magic?" In this connection, Montaigne's discussion of "the force of imagination" is worth reporting. "I am one of those that feels a very great conflict and power of imagination. All men are shocked therewith and some overthrown by it. . . . Simon Thomas was a great physician in his days. I remember upon a time coming by chance to visit a rich old man that dwelt in *Tholouse,* and who was troubled with a cough of the lungs, who discoursing with the said Simon Thomas of the means of his recoverie, he told him that one of the best was, to give me occasion to be delighted in his companie, and that fixing his eyes upon the liveliness and freshness of my face, and setting his thoughts upon the jolitie and vigor wherewith my youthful age did then flourish, and filling all his senses with my florishing estate, his habitude might thereby be amended, and his health recovered."

Doctors should remember that "liveliness and freshness" of face are contagious and that "beams from happy human eyes" may drive the clouds from heavy psychological skies.

Plato said, "The great error of our day is that physicians separate the soul from the body." The following couplet from the fifteenth-century *Regimen Sanitatis* indicates a firm medieval belief in the power of mind over body:

> *Joy and temperance and repose*
> *Slam the door on the doctor's nose.*

With rare exceptions, the tuberculous patient needs only a wise phthisiotherapist (specialist in the treatment of tuberculosis) who knows that mind and body are so interdependent that there can be no life when they cease to function as one. Some psychiatrists believe that when labor begins, the unborn babe feels the pressure of the womb and experiences a psychic reflex which initiates a prenatal anxiety complex. The scope of this discussion is too limited to permit a consideration of the genesis of all psychic conflicts, but this one reference indicates that the complete life cycle of the tuberculous patient must be explored.

Conscious of the human organism as an indivisible whole and of the necessity of equable balance for adequate living, involuntarily the phthisiotherapist pursues the psychosomatic concept as did Hippocrates of old without being fussed by this high-sounding new term for a time-tried practice.

In a discussion of this subject it is well to remember that under the stress of modern life it is difficult for us to escape psychic conflicts. Potentially even the best of us are in line for the madhouse. Also, we should remember that there is no straight line dividing sanity and insanity. Even those who think they are on the beam daily are being dragged back and forth across the imaginary line by their response to conflicting emotional currents.

Sixty-five per cent of the Veterans Administration's sickload is in the realm of neuropsychiatry. Some authorities claim that we need 6,500 additional psychiatrists to take care of the nation's mentally sick. No wonder that Day of Mundesley Sanatorium (Great Britain) attributes a large percentage of pulmonary tuberculosis to "dis-ease in their psychological environment." He thinks 30 per cent of the whole sanatorium population are sick in mind as well as in body. On a broad psychosomatic interpretation we can raise the ante to 100 per cent and not go astray.

With mental instability clinging to a vulnerable soma, it is not surprising that the imbalance occasioned by disease often leads to disturbing psychic conflicts. As a rule these are not insurmountable, and so far as possible they should be resolved by the patient with the help of the attending physician. When this can be accomplished without the aid of a psychiatrist, the patient's interests are not divided between doctors and his confidence disturbed. To the average patient the suggestion of a psychiatrist in the management of his case would spotlight his mental aberrations and aggravate his psychic conflicts, which otherwise he might have resolved in the course of time almost, if not quite, unconsciously. In the patient's life pattern, tuberculosis often comes as a great catastrophe, representing a formidable obstacle to a normal existence. He is in need of a physician he can tie to until the storm passes. Often the art of medicine becomes the simple art of being merciful. The assurance of genuine interest and sympathy captures the patient's confidence and secures his co-operation. Telling the patient bad news is not easy. It is a poor doctor who precipitates a hurricane and fails to anchor the storm-tossed soul.

No field in the whole realm of medicine offers such exacting, intriguing, and stimulating opportunities for service as that encompassing the management of pulmonary tuberculosis. Naturally, tuberculous patients, representing a cross section of humanity, run the full psychological scale.

The physician who hopes successfully to walk the ward and win the respect and confidence of his patients and see them safely on the road to recovery must tap the seat of reason, appraise the patient's character, and analyze carefully his psychic response to disease. To dissipate fear and resolve conflicts, he must possess a rare personality with exceptional qualities. If I were asked to enumerate these qualities I would name the traits Goethe attributed to Voltaire, but not without self-depreciation and apologies to all fellow physicians. The list is too long for enumeration—suffice it to say they pyramid perfection.

Often the apparently well-poised patient, upon being apprised of the presence of tuberculosis and the necessary therapeutic requirements, may, through the exercise of cultivated inhibitions, artfully conceal mild psychic conflicts. Nevertheless, these emotional upsets may initiate an imbalance resulting in functional disturbances with the possibility of organic changes. The wise physician may anticipate such an eventuality and employ preventive psychotherapy, or, if he does not immediately sense the psychic difficulties and the patient is not exhibiting satisfactory response to management, he may be able to penetrate successfully the veil of graceful acquiescence and discover existing conflicts.

Moderately stable victims of the disease with obvious mild psychic conflicts represent a large percentage of the patient load. With a favorable environment, a skillfully applied educational program, and well-chosen therapeutic methods, almost without exception their conflicts are resolved, and they make good patients.

More emotional and less stable persons, upon being informed of the presence of tuberculosis, may immediately burst into tears, spurning all efforts to reconcile them to the disease. In many cases, this distressing complex may be gradually modified through education replacing exaggerated ideas with consoling facts artfully presented by a sympathetic, far-sighted physician, who must at the same time compose distraught relatives. Occasionally patients stricken with even more serious psychic conflicts seek the protection of silence. These individuals are in dire need of neuropsychiatric help, and prompt measures should be directed toward a better understanding of their physical condition, its therapeutic implications and prognostic possibilities. Well-planned educational efforts on the part of the attending physician may succeed in making a good soldier of a whimpering coward. Because of the hopeless instability of the nervous system in certain patients, the obstacles may be insurmountable and the end hastened by continued anxiety. Fortunately this course is rarely experienced, especially if the attending physician is reasonably competent and exceptionally patient.

The patient's domestic and social situation is very important. For parents, the mental strain of exposing their children by being in contact with them or of being separated from them is always a factor influenced by the age, character, and temperament of the patient and the children and by the environmental conditions. Adoring mothers who cherish an abiding sense of sacrificial duty in the home cannot surrender their position without psychic conflicts which may, in some cases, prove a serious handicap. Such difficulties may be overcome by convincing the mother that contact with children should be broken and management graciously accepted in order that she may later safely resume her place in the home. Out of his experience the physician may be able to assure the anxious mother that in all probability her children will be protected physically and benefited psychologically by her temporary absence.

Separation of husband and wife may occasionally lead to serious psychic conflicts. Here the range and scope of evil possibilities hinge upon the character and temperament of the respective personalities and their ability to maintain equable social and moral standards under abnormal conditions. There is nothing so discouraging as domestic infelicity, especially when accompanied by an incapacitating disease and the haunting fear of inconstancy. Not infrequently, an irresponsible personality with sharpened psychic susceptiblities may manifest serious conflicts because of imaginary dangers. Such evil fears spring from groundless illusions which may be aggravated by isolation and physical inactivity. On the other hand, the attending physician occasionally finds an unsuspecting soul "singing at her grinding" suddenly shocked by the deadening consciousness of a faithless spouse. Nothing leaves one so inert, so devoid of psychological competency, so unfit for disciplined battle.

Unmarried lovers may suffer similar conflicts, often magnified by the fact that chronic invalidism may cool the ardor of a coveted lover. Such fears may lead to the precipitate negotiation of matrimony with all the hazards of such an untimely union.

These problems of the heart place upon the attending physician varied responsibilities. Some may be successfully executed through the exercise of ordinary skill, while others may require the wisdom of Solomon. But, with openness of mind and keen observation, the physician learns in the school of life and develops a certain skill in giving more than is demanded by strict measure. Through such giving, tolerance is broadened, understanding enlarged, perception sharpened, and initiative finds its appointed course. The exigencies of each case must suggest the method, which will necessarily depend upon "the character of the metal, the heat of the forge, and weight of the hammer."

The resourceful physician, with plenty of time, sincerity of purpose, and straightforwardness of action, may succeed in bridging gaping chasms and in healing sensitive wounds of the soul. As may be said of physical scars, psychic scars often memorialize heroic deeds. Such memorials should rest securely among the unheralded satisfactions of both patient and doctor.

Obviously the wide range of psychic manifestations makes adequate discussion impossible. The attending physician must be ready to meet the needs of his tuberculous patients as they come from every level of society, psychically geared to this fast-going, highly scientific, mechanistic age, in which mankind has modified his religion in favor of the less satisfying guidance of science and reason. When faced with what they consider serious life hazards, patients, almost without exception, seem to suffer from an obvious sense of personal inadequacy and a need for an abiding faith in some unseen power. No doubt Ibsen had this in mind when one of his characters, under emotional strain, said; "Without a fixed point outside myself, I cannot exist!"

Even un-Christian, self-sufficient Goethe, when threatened with destruction by a storm on the rocks of Capri, quieted his terrified fellow passengers by urging them to pray and by reminding them of Christ walking on the water.

Henry C. Link's book *The Return to Religion* was inspired by a study of psychology as influenced by a long financial depression. He feels that the Bible remains one of the most promising texts for the solution of fundamental psychological conflicts. It is reported that shortly before his death Dr. William J. Mayo said that regardless of what people think of religion, he had found that patients with some anchor outside themselves made life much easier for the doctor.

The wise physician knows that in certain types of people the religion of Christ and the obstinacy of human frailties may come together with such odds as to create grave psychological conflicts or to aggravate those already existing. Advisedly, in cases where remorse overwhelms the seat of reason, the physician may venture to cite Mark Twain's opinion of conscience: "Your conscience is a nuisance. A conscience is like a child. If you pet it and play with it and let it have everything it wants, it becomes spoiled and intrudes on all your amusements and most of your griefs. Treat your conscience as you would treat anything else. When it is rebellious, spank it—be severe with it, argue with it, prevent it from coming to play with you at all hours, and you will secure a good conscience; that is to say, a properly trained one. A spoiled one simply destroys all the pleasure in life."

A broad knowledge of nature, literature, history, and biography will enable the physician better to interpret his patient's psychic needs and to direct his reading along lines psychically helpful. Often the most essential initial educational adventure is teaching the patient the plain truth about tuberculosis. The story in language he can understand is often a source of great comfort and seldom is it wholly discouraging. Rarely is a patient's condition so serious as to preclude the possibility of a ray of hope. But to many patients the truth should be given in graduated doses, never exceeding their psychic tolerance. It is well to remember that there is no swift approach, no short cut, no possibility of sudden arrival.

The more nervous and fearful the patient, the more important the sanatorium becomes in the management. The daily contact with physicians, nurses, and other patients in a well-ordered sanatorium serves as a revelation, inspires confidence, increases knowledge and dissipates fear, thereby creating the best possible conditions for progressive improvement. For many there is nothing more hopeless than to lie down at home with the shocking consciousness of the intimate presence of a dread disease, fully aware of the partially concealed anxiety of poorly informed, sympathetic loved ones, obviously ignorant of the patient's most urgent needs. Genuine poverty and the necessary household penury often serve as aggravating factors. Such an environment encourages dangerous introversion and may cause the patient to hug silently his own burden of bitterness through long days and nights, tortured with a hopeless sense of fear and uncertainty and possibly harboring the spirit of rebellion common in the course of a great catastrophe.

A misplaced word may cause a great deal of unnecessary worry. A passing remark of a friend or another patient may result in a wakeful night or days of useless anxiety. The educational program and the daily routine should be designed to prevent or to meet such psychic events. Through the patient application of the attending physician or the well-trained public health nurse, the acquisition of knowledge and understanding on the part of the patient may replace doubt, fear, and rebellion with hope and its attendant virtues.

The physician who loves people and has the gift of getting on with his patients can penetrate the well-planned defenses of the shrewdest pachyderm. There is a rich reward in the pursuit and discovery of that spark of response hidden beneath the crust of certain reserved personalities. This spark may be fanned into a warm glow of great mutual value. Confidences are to be treasured not only as evidence of therapeutic success but because they open avenues through which curative suggestions may travel to their coveted goal.

The physician who does not gain access to the sacred precincts hidden beneath his patients' skull cap is missing one of the most fascinating functions of the patient-physician relationship. He is forfeiting the opportunity to harness the energy which generates the storms of frustration and motivates behavior, and thereby he is sacrificing a vital therapeutic force.

Through proper education the patient must be directed toward self-expression and the execution of enlightened responsibility. As far as possible the physician should impress upon him the importance of a partnership in the difficult task of getting well. It should be understood that this happy union cannot give birth to good health without mutual participation in a courageous campaign. Early in the course of treatment he should be impressed with the fact that both mind and body must be wholly committed to the task of getting well and that there should be no respite. Finally, he must learn with Carlyle that "the duty of being brave is an everlasting duty," even though it may lead to the last great mystery.

CHAPTER XXIV

Lights and Shadows in the Sanatorium

TO illustrate some of the problems referred to in the preceding chapter, here are a few cases representing different psychological types. First we pass thousands of well-poised patients without serious psychological conflicts, and almost without exception we may safely pass those who are moderately stable. As a rule their mild mental difficulties respond to the sanatorium environment and the planned approach of the physician and nurses.

The more emotional patients may spend days or even weeks in tears, taxing the ingenuity of everybody concerned. But with rare exceptions ultimately these, too, may come safely under control regardless of therapeutic requirements.

In this group we recall a well-nourished, handsome woman with many good reasons for a continuing life, but she was obsessed with the fear of death. In spite of this complex she demanded much attention from all possible sources and seemed to think only of her own comfort. Every day when I made rounds, she opened the conversation by saying, "Doctor, you know I am going to die; you just want to make it easy for me, and you won't tell me the truth." After patiently listening to this statement every day for weeks in spite of my avowed belief that she had a good chance to get well and that she could save time by accepting that judgment, I decided upon a rather radical course.

One morning after listening to the same old story, I said, "I have decided you are right; you are not going to get well. Since you insist that death is your inevitable lot, all my efforts to help you may be in vain. But once more I urge you to discard this fatalistic attitude and leave a better record for posterity no matter when you die." She was furious, and I, knowing that she would need time to collect her thoughts and formulate her policy, silently slipped away with the hope that a good dose of anger might bring a change of heart. The next time I made rounds she was psychologically sound. She became a good patient and achieved a complete recovery and socioeconomic competency. Seldom does the attending physician find it necessary to employ such heavy pressure, but in this case it was chosen as a last resort.

As an example of one of the rare exceptions I am reporting the case of a young woman who came with very little trouble in her lungs but with a heavy weight upon her mind, which she could not be induced to lay aside. The knowledge of tuberculosis in her own body was more than she could bear. After two or three weeks during which I had been unable to fathom her mental conflicts and to bring about a satisfactory adjustment, I was contemplating the advisability of calling upon a psychiatrist for help. But before this could be accomplished, the superintendent of the sanatorium called me to say that the patient claimed that an emergency had arisen and she wanted permission to go to town for two or three hours in order to take care of it. In fact, I was informed that she was going with or without permission. In truth, the emergency was the child of her own distraught brain. She went to a hardware store, purchased a pistol, and a few hours later the police found her locked in a hotel room with a bullet in her brain. This is very unusual. As a rule, tuberculous patients are hopeful, and often the faith in the future is remarkable even though in some cases it may be unwarranted in the light of the hopeless physical possibilities. In this case, perhaps I should have achieved a more enlightened penetration of her brain before she decided to lodge a bullet there.

In the latter group many cases clamor for attention in this necessarily brief story. A striking example can be reported with the cost of only a few words. A young doctor who knew he had tuberculosis worked at his practice until he was in a hopeless condition. As a rule, when death is inevitable, physicians try to spare mental suffering. With occasional exceptions it is thought best to tell relatives the truth but encourage the patient when possible. Fortunately time often mercifully brings a gradual awakening and the inevitable fact of death is less cruel than if suddenly revealed by the doctor or by members of the patient's family.

But this young physician, after months in the sanatorium with obvious loss of ground, needed no encouragement. On the other hand he manifested that strange euphoria which often occurs in those with exceptional mental qualities. In mild form this strange mental excitation may be described in the words of Katherine Mansfield as ". . . the faint glitter on the plant that the frost has laid a finger on." Or as in this case it may be that both soul and body ". . . burn as in oxygen gas." On the last day of this young man's life he awakened with a shining face; his nurse prepared him for breakfast, served his tray, and tarried to hear his breathless plans for pleasure and travel as soon as he was strong enough. She urged him to quit talking long enough to regain his breath for breakfast and then departed for the care of other patients. When she returned for his tray, she found that he had gone on a long journey from which he would never return. Apparently, after drinking his coffee, he had peacefully entered upon his eternal sleep. Silently we contemplated his flushed cheeks, his bright eyes, his scintillating mind, his confident soul, and his unfailing hopefulness, and we were glad to know he was on his way.

After all, Diogenes may have known more than we are willing to believe when he said, "the only way to freedom is to die with ease." O'Henry, dying of tuberculosis, seemed to know his fate and had the courage to say, "Pull up the shades. I don't want to go home in the dark."

This reminds me that C. McLaurin in *Mere Mortals* indicated that it is helpful to have patients who want to "get on with their dying." While this seems a bit cruel, such an attitude would lessen the present interest in euthanasia. Apropos the above, there have been times when I wished for patients like Queen Elizabeth, who, according to reports, once said, "To hell with melancholia."

When I was subsequently dean of the University of Oklahoma School of Medicine, a young chap was placed under my care because there was a question whether or not he was physically qualified for such an exacting task as medical education and because of my friendship for his remarkable father and mother. While there was something in his appearance and his personality peculiarly ethereal, it was obvious that his feet were on terra firma. During his second year in school, while playing golf, he developed a sudden severe pain in his left chest. He was placed in the University Hospital where the diagnostic study revealed spontaneous collapse of the left lung, possibly due to a tuberculous lesion. He was moved to the sanatorium, where he remained until his trouble was well under control. When he was convalescent, we made rounds together and planned special studies and statistical records which he could further pursue while resting. His disease was responding under artificial pneumothorax which had been continued in order to rest the affected lung. He had learned much about the management of the disease and could be trusted to watch his step. Because he was an educated patient in every sense and because of satisfactory response to treatment, he was permitted to return to school with the understanding that he would continue to live in the sanatorium where his physical well-being could be guarded and our mutual studies continued.

When he was graduated, we negotiated plans for intern service in Boston. Leaving out many interesting details, it is enough to say that his progress was phenomenal. His work attracted attention, and he was invited to accept special training in the highly specialized field of neurosurgery. A three-year scholarship with one year abroad was made available. While he was on this scholarship at the Neurological Institute in Montreal, war between Great Britain and Germany was declared. He joined the Canadian neurosurgical unit and went overseas as a medical officer in the service of the Canadian Army. He was on duty to help take care of the mangled Dieppe casualties suffering neurological injuries. Continuing with this unit, later he was stationed at the neurosurgical hospital established to take care of casualties returning from combat across the Channel. Finally, he was left in charge of the unit when his chief returned to Canada, and during the Rhine campaign the load was exceptionally heavy. Two of his men were off duty because of illness; forgetting the "way you live" concept under the exigencies of war, he worked day and night and sacrificed the health he had learned to guard while in the sanatorium.

One night after tossing with fever and coughing with a restrained consciousness of the significance of such symptoms, he sought an examination. A cavity was found in the right lung, and tubercle bacilli were discovered in the sputum. His skills were halted, his presence in the operating room and on the wards was discontinued, his ambitions thwarted, his career ended, at least for the time being. He was told what he already knew better than his medical advisers and was invalided home on a Canadian hospital ship. Sanatorium care failed to bring arrestment of his disease; surgical collapse of the right lung was recommended and accepted. With limited breath and abiding hope, this lieutenant colonel in the Royal Canadian Army Medical Corps fights on with honor and the gratitude of all nations because of his contributions to those who suffered in World War II and all potential victims of wars to come. His case stands among the saddest of war casualties. His mission was to save, not to destroy, life, and all the world prays for his recovery.

Putting an Indian to bed in a sanatorium poses special problems not commonly encountered among white patients. His love of open spaces and undisciplined habits of living relatively free from the inhibitions necessary for the successful management of tuberculosis make the restricted life of the institution an incomprehensible burden—an imposition not to be lightly tolerated. Also rankling in his heart is the isolation from his own kind, the restrictions upon his biological propensities, and in some cases the curtailment of accustomed alcoholic bouts. Often these difficulties are insurmountable, and disaster is inevitable. Chasing the cure is contrary to the Indian's way of life, and attempts at control and discipline often are futile.

The above serves as a fitting introduction to the following brief references to the Indians' psychological responses to the doctor and the discipline of disease. When it becomes necessary to consider sanatorium care for them, their personality traits, the vestiges of their primitive habits, and the resulting psychology which defies the psychoanalysts, must be considered. It is difficult to penetrate the defensive crust arising through eons of savage existence and often impossible to tap the spiritual and intellectual values concealed by their masklike faces. Naturally they are disciplined by the days when revelation of thought or design through the least change of expression might have meant death and destruction. In many respects, while trying to give the Indians the benefit of the white man's culture, we fail to profit by what they have to give us. Often as I have sat at the bedside and seen them recklessly passing to the Happy Hunting Ground, I have wondered whether they have not retained their primitive price on life. Their valuation is not the same as that marked up by the average white man. And this difference may account for the fact that they are not so reluctant to exchange the restrictions imposed by the Great White Father in Washington for the free life offered by their conception of the Great Spirit. In the past, often their people were buried upright, with food, clothing, the implements of warfare, and their favorite pony standing by ready for the journey. Almost we could exclaim, "God speed their flight!"

After this discussion of the Indians' psychology I hasten to admit there are many exceptions and to note that in Oklahoma, which contains about one-fourth of all the Indians in the

United States, they have fared relatively well. They attend the public schools, they speak the white man's language, and gradually they have accepted his way of life. In short, for the most part, they are being assimilated into the general population of the state.

In the field of medicine they accept the most approved scientific care. This means that in the short span of sixty years they have discarded their magical and ritualistic methods—methods which Hippocrates broke away from in the fifth century B.C. Thus many doctors still living in Oklahoma have had the unique experience of witnessing a transition in medical practices among the Indians corresponding to a period of twenty-five hundred years in the recorded history of medicine. The rapid decline in the death rate among Oklahoma Indians from tuberculosis alone (300 in 1940 to 120 in 1949) indicates a profitable adjustment.

One of my first sanatorium patients was a beautiful Osage Indian girl with all the fine befeathered, elegantly beaded trappings of her tribe, plus civilization's richest ready-to-wear, with a white maid-in-waiting. She came in a Cadillac sedan with a liveried white chauffeur. In spite of the fact that I tried to temper the necessary rest cure to her limited tolerance, she could not be convinced that the Cadillac and the cure were incompatible. After a short, unhappy stay she left against medical advice. Her father, a wise old Osage, knew that she was an innocent victim of civilization and its "black gold" and that he stood helpless before his own willful child. At that time the Osage people represented the richest nation per capita in the world because of the oil that gushed from beneath their luscious pasture lands. Nature with the aid of Uncle Sam had provided something which was not good for them. No doubt it would have been better if the discovery of Osage oil could have awaited eons of evolution. The white man, with few exceptions, is equally too primitive to withstand the luxuries made available by oil's fabulous fortunes.

Eleven months later this young lady returned pale, emaciated, haggard, and hopeless. In a few more months of inconsolable confinement she fretted and coughed her life away. I have always hoped that her spirit reverted to the blanket and that after shedding all her so-called civilization she joined her progenitors in the Happy Hunting Ground.

Old John (her father) and I understood each other and charged this sad loss to premature sophistication resulting from unwonted wealth. John was an official interpreter for his tribe. Often in this capacity he went to Washington to help his people plead for more money in order that some of them might make more whoopee. One time when he was before the Land Commission in Washington one of the old aborigines had spoken two hours in his own tongue. When John got up to act as interpreter, a member of the commission said, "Mr. Abbott, if you can interpret that speech, you are a good one." He replied, "I can do it in just four words. He wants his money."

This economy in words is characteristic of most of the Indians I have come to know. Occasionally he sent postcards to me from Washington. I remember one picture card of the Capitol steps, on which he had written, "Dear Doc, I am here—John." When he died, the newspapers carried a story which indicated his consciousness of the evil changes civilization had wrought and suggested a nostalgic longing for the hard but good old days. This sentiment is reflected in the following from a Muskogee paper: "Money Good, Is Poison too, Indian says—At a meeting of Indians who came to hear John Collier, Indian commissioner, explain why they didn't receive enough money, there was one Indian who complained of too much money. He was John Abbott, Pawhuska, member of the wealthy Osage tribe, 'Young folks now get drunk, cuss, act bad. We got high sheriff at our town, but we got firewater all same and boys and girls drink it.' Abbott said in broken English.

" 'Money do good but money poison, too. Money ruin our boys and girls. Five die last month; they die young. Old men live long time. We don't need so much money. We need more boys who work—not play.' "

THE SANATORIUM

Many years later I sat at the bedside of an attractive dark-complected woman who possessed beautiful features of remarkable symmetry. The beauty of her face was slightly marred by the anxiety accompanying an attack of blood-spitting. In keeping with their primitive instinct, her sister, equally attractive, was standing by to proffer any needed aid. Recognizing the faint copperish Indian complexion, artfully I inquired about its origin. They were proud of a few thirty-seconds of Osage blood and a little more of Kaw. They said that during the peak of Osage oil prosperity their income was approximately five thousand dollars quarterly. Now they receive only twelve hundred. Having readily learned easy living under the twenty-thousand-dollar annual income and having failed to save for a rainy day, they were finding the adjustment very difficult.

A few years ago I had under sanatorium management a young Indian woman who was well educated and willing to follow the established regime. At her bedside were all the current selections of the Book-of-the-Month Club, Thomas Edward Lawrence's *The Seven Pillars of Wisdom,* and the Holy Bible, yet she was having her beautiful long braids cut off in order that her mother and father might offer them in flame to the Great Spirit. She was not sure this would hasten her recovery, but her less civilized mother and father considered it a necessary sacrifice, and she made the offering in line with duty. No doubt her acquiescence was conditioned by the ingrained primitive urge to appease the Indian's God.

An Osage who was a periodic drinker was referred for sanatorium care. His attending physician was good enough to report his alcoholic proclivities with a timely warning. The young man was placed in a private room; and after spending much time on the psychological side of the psychosomatic complex, explaining the absolute necessity of co-operation and impressing the danger of unfavorable reactions to treatment if he did not literally toe the mark, we were surprised that he proved to be an ideal patient. But we never let him out of sight. If he needed a haircut or wanted to make a trip to the jewelry store, we sent a nurse along to guard against the bottle and get him back sober. At one time he spent several hundred dollars for a ring and a watch. This was considered a good investment since the cash was frozen, at least for a time, while the Indian psychology toyed with the new-found possessions. But we knew that with a little freedom his inbred propensities and his desire for firewater might lead to the pawnshop and, inevitably, the police station.

When it became necessary to close the farm sanatorium, this young man was carefully domiciled in another institution. Apparently the change disturbed his morale, and he became restless and was overwhelmed by an uncontrollable urge for alcohol. Finally he slipped away, and in spite of a glorious drunk he was able to evade the police for three days. Ultimately he came back in the custody of a friendly taxi driver. But he had pawned his watch and ring and had not enough money left to pay the taxi fare.

From this time, periodically he found a way to get out and go on resounding benders. Unfortunately he was not particularly discriminating about his drinks, and one fateful morning he came in with a heavy trace of bay rum on his breath. Following this, his last bout, he developed a toxic condition accompanied by dilation of the stomach and an acute congestion of kidneys, which, in spite of all that could be done, resulted in death. As I stood at the autopsy table contemplating his tuberculosis, the enormously dilated stomach, and his acutely congested kidneys—all representing his heritage from the Great White Father's civilization—I looked upon his fine physique and the beautiful convolutions marking the surface of his exposed brain and thought how happy he might have been if his life had been launched upon the four hooves of his pony in primitive fashion instead of the four wheels of his automobile which helped to launch his fatal marathon for psychobiological satisfactions.

In the summer of 1924 an Indian named Bill came to my private sanatorium because of tuberculosis. Under routine management he became a very good patient. In time the disease healed, and he was permitted to return home. But also he was well heeled with the proceeds from Osage oil, and he had developed confidence in the sanatorium as a shelter in time of storm. With this feeling of safety firmly fixed in his oft-disturbed mind, he would call a taxi and make use of this haven when warned by alcoholic whisperings. He had an uncanny way of making this decision just in time to evade the police. The practice was tolerated for a while, but frequent repetition caused alarm. While we were contemplating some defensive action, he came in a little too drunk and tried being rough with the night nurse, and the next day we read the law to him.

He never came to the sanatorium again, but one night during our "Jake" paralysis epidemic (poisoning from accidental contamination of Jamaica ginger sold in drugstores and sometimes imbibed by alcoholics) I received a telephone call. A woman said: "I am calling for Mr. Bill. He is sick and wants you to come. He's down in bed and can't get up." Instinctively I accepted the call. I found the patient in bed complaining of loss of power in his lower extremities. When I stripped his magnificent body for examination, I was shocked to find that his lower extremities were completely paralyzed.

I said, "Bill, what have you been drinking?"

"Doc, I drink everything I can get my hands on."

"Have you had any Jamaica ginger?"

"Yes, Doc, I have."

"Can you let me have some for laboratory tests?"

"No, Doc, I never leave any. There's a garbage can full of empty bottles in the back. You might find a drap or two."

After looking through a half-bushel of bottles, I gave up. Resuming my place at the bedside, I said, "Bill, if you don't quit drinking everything you get your hands on, some day you'll get your knock-out dose."

In naïve fashion with candid flashes from his guileless eyes he said, "Doc, drinking ain't hurten me. I jest can't use my legs."

Two years later a liveried chauffeur came to my office to

announce that Mr. Bill was in his car down in the parking lot and wanted to see Doctor Moorman. I yielded to my curiosity and went down. Sitting limp in the lap of luxury, Bill opened the rear door to the Cadillac sedan, revealing a flashy young woman in silks, and said, "Doc, I want you to tell this young lady my paralysis is due to Jake and not syphilis." I have never learned whether or not my response cinched the match. Later I received a friendly postcard from a distant city, but the message, in keeping with Indian brevity, was not informative.

In the sanatorium, I now have charge of an Indian youth whose body, when stripped for examination, reminds one of Tait McKenzie's, "The athlete modeled from the average of 400 Harvard students." Yet this boy has tuberculosis and, unfortunately, an alcoholic urge, which, of course, is incompatible with the cure. Fortunately he is responding to streptomycin. As I have suggested, this new therapy may prove to be a great boon to these impulsive, unstable people who cannot coerce a recalcitrant psyche and a rebellious body into a state of happy psychosomatic equilibrium. God grant that this may be true. Many of these unstable individuals have passed to the Happy Hunting Ground on the wings of an inadequate will.

A frail young white woman with pallid cheeks, flashing eyes, and an intellect remarkably keen was referred to me by a doctor friend, now deceased. Though she and I worked along with a more perfect understanding than either would dare admit, we finally came face to face with death. For days I had dreaded the last encounter with this woman's gleaming eyes, definitely lighted with that strange effulgence tuberculosis occasionally bestows upon those who are on the last lap of life's incomprehensible course. I had given much thought to this inescapable duty and wondered what I could say when faced with the last encounter.

One morning I found her with eyes exceptionally bright and searching, but with no audible question. Knowing the issue was at that moment in the hands of God, I summoned courage for a pleasant greeting and passed on to see other patients with an uneasy conscience and a cowardly feeling because I had evaded conversation so obviously suggested by the quizzical gleam in the windows of her soul. Soon a nurse called me aside and said she wanted me to come.

Alertly and gravely with piercing prescience she looked beyond my wavering defenses, as though searching the very depths of my consciousness with an appeal for a frank statement of the truth. "Doctor, this is the end, isn't it? I don't believe you would try to deceive me. If this is the last, I must talk to you." With a clear voice under perfect control, she said, "You know I am not afraid to die, but please don't let me go without a chance to thank you once more for everything you have done for me. I know you have tried and that you have done all that any doctor could do. My husband is on the way, but I'll be gone before he reaches me. His means are limited. Please tell him I want my doctor's bills paid first." Placing a slender hand in mine, she said, "I must say good-bye now." In less than thirty minutes she was dead. I thought, "Poor splendid wings, so frayed and soiled and worn," and yet how ready for the unknown journey.

My dear old friend who had treated her in New Mexico sent me a copy of a letter he had written to her, which illustrates the true physician's interest in his patients. I quote one paragraph: "I am leaving on my vacation the last of this month, and it would be much better to start this [new treatment] in Oklahoma City than to come back to Albuquerque. Be a good girl and do what I tell you. You have always been a good patient, and I want you to follow my orders now the same as you did while at the Presbyterian." Furthermore, this physician's professional loyalty is exemplified by the following sentence from a note, accompanying the copy of his letter to the patient, in which he had given me an undeserved boost in order to bolster his patient's morale: "If you need a new hat after what I said about you, let me know."

It was a beautiful afternoon in late September, 1944. I was working overtime, but it was impossible for me to do less. When my young colleagues went to war, I volunteered to help hold the home front. This much I was determined to do even at the risk of my coronaries.

My last patient was a beautiful young woman with the gift of joyous laughter in her eyes, now subdued by the weight of war on her heart. Her lithe figure followed the lines of youth and her sparkling countenance betrayed her love of life, yet there was something in her manner suggesting unusual courage and pertinacity. Here was the very essence of heroic young womanhood making war a thing well worth winning. Her husband was in the artillery overseas awaiting hazardous assignments. The separation and the ceaseless anxiety had lowered her resistance. Fatigue, cough, and loss of weight had driven her to the doctor. She was seeking medical advice because of the conviction that for her husband's sake she should keep well. Examination revealed the evidence of a treacherous disease. Tuberculosis was doing its deadly work.

It was obvious that I was facing a difficult task. Under such circumstances telling the patient is not easy. But the conscientious physician never runs from duty. Fortunately, I had learned that even the plain hard truth can be shorn of its sharp corners. The assurance of genuine sympathy captures the patient's confidence and secures co-operation. The truth in graduated doses may develop a lifesaving tolerance. While entering into a partnership for the purpose of fighting a deadly disease, we both understood that there were two wars to win. I agreed that the Captain of Artillery should not be handicapped by this battle on the home front when she insisted that he should not know of her difficult encounter with disease until his war was won. With a remarkable display of courage, this young volunteer determined to prove her mettle, win her spurs, and claim victory in her own right. There was not a better soldier anywhere on the foreign battle front.

She entered the sanatorium, marshaled her forces, and remained on the firing line while her husband was giving the enemy hell on the way to Berlin. Her abiding hope was that she might be physically fit when her Captain came marching home. Her courageous letters to him were relayed through her home town to be postmarked there before going overseas. His were received there and forwarded to her own battle front.

Consistently we made our plans, and as time passed, we discussed our losses and gains, determined our strategy, and established our lines of action. Ultimately the fighting was furious on both fronts. The hazards abroad were shocking, and the defenses on the home front were being shattered. The tubercle bacilli were on the march, leaving gaping craters in the lungs. In order to close the breach and form new lines, it became necessary to advise major rib operations in successive stages. Eagerly she met the knife and emerged from each trying experience with a shining face. In spite of her wounds, she exulted in the thought that the Captain of Artillery was pouring lead on the enemy abroad.

The small-town post office, accommodating the two fronts, kept the missiles moving. In time there came a day when progress was good on both sides of the sea, and the god of all true lovers gathered up these identical supplications and vouchsafed victory, physical fitness, love, and home.

With the news of unconditional surrender of Hitler's hordes, the truth from the home front was flashed overseas, and the services of the Red Cross were engaged with the hope of securing speedy leave and prompt passage home. The young woman, worrying about the scars of battle, was reassured about her physical handicaps. She was urged to think only of the happy reunion with the privilege of sharing the glory of battle and the reward of victory.

With the knowledge of the doctor's appeal through the Red Cross and of pending negotiations for his return to the States apparently bogged down in red tape, the young captain by-passed local authorities and appeared at Regional Headquarters. After a scathing rebuke, his story was heard, his papers examined, and immediate leave granted. He was sent to Paris with instructions to catch an army plane for New York.

Arriving at the airport, he was informed that all passenger space was taken, but there was room for 185 pounds of additional baggage. Tipping the scales with his luggage in hand at 180 pounds, he alleged that he begged for special consideration and insisted on being loaded as baggage. The connections in New York were good, and in a relatively short time the young volunteers were in each other's arms sailing the sea of love, halfway between the Atlantic and the Pacific.

It was a glorious Sunday afternoon; the telephone rang and the charming young patient said, "The Captain of my life is here, there is no room in the hotels, what can we do?" Treasuring the inclusiveness of her euphonious "we" and realizing she had been taught to look to her doctor for the solution of all her problems, I told her that the guest room in my home was awaiting her hero. When I knocked at the young man's door to say "good night," I found the Captain of Artillery between immaculate sheets. On the floor beyond the comfortable bed, the boy's battered duffel bag appeared, and in imagination I saw the fox holes of France only a few hours away and went to my room silently exclaiming *"Gloria Victis."* With the lucky lovers in my heart, I fell asleep, planning their second honeymoon.

Shortly before this writing I received a letter from this happy couple indicating that the intervening five years have been crowded with joyous living and crowned by material success.

Such reporting as this must suggest to the reader the physician's rewards. They are legion and often too personal for publication.

I cannot repress the temptation to give an example of the humorous experiences constantly occurring with varied ramifications. I had a delightful female patient who had waited weeks upon weeks for a negative sputum. One morning I walked into her room and found her in silk pajamas sitting on the side of the bed in a flood of sunshine. With the aid of a silver hand mirror, she was adjusting her jaunty little curls. She presented a picture well worth preserving, but when I announced, "There's good news for you," I was glad there were no photographers in the room. She slammed the mirror down, tossed her curls to the wind, sprang to the floor and clasped her doctor in the innocent, spontaneous embrace which comes only from high elation and genuine appreciation. Immediately I looked up and down the hall for nurses, patients, or possibly her husband who came daily about that time. My solicitude meant nothing to a young woman who had achieved a negative sputum. With no compunction I consider this among the lights which help dissipate the shadows of a doctor's life. Since there were no witnesses, the reader is requested to accept the story and consider it only as incidental among the doctor's rewards.

While this manuscript was in preparation, I heard from a one-time vivacious young woman who came to me soon after the birth of her only baby. She was surprised and shocked to learn that she was suffering from advanced tuberculosis and exposing her baby to infection. Like the good sport that she was, she committed her child to the care of others, entered the sanatorium, and in the face of grave handicaps carried on from month to month. At times it seemed that she could not survive, and though realizing her plight, she bravely persevered, even when I suspected that hope was running far below her courage.

The message I received indicated that this woman was still vivacious and courageous in spite of the intervening years. She was happy to report that her daughter, having missed massive infection, was sound and well, and her granddaughter was reveling in a healthy, joyous childhood. Such reports augment the physician's abiding satisfactions.

Although I have discussed foolish virgins in previous chapters, these are reported here because they had tuberculosis and because of the interest, educational value, and warning their stories carry. These are city girls, and while milk-maids on the prairies and sophisticated young women on paved streets are the same biologically, apparently city life releases inhibitions and unfavorably conditions them to temptation.

Twenty-odd years ago a doctor from a large city a thousand miles away wrote to me pleading favorable consideration of a problem he was trying to solve without a serious shock to two gentle old people already failing in health. A refined young girl of good family previously unblemished by moral turpitude had yielded to temptation and had awakened to the fact that she must pay the fiddler. She was willing to make any sacrifice rather than shatter the faith and happiness of her mother and father for the remainder of their years. Her physician could find no just cause for the interruption of her pregnancy, and in any case a clandestine service would have been foreign to his medical traditions. Fortunately, she was suffering from minimal tuberculosis and a change of climate could be arranged with relatively little mental anguish on the part of her parents as compared to that which would have been occasioned by a knowledge of the unfortunate departure from the straight and narrow path. This could be negotiated without undue strain upon her doctor's conscience. Although it was somewhat embarrassing for me, I acquiesced in the family doctor's plan.

While chasing the cure in the sanatorium, the young creature's moral reputation was carefully guarded. She was known as Mrs. Q, and because of her disease it was thought that the baby should not be in contact with her. When the time came, according to our preconceived plans, she was transferred to the lying-in department of a good hospital. She had an excellent obstetrician, who generously lowered his fees and accepted monthly payments so that they could be unobtrusively blended with the sanatorium charges and thus obviate suspicion on the part of the unsuspecting parents. After a serious conference the prospective mother agreed that it would be best for her never to see the baby. With this understanding we were able to negotiate adoption in a fine, well-to-do family. The mother was never to know the identity of the people who adopted her child or their place of residence.

In time, the tuberculous condition was arrested, her girlish figure restored, and she was permitted to return to her happy mother and father.

THE SANATORIUM

She came to us like a soldier with two battles to fight, she behaved like a good soldier, and she developed the philosophy of a stoic. Apparently there was no bitterness in her heart. Yet, psychologically she had walked the streets of hell, while on the way to heaven. What a price she paid! What sustained longing she has endured. Even yet, occasionally she writes to one of the nurses hoping to get news of her daughter who is now a mother herself. This faraway mother and grandmother must go about her daily duties harboring the secret of maternity and the burning sense of unrequited love while hanging on every word from the wise nurse who, according to her training, faithfully withholds identity and location. Though there may be much romance and biological excitement in social and moral nonconformity, there is a price, and the crucible burns long and at times becomes very hot. For the moron who does not conform there may be little remorse, but those who have the capacity for great enjoyment usually are endowed with a keen sense of guilt and may expect to reap the stuff that sorrow feeds upon.

An ambitious, fair young creature from a distant university in the Far West was suddenly seized with an attack of bloodspitting. She was referred for sanatorium management. Examination elicited signs of advanced tuberculosis in both lungs. While bed rest was being pursued and the lungs were showing some improvement, the signs of pending maternity gradually developed. The possibility of tuberculous peritonitis with abdominal fluid to cause enlargement of the abdomen was considered. In this case, such a tentative diagnosis furnished a reasonable screen behind which the doctor could hide his suspicions while awaiting the truth either from the lips of the patient or from nature's cue. Many hundred miles away this charming creature had a fond mother and father who would resent the least insinuation of immorality. This and the girl's obvious refinement conditioned the doctor's strategy, yet it was quite necessary to get on with the diagnosis.

One morning after pleasant greetings and a frank discussion of people's foibles and frailties admittedly universal, but varying in pattern and degree, her bright face clouded, the need of confession pricked her soul and released her tongue, and she poured her pent-up troubles in her doctor's lap. A normal biological phenomenon progressing in the diseased body of this young woman presented serious problems. Suffice it to say that a happy solution was found, and the baby lived to participate in the late world war. It should never be forgotten that sooner or later nonconformists pay, though the deed may be registered only with the doctor and in the secret recesses of their souls.

Those who are troubled about the question of deception necessary to achieve such ends are referred to the Great Book where the criteria of service are laid down and forgiveness of sin is recorded. Through experience, physicians learn to do the best they can with human foibles, to accept the inevitable, and to make the most of what comes. In his delightful monograph, "In Defense of Fishermen," Grover Cleveland quotes the following: "Uncle Toby, overcome with tender sympathy, swore with an unctuous, rotund oath, that his sick friend should not die; and we are told that 'the accusing spirit which flew up to heaven's chancery with the oath blushed as he gave it in; and the recording angel, as he wrote it down dropped a tear upon the word and blotted it out forever.'"

Doctors who are trained to accept patients as they come and to do their best to help them, and patients who have erred and are penitent need just such an angel to blot out all evil thoughts, words, and deeds and to give credit for all good intentions.

I have chosen to relate in this chapter stories of interesting or unusual patients and their problems. Not all people who get sick have arresting histories or even noteworthy personalities. Truly Dr. Logan Clendening is right when he indicates that only Dickens divined what all doctors know—that patients can be bores.

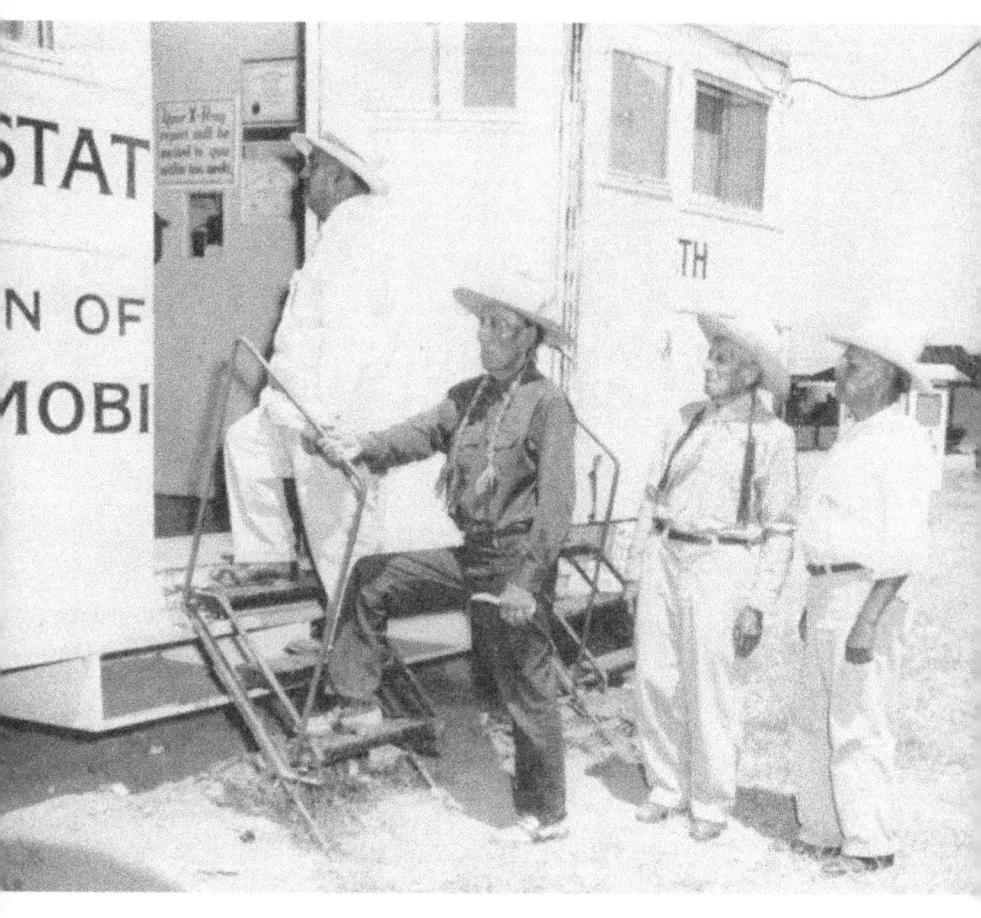

Indians are eager to co-operate in tuberculosis detection

Courtesy Dr. Grady Mathews
Oklahoma State Board of Health

CHAPTER XXV

Medical Education

IT was in the first decade of this phenomenal half-century that I came from country practice to Oklahoma City, where I was destined to participate in medical education. Those who may consider country practice a poor preparation for teaching should remember that this was before the days of X-rays and cardiograms, when diagnosis was dependent upon the exercises of the five senses, always available and often incredibly keen. Doctors still believed in inspection, palpation, percussion, and auscultation, and sometimes they gained valuable information through the exercise of taste and smell. Wholly dependent upon my own resources, I had found it necessary to develop these senses, which in the present-day practice are to some extent replaced by more modern methods, but not without a distinct loss to both patient and physician. History-taking and physical examination constitute an important psychosomatic link in the patient-physician concept which must never be completely discarded. I have not followed some of my professional friends who have said this is the age of Roentgen (the X-ray)—the age of Laënnec (the stethoscope) has passed.

With these limited qualifications I found that the best way to learn is by teaching. The task was exacting, the responsibility challenging, and contact with the students stimulating, making of the whole an exciting adventure. I am forever indebted to the medical school for the experience and the accrued benefits.

After teaching physical diagnosis in the University of Oklahoma School of Medicine for approximately twenty years, I was made dean of the school in 1931. Although I had learned much about medicine by teaching, I was totally unlearned in the administrative problems of a medical school and the ambiguous ways of governors, legislators, politicians, and regents until the deanship was thrust upon me. This position with its varied problems and responsibilities was truly revealing and highly rewarding. In spite of the difficulties sooner or later confronting every tax-supported medical school, progress has prevailed. Through increased facilities, student capacity has been increased with corresponding advantages to the state. The Oklahoma Medical Research Foundation—conceived by Dr. Tom Lowry, then dean of the University of Oklahoma School of Medicine, approved by the council of the Oklahoma Medical Association, and developed by the alumni association of the School of Medicine—is making available a great research institute which should augment the school's opportunities and stimulate scientific progress.

Though having long since reached the retirement age, I am honored with an emeritus professorship in medicine and blessed with the privilege of teaching medical history.

Everyone should know that the one goal of medical education is the prevention of disease, the treatment of the sick, and the preservation of health.

If space would permit a comprehensive account of what is known about medical education, the average reader would have a better understanding of the mutual problems confronting the medical profession and the public, from the patient-physician relationship up to the deans of medical schools, the Association of American Medical Colleges, and the Council on Medical Education. Since the health and happiness of the people are largely dependent upon applied medical knowledge, what could be more interesting than to study the principal sources of this knowledge? Even the confirmed devotee of fiction could find no fault with the fabulous story of medical progress arising through the unceasing efforts of the medical schools, made possible by funds from the pockets of the people.

MEDICAL EDUCATION

On this continent the medical schools of Canada and the United States have generously co-operated and shared in this progress. Such a fortunate situation exists not wholly because of common interests, but in part because of the influence of great personalities in the field of medical education. Apropos this challenging experience, it may be said that medicine is endowed with the enviable freedom to strike across international boundaries. Because of its merciful mission in peace or war, it overrides all enmities and prejudices and finds a welcome wherever there is human suffering.

In a broad sense the welfare of the world is within the purview of every legitimate medical school.

While we cannot indulge in historical detail, it seems wise to tell the people who are interested and concerned about many phases of medical education something of its accomplishments, ideals, and purposes, and to point out some of the obstacles to its progress. Perhaps the best way to accomplish this end without divorcing the bare facts from the pulsating elements of human interest is to refer briefly to the textbooks of some of our great American medical teachers and writers, who have tried to keep before the student and the teacher those facts and principles considered fundamental in medical education and therefore essential to individual and national welfare.

The first edition of Sir William Osler's *The Principles and Practice of Medicine,* dedicated to his teachers, was printed with a very simple preface in 1892. There was no intimation of even potential problems ahead. He must have exulted in his achievement, especially since the interminable demands of the task delayed his proposal to the charming young widow of Dr. Samuel W. Gross, who, having lived with a doctor, should have known how to make allowances. According to a note in his working copy of the text, the first volume that came from the press on February 24 was tossed into her lap the morning of February 25 with these words, "There it is—now what are you going to do with the man?" They were married in the succeeding May, and Grace Revere Osler learned that the finality with which he popped the question, based upon completion of his text, was premature and wholly unwarranted.

Nevertheless, Osler had the wisdom to follow the dedication of the text with this famous line from the first great modern medical writer and teacher, Hippocrates: "Experience is fallacious and judgment difficult." As we have learned, this remarkable first edition of Osler appeared in the second decade of an era representing unprecedented medical progress. His wife, who had patiently awaited the consummation of his great work, soon learned with equal patience to shield him and conserve his time for the engrossing task of keeping up with the march of medical science and recording its essential features for the successive revisions of his text in order to keep teachers and pupils abreast of progress.

In the preface of his third edition in 1898, only six years after the first and the one I studied at the turn of the century, he said, "At the rate of progress in all departments, a textbook six years old needs a very thorough revision." As his gifted wife continued to conserve his time and energy, one edition after another came from the press until his death at Oxford in 1919. After helping complete the work he planned and after having helped to prepare his great library for its final depository at McGill University in Montreal, she died dramatically of apoplexy in a few minutes after being seized with a severe pain in her head. The books were boxed, her courage intact, and all was ready.

In the preface to the tenth edition, Dr. Thomas McCrae of Philadelphia, who was assigned the duty of keeping the text up to date, found it necessary to make many changes in order to include the developments of established value. In the first paragraph of his preface to this edition McCrae says, "Those who have read the biography of Sir William Osler by Harvey Cushing will have noted the large part which this textbook occupied in his life. It was one of his great interests and, as has been shown, played a large part in various ways in the advance of medical science."

MEDICAL EDUCATION

In the preface of the thirteenth edition, in 1930, McCrae's successor, Mrs. Moorman's esteemed uncle, Dr. Henry A. Christian of Harvard Medical College, indicated the sound sequence of purposes and principles in the following words: "A pupil of Osler, a friend and colleague of McCrae, I welcome the opportunity of continuing the medical traditions of this book, which for so many years had the guidance of these master clinicians. In this, the thirteenth edition, my purpose has been to continue its traditions, attuning them to such newer knowledge in the field as recently has developed. To this end there has been rearrangement, rewriting and the addition of new material."

When the sixteenth edition was being prepared for the press, again Dr. Christian was troubled about the matter of rapid progress and the necessity for revision, even though his fifteenth edition was hardly off the press. The following from the first paragraph of his preface will reveal his problem and his logical approach: "Medicine progresses rapidly. Practitioners and medical students naturally seek knowledge not alone of the long known in medicine but also of the new, when the correctness of the new seems established. Also some of the new knowledge consists of the disproof of things previously considered demonstrated. It is the task of the author to add what in his judgment seems acceptable as positive additions to our knowledge and also to change, to delete what seems to have been proved incorrect or improbable. Neither addition nor deletion is justified until competent authorities have given evidence enough to guide safely the task of the author in keeping descriptions and discussions in the text consistent with what is known or at least strongly believed in at the time of making a revision of or writing a new medical text."

Apparently Dr. Christian was so impressed with the onward march of medical science during the period covered by the Osler text that he included in this edition the history of medical progress from 1892 to 1947 prepared by another great teacher, Dr. James G. Carr. It is clearly shown that, in the original preparation of his text, Osler was launching six decades of the world's most remarkable medical progress and initiating an evolutionary medical educational program in keeping with progress. His contribution through the textbook and other important writings, both scientific and cultural, and his bedside teaching at the Johns Hopkins Medical School and Hospital, with its human touch, is beyond comprehension. Harvey Cushing's remarkable biography of Osler clearly reveals not only the man's incredible influence upon medical thought and bedside teaching in the United States with the patient's interest always uppermost, but also the impress of his personal charm and his unusual erudition upon three great nations. Today in this disturbed world his humanity, his moral philosophy, and his ethics are reassuring, and their influence upon medical education is of great importance.

The authors of other great texts on the practice of medicine represent similar ideals, reflect a corresponding consciousness of progress and experience the same problems with reference to revisions.

To mention only one of these, Jonathan C. Meakins introduces the fifth edition of his fourteen-year-old text with these significant words: "The task of writing a new edition of the Practice of Medicine is becoming increasingly difficult. This is so for a number of reasons, of which the most specific is the upsurge of specialized technics. In other words, the wide view of medicine is being clouded by a multiplicity of minutiae which are beyond the technical capacity or facilities of the general physician. Indeed, the requirements of medical practice are becoming so complicated that there must be, in the near future if not immediately, some organized effort to bring these diagnostic and therapeutic facilities to the doctor and the patient. This general absence, however, does not afford an excuse for neglecting to include or even emphasize them in the present text. The fortunate patients who have access to metropolitan clinics have these facilities readily available. However, they make up a comparatively small percentage of those who suffer from ill health. Furthermore, human disabilities do not in the main come from rare or exotic diseases, but are due to more obvious and too often neglected causes such as economic, social, and emotional situations."

What has been said of medical textbooks applies in the field of surgery and, to a great extent, in other important departments of medical education. It may be said that teachers and medical authors in all the fundamental branches of medicine, including the specialties, have witnessed phenomenal progress and have made the best possible adjustments. In addition, the deans of medical schools have been swamped with requests from representatives of the various specialties for more time on already overloaded curricula, while being criticized by the public for not turning out more well-rounded general practitioners clamoring for a location in the country. This situation is in keeping with Dr. Meakin's reference to the "upsurge of specialized technics" and the "multiplicity of minutiae which are beyond the technical capacity or facilities of the general physician." Deans of medical schools and curriculum committees are conscious of the danger of giving too much time to the less frequent diseases and to highly technical procedures.

Fortunately, there is now some hope that the pendulum may swing back toward the common conditions and diseases occurring in country and town, constituting 85 per cent of medical complaints and yielding to a wise combination of common sense and simple remedies of moderate cost. Unfortunately, the teaching hospitals are full of the 15 per cent group requiring the highly technical diagnostic and therapeutic care. While taking care of the few who are really in need of medical skill, we must not neglect the 85 per cent who, though not badly in need of medical care, would have a hard time psychologically if they could not have the satisfaction of medical advice. Somebody must see them and make sure they are properly cared for. They are at least psychologically in need of a doctor and have a right to demand his services. He must give them patient care, differential diagnostic consideration, and mentally stabilizing attention. He must know at least enough about the more difficult 15 per cent group to give careful appraisal and to choose a specialist wisely when special care is indicated.

Today this is the broadest field for constructive service open to the medical profession. This fact is known to medical educators, and many of the schools are trying to prepare their pupils for this type of service when they graduate. They are meeting this special need by building up large Outpatient departments, and some of them are even developing preceptorship plans under the good offices of worthy country doctors, with the sole purpose of bringing the student into contact with those belonging in the 85 per cent group where the common everyday problems of the people may find solution.

Having gone so far on the trail of science, we are now awakening to the fact that we have suffered a distinct loss in the art of medicine. We are learning that one mind cannot comprehend all that medicine encompasses and that medical schools must prepare doctors for general practice as well as for research, for industry, for public health, for the specialties, and last, but not least, for the teaching of medicine. Perhaps medical schools have failed to keep in mind the vital relationship between general practice and the teaching of medicine. The trend toward full-time clinical teachers and full-time occupancy of teaching hospital beds with the 10 to 15 per cent group of patients in need of highly specialized diagnostic and therapeutic care is not conducive to the preparation of physicians for general practice. If this important function of the medical schools is to be properly performed, much of the teaching should be done by physicians in general practice who see the people in complete cross section, in the hovel and in the palace, where the 85 per cent suffering from common but genuine afflictions are found. This group, not yet having fully surrendered to the exigencies of disease, likewise stands in need of exceptional skills, often wanting in the minds of physicians whose full-time experience is bounded by the walls of hospital wards. Such teachers are missing the most rewarding experiences in practice. From lack of broad experience they are wanting in the art of medicine which must meet the varied psychological needs of the masses seeking medical care. The successful general practitioner, whether he knows it or not, must become a good neuropsychiatrist. Formal education in psychiatry can never quite replace the physician's experience arising through contact with his patients and their relatives and friends.

These considerations point to the need for careful selection of teachers, both full and part time, and perhaps the wisdom of providing some type of special training for medical teachers.

Long ago, Sir James Mackenzie said, "The pursuit of medical knowledge tends to assume ever more and more academic character, with little reference to the problems confronting the doctor who practices medicine." How pertinent this statement is to our purpose. We must get back to the fundamental care of the sick while doing what we can to advance medical science, with the hope of ever limiting the need of such care. In recent years often science and distrust have traveled together. Amiel has said, "The fire which enlightens is also the fire which consumes; the element of the gods may become that of the accursed." We must halt this trend in the field of medicine.

Perhaps too much money is being spent in research, especially when none of it goes for the direct solution of the present problems of the general practitioner and his patients. A careful survey of these problems, including socioeconomic conditions, is long overdue. Medical schools might well pursue such a study in search of data upon which to build a balanced curriculum. The wide discrepancy in the per capita cost of medical education in different schools and universities suggests that in some instances too much money is being spent in the highly technical fields or perhaps the building of teams in highly specialized departments. Thus a similar survey of the schools may uncover facts of curricular value.

Considering the obvious problems confronting the medical authors and teachers and the deans of medical schools who have the considered aid of the Council on Medical Education and the Association of American Medical Colleges, is it surprising that an aroused but uninformed public finds it difficult to understand the limitations, policies, and practices of medical schools.

Perhaps the most serious current difficulty is the matter of costs. The nature of scientific progress has multiplied the cost of medical education, and the changing socioeconomic conditions have resulted in diminishing returns from private donations, endowments, and foundations. In addition to the life and death values in medical education, the people have a more possessive interest than they realize. It is by far the most costly of all types of education. The student capacity of medical schools is limited largely by physical facilities which cannot be increased without large sums of money. More buildings, more equipment, more laboratory space, more hospital beds, and more outpatient facilities are among the requirements. The tuition and fees can never approach the necessary costs. The people who clamor for more doctors must realize that the first requisite is more dollars. Today our chief concern hinges upon the increasing costs. Up to now the schools have been able to meet the high costs, but how to meet still higher and higher costs is a difficult problem.

This naturally leads to a discussion of admissions to medical schools. Out of the thousands who apply, only hundreds are accepted. Even with a catastrophic lowering of standards it would be impossible to take all who apply or even all who are scholastically qualified. While this great problem is being seriously considered by medical educators and the regularly constituted agencies interested in medical education, the schools are being blamed by the public for not admitting more students and turning out more doctors. If the popular advocates of more doctors only had a full knowledge of medical education, plus one year's service on the dean's admissions committee, they would forever hold their peace. In the light of present-day propaganda, much of which is unwarranted, this popular attitude is easy to understand. An erudite young friend of mine who is politically and socially conservative, a great believer in free enterprise, occupying a high position in educational circles, believes that "A person who desires to study medicine ought to be allowed to go to hell in his own way. That's what should happen, we insist, in practically every other field, including the legal and engineering professions, where there is really no restriction on numbers."

Even with the present methods of selection, comprehensive in appraisal and meticulously applied, one student out of five goes "to hell," and one physician out of five drops out of practice. If the bars were entirely down, the lowered standards and the increased mortality would promptly put the medical schools on the road to hell and drag the public with them.

It should be remembered that medical schools are not in every way comparable to the schools of law and engineering. And it should be known that much of the propaganda for more doctors, particularly for rural communities, comes from those who have deserted the country for the overcrowded urban centers. The people who have spurned the soil and put aside the plowshare and the shovel should not expect their sons and daughters to become militant in behalf of those who are left behind. This demand for better medical care in rural communities would be less unreasonable if it were not for certain mitigating circumstances. If the young doctor had not spent a good part of his life and a small fortune in preparation for a type of service which cannot find satisfactory expression in remote localities without the immediate expenditure of a goodly sum for office, laboratory, and other necessary facilities, the situation might be different. These obstacles, with community help, are not insurmountable, and in some locations they are being overcome through co-operation of the people and the doctors.

Since better distribution of medical care is to a large extent a matter of education, it is well for people to know that there are some very good additional reasons why doctors are not locating at the crossroads in rural communities as they did fifty years ago. Before the turn of the century the country doctor could make a living on typhoid fever, diphtheria, pneumonia, and summer complaint. Immunity measures provided by medical discoveries have virtually eliminated typhoid and diphtheria. Sulfonamides, penicillin, and aureomycin and other new drugs have rendered pneumonia much less ominous for the patient and much less profitable to the doctor. Refrigeration, sanitation, and improved medication have almost eliminated summer complaint. Improved roads, automobiles, and transportation by air, plus education with reference to clinics and hospitalization, tend to whisk the patient past the country doctor while he is being penalized through the modern medical publicity and motorized psychology. Considering present modes of transportation the country patient fifty to one hundred miles from the nearest city, relatively speaking, is much closer to medical care than the patient living ten miles from his country doctor fifty years ago. Under these circumstances, it is hardly fair to expect the well-trained doctor to invest $30,000 to $50,000 for sufficent modern facilities to stop the motored marathon toward city practitioners. Are the people and the trend of the times to blame, or must the medical profession be held responsible for the dearth of country doctors?

The communities in need of good doctors and desirous of scientific medical care should consider the feasibility of providing modern facilities for a well-trained young doctor when one is available. Before leaving this subject I should add that because of improved therapeutic methods and other short cuts which, directly or indirectly, have come through medical education and improved transportation, one doctor can now cover a community that would have required three or four doctors in the horse and buggy days.

Furthermore, the alleged shortage of doctors has been greatly exaggerated. In this connection it seems reasonable to include in the calculation the health and physical competency of the nation. The population of the United States has been doubled since 1900. Average longevity is increasing at a rapid rate, and the health level is higher than ever before. The United States has more physicians in proportion to population than any other country in the world except Palestine, where the profession is surcharged with refugee doctors. We have the best system of medical education and the most nearly adequate medical school facilities in the world. The fear of a serious shortage of physicians in the future is obviously unfounded unless we enter upon another full-scale national emergency. During the past few years, seven four-year medical schools have been added to those already in operation and five more are being contemplated.

In the light of a widespread consciousness of the importance of medical education, it is worthy of note that the only people who are really conscientiously working for improvement are the medical educators, the Council, and the colleges. The recent annual addresses of the successive presidents of the Association of American Medical Colleges have reviewed the course of medical education in the light of scientific and socioeconomic progress, in order to lay a sound foundation for their expressed concern over the present problems and the future of medical education. After sixty years of concerted effort, this association in annual session in 1949 found it necessary to devote special attention to student-selection problems, curriculum planning, making the internships a planned educational experience, and the training of general practitioners. For years many medical schools have been concerned about preparing doctors for country practice and devising ways and means of inducing them to locate in rural communities. Loans, scholarships, preceptorships, and other educational experiments and inducements have been employed, but it is difficult to turn the tide which has been rising with each new generation. At least the physicians engaged in medical education have tried. Through this influence and the possibility of a changing mass psychology, there seems to be a new hope. In this respect the problem of the medical schools might be partially solved if the various specialty boards required every applicant to have three to five years in general practice before official certification. Through such a mandate the knowledge of medicine and the patient would be more equitably balanced, and there would be more general practitioners and more genuinely qualified specialists. In sequence, a better understanding of the patient-physician relationship would be achieved and a more equitable distribution of medical services would result.

Conscious of many imperfections and many unsolved problems with undetermined potentialities, medical schools under the direction of the Council on Medical Education and the Association of the American Medical Colleges are sponsoring a three-year survey, with the avowed purpose of building a medical curriculum that will meet the needs of the American people.

In addition to continuous striving for better service, this plan is representative of periodic organized efforts to bring about improvement since the first self-imposed housecleaning accompanied by the Abraham Flexner investigation in 1907 of the 155 existing medical schools. Flexner was working with the Carnegie Foundation for the Advancement of Teaching. His report resulted in the closing of many schools and the elevation of standards for those remaining in the field. Since the reforms set in motion at that time, there have been no radical changes, but surveys, reports, and recommendations have helped to establish minimum standards, methods of procedure, and desirable goals. Those who read these reports must be impressed with the purposes and ideals which invariably champion the public weal.

It is hoped that this brief discussion may help those who read to realize that the task of medical education is a complex one, and that many unselfish medical teachers and deans of medical schools with the help of two great volunteer agencies, the Council and the Association of the colleges, are continuously striving to fathom the complexities and to apply effectively the accepted principles and practices.

CHAPTER XXVI

Medicine in Retrospect and Prospect

IF medical education is sometimes misunderstood, equally the drama of medicine wrestling with scientific progress in a changing world is difficult to stage. It concerns not only the medical profession but the people as well. It has much to do with their way of life, the government under which they live, and the world of which they are a part, with its frequent social and economic upheavals and its ever recurring wars.

In primitive times when, in all probability, our savage progenitors used pebbles instead of pennies to close dead eyes, medicine was rudimentary and its practice relatively simple, with responsibility resting chiefly upon the gods. If a cure was achieved, the medicine man was extolled. If death ensued, the great spirit was appeased. Through an evolutionary process with scientific thought leading intellectual development, ultimately medicine moved into this phenomenal twentieth century.

When I located at Jet, the practice of medicine among the homemaking pioneers was still relatively simple. Almost without exception the conscientious physician was well grounded in the principles of practice and committed to the task of doing his best for the patient and the community, making his own interests secondary to his professional ideals. As a result he was accorded implicit trust with full appreciation of his skills. Where accident, injury, or illness called, first aid and home remedies were put aside when he appeared. Everbody made way for the doctor and stood ready to do his bidding. He was entrusted with the most vital issues and the most sacred family and social secrets with the utmost confidence. He was physician, counselor, and friend. The position he held in the hearts of his people was not altogether out of deference to the physician himself, but in part out of respect for a profession devoted to service. This respect and confidence made each case appear as a sacred responsibility, spontaneously calling forth all that the science and art of medicine in a rural community could command.

If it seemed wise to put out the cat and the dog, unchink the cracks and the keyholes, send the neighbors home and raise the window of the sick room, often the only room, the response was eager and prompt. The doctor's authority was respected and his wishes anticipated. If it was deemed advisable to discontinue the skunk oil and kerosene, to remove the onion poultice, or discard the asafetida, there was no dissent. Always good country people were good patients. They were not self-opinionated, not endowed with fixed notions about therapeutic procedures, not sensitive and fearful, and consequently not difficut to please. Recovery, which was usual, redounded to the doctor's credit, and when death became inevitable, it was accepted as a stroke of Divine Providence, the doctor held blameless and idealized because of his faithful services.

Fortunately there is a professional devotion which puts duty above privilege and rewards both the physician and the people who place their trust in him. This reward has always been among the good doctor's abiding satisfactions. Fees were small and easily fitted to the patient's purse. As a rule the prairie homemaker's financial status was like an open book. There was no surplus income, no hidden assets to trouble the soul of the man who tilled the soil. Always the cards were on the table. The patient and the physician were free, and their dealings were straightforward and aboveboard. In fact, they could look anybody who questioned their relations in the face and tell him to go to hell. This was just plain unadulterated freedom arising

DR. FRANCIS ADAMS
This photograph was given me by his granddaughter, Mrs. Jessie G. Syme

from the grass roots. It was not comparable to the so-called freedom of capital and labor. Today the same one-time free men are hedged about by rules and regulations, executing directives, filling out blanks, and often signing their liberties away.

In those early days making a call was a pleasant experience. There was a world of nature along the way, a rhythm in the atmosphere, a song in the sun, a serenade in the stars. There was silence, solitude, and mystery, and a strange fascination in the task, with a mission of mercy as its objective. The leisurely pace, with horse sense animating the rein, did not run blood pressure up and longevity down, as does the steering wheel, vibrating with powerful but inanimate energy. In the merciless machine there is no motivating intelligence, no flesh and blood response to tone down the ominous tension. The grim grip upon the wheel must never slacken. The mind that governs the grip must never give up its hazardous task. There is no time for contemplation, no silence, no solitude, no surcease for appreciation of the sun or the unlighted darkness of the night, yet beyond the arc of the headlights there is the mystery of the stars. Our civilization, particularly in urbanized, commercialized, mechanized populations has robbed us of these stabilizing influences. We must be kept within the line of progress if we are to measure up to the world's estimate of success. The leash of nervous tension will not let us go. What would old Horace say if he could have a look at our present mode of travel? It is said that when he grew tired of the sordid city of Rome, he mounted his mule and urged him to shake the dust from his feet. Yet, while spurring his mule to greater speed he was critical of the wheel, perhaps conscious of its potentialities.

> *Others the heated wheel extol,*
> *And all its offspring, whose concern*
> *Is how to make it farthest roll*
> *And fastest turn.*

There is a great difference between practice now and fifty years ago. Some people who accept life without thinking may be surprised to learn that the difference is not altogether attributable to the medical profession. The people likewise are subject to the tensions of modern life. They, too, have been caught in the maelstrom of this mechanistic age and are being conditioned by the swift pace of the socioeconomic whirl. There is little time for measured contemplation and mutual understanding. The resulting confusion supplies tinder for the smoldering fires of suspicion and mistrust. Again Horace epitomizes our vague idea of what is happening—"Something mixed with something else makes something worse." And again those who are not thinking may say how can this be, when, thanks to medical progress, we live twice as long, and through scientific ingenuity we are much more comfortable than ever before, and many times as clean.

Admitting all this and noting that we have minimized the vastness of continents and the breadth of intervening seas, we cannot escape this disturbing query: Can we be sure we are not soaring on wings of wax? In this age of atomic energy it is well to remember that in the last analysis these achievements are relatively unimportant. Even longevity is not the measure of life. Deeds not days determine our usefulness and our satisfactions. Amiel says, "Life has been lent to us, and we owe it to our traveling companions to let them see what use we make of it to the end."

Fortunately all these differences revolve around the functions of a profession founded upon the principles of service. Essentially it is based upon a patient-physician relationship, which in spite of required revolutionary adaptations, must not be lost. It is as fundamental as the family, as sacred as the church, as essential as free speech, and as right as anything in the Decalogue. Though we travel far and fast, we miss the safety, the companionship, the leisure, the faith, and the helpful cooperation once found at the family fireside. The passing of these phases of life affects the practice of medicine.

The mental and physical strain of meeting the multiplied and widely diversified opportunities and responsibilities of modern existence have created medical problems, both physical and psychological, which did not exist fifty years ago. No matter how swift the current of life, the doctor must be in the middle of the stream. Sink or swim, he must stem the flood, safeguard the journey, support the weary, rescue the drowning, and succor the dying.

In the light of what has been said about the doctor, it is reasonable to inquire: Why is he not still the old-fashioned family adviser? The rapidly developing changes mentioned above, with multiplied facilities for hospitalization, the revolutionary improvements in diagnostic and therapeutic procedures, the obvious necessity for medical specialties, and the rapidly increasing radius of family contacts and popular concepts have created an unwarranted breach between the family and the family doctor.

Neither the family nor the doctor is wholly responsible for this unfortunate situation. Our psychology is unfavorably conditioned by the almost hopeless effort to keep up with the too rapid progress. Daily we go about our pressing duties, buffeted by the exacting rules of a heterogeneous, overorganized, overstandardized mode of existence.

Doctors not only suffer with society as a whole, but in addition they find it difficult to follow the phenomenal stride of medical science with the necessary adjustments and the demands of an exacting public, armed with a little medical learning gleaned from lay publications. The old adage, "Where ignorance is bliss, 'tis folly to be wise," was once very comforting, but now that all are relatively wise, medical ignorance may indeed be fatal.

Ambitious, conscientious members of the medical profession are now straining every nerve under the merciless spur of advancing knowledge. The field of medicine has become so vast, and available scientific learning so boundless, that the mind of the average physician is staggered by the increasing weight of his responsibility to his patients.

To emphasize this responsibility the following quotation

from the writings of the erudite S. Weir Mitchell, America's first successful neuropsychiatrist, is pertinent. In 1887 he said: "Within but a few years the instruments of precision have so multiplied that a well-trained consultant may be called upon to know and handle as many tools as a mechanic. Their use, the exactness they teach and demand, the increasing refinement in drugs, and our ability to give them in condensed form, all tend towards making the physician more accurate, and by overtaxing him, owing to the time all such methodical studies require, have made his work such that only the patient and the dutiful can do it justice."

If he comprehends the fundamental facts and principles involved, if he becomes proficient in the application of the common mechanical and laboratory aids to modern diagnosis, if he learns to employ the many technical therapeutic procedures now practiced in the hospital, the office, and at the bedside, if he knows when and how to refer his patients for highly specialized services, if he maintains his poise and presents a shining face regardless of the day's work—if, in all these, he has steadily moved on to a higher position, he may not qualify as the old-fashioned doctor, but he can still be the family's best medical adviser.

Every family should find such a doctor and look to him for advice in the prevention of disease and for medical care in time of need. The physician's response should be such as to justify the utmost confidence. Since there are no old-fashioned families, there is no place for the old-fashioned doctor, but every family is entitled to the satisfaction and the security of a family medical mentor.

No decision having to do with individual or family health should be reached without his knowledge and advice. The need and choice of a specialist should always have his consideration. The various services offered by health departments, schools, and other health agencies should come to him for careful study and approval in the light of individual family needs.

Although the time-honored relationship between family

and family doctor has been rudely strained by the rapid development of medical knowledge and by inevitable changes in society, it is doubtful that there has been a period since the time of Hippocrates when humanity, though blessed with the gift of science, has been so in need of the art of medicine. Sir William Osler insisted that medicine is of the heart as well as of the head. After science, in cold calculation, satisfies the head, there is something wanting, unless the doctor has found a fallow spot in the heart of his patient. While both patients and physicians are being tried and possibly hardened by the present ominous realities of human existence, they must not lose their medical birthright. They must learn to give and take and find a way to hold fast the fundamental principles of life, while their once delightful world is slipping away. Is it not time for the people and their professions to assay their souls, fit their standards to the needs of an exigent world, and set their wills against the trends that would destroy our civilization? As we stand between hope and fear, knowing that the creeping paralysis induced by the drive toward a false security is threatening our freedom, we must guard the citadel within where no unholy influence can enter uninvited. The goal of medicine, as of man, is a pure spirit, not a bellyful.

Judging from what has happened in other comparable countries where true democracy has been supplanted by statism, the preservation of medical practice according to its American traditions represents the first principle of survival. This must come about through society's only salvation, man's individual freedom and integrity. Hesiod's lament (700 B.C.) offers no solution, "Would that I did not live in this time. Would that I had died before, or was born much later." Obviously Hesiod was no prophet. If he lived today, he might repent that lament. Since there is no escape for those who make up the warp and woof of each generation, we must take life as it comes. We must try to preserve our equilibrium by not being the first by whom the new is tried and possibly save our souls by not being the first to cast the old aside.

Since it is doubtful whether the American people ever lived in a time so precarious, when decisions were so difficult, and responsibilities so great, it is imperative that we foster the integrity of the individual, the family, the home, the church, the state, and the nation. One of the most fundamental of all the services required for the normal functioning of these units of society is medical care. This being true, nothing can be more important than the future of medicine. Wherever medicine has become a state enterprise, the cost of medical care has soared and the quality has unquestionably suffered.

It may surprise some to know that in this country we have approximately twenty-five million people now under a form of socialized medicine. Medicine under the Veterans Administration is in reality socialized medicine. While the V.A. medical service has been greatly improved, the change for the better came only when General Bradley and General Hawley decided to restore it to the principles and practices of civilian medicine so far as possible under government control. We owe a great debt of gratitude to the Veterans Administration physicians who have courageously cut much of the government red tape and removed many of its devastating restraints in their hopeless struggle for professional freedom.

Perhaps the best example of the failure of government medical service is to be found in the Indian Service under the Department of the Interior.

After having a free hand for many years in the matter of giving medical care to the Indians, the administrative service in Washington and on the reservations, bound as it is by red tape and political expediency, is shockingly inefficient. I say this from first-hand experience, having recently made a survey of the Navajo and Hopi tribes at the invitation of the American Medical Association under the sponsorship of the Department of the Interior. With few exceptions the quality of medical care is deplorably low and the coverage wholly inadequate. Preventable and curable diseases run rife because of indecision, inefficiency, procrastination, and numerous inexcusable inadequacies. While it is true that good medical care for the Indians presents many difficulties, few if any of them are insuperable. Unfortunately disease marches on while the government marks time. Although space will not permit a detailed account, the over-all picture has been thus summarized in order that those who think government control is desirable may be forewarned. Everyone who looks with favor upon the prospect of government medicine should carefully consider the debacle of the nationalized medical adventures already in hand. Considering its possible uses and abuses, its quality, its costs, and its questionable compensations, government medicine is something to be assiduously eschewed.

In spite of this heavy load upon the taxpayers with relatively inadequate returns, the people and the profession are fortunate in that, with these exceptions, medicine in this country has remained relatively free. In other nations where physicians have found it necessary to accept government regimentation, general socialization has prevailed, with disregard for the individual and a mediocre socioeconomic ambition, striking an average level which cannot rise except at the expense of much that is great and good. Exactly one hundred years ago, as though anticipating the problems of this generation, Amiel said: "The statistician will register a progress, and the moralist a gradual decline; on the one hand, a progress of things; on the other, a decline of souls. The useful will take the place of the beautiful, industry of art, political economy of religion, and arithmetric of poetry. The spleen will become the malady of a leveling age."

When we embark upon the philosophy of the socioeconomic leveling process, we are heading back toward the dawn of creation when there was a state of almost complete equality without a clear-cut differentiation of things and forces. Then we were a unicellular bit of protoplasm groveling in slime, hoping to get ahead. On the presumption that this is not our present ambition, I am of the opinion that, at least in America, we can find a way to amalgamate our differences, retain our freedom, treasure our mutual dependence, and gladly share its benefits.

Already, in medicine, there are signs of compromise, of a better understanding, and a change of heart with added emphasis on the patient-physician relationship in spite of the changing picture. There is an obvious trend toward general practice and the reclamation of the doctor's realm in rural communities, but with streamlined methods to meet modern conditions. Emphasis upon neurophsychiatry is resulting in a revival of interest in the patient's mental demands, and the present enthusiasm about prepaid insurance to help meet catastrophic illness has focused upon the mind of the doctor a more charitable understanding of the patient-physician-fee situation. The occasional hardship suffered because of questionable fees, combined with other abuses and misunderstandings, has led to the appointment of grievance committees by medical organizations in a number of states. The representatives of organized medicine want to make sure that the people receive good medical care on an equable basis, and they stand ready to hear complaints when the occasion arises. Perhaps increased confidence because of this conscientious gesture in behalf of aggrieved patients represents its greatest accomplishment.

The organized profession is now embarking upon a wholesale educational campaign with the hope of a better understanding between the public and the profession and between the individual patient and his physician. It is designed to reveal medicine's function and how this function may best be performed. The importance of this plan is emphasized by the pro and con nonprofessional or so-called lay publicity with which the public is constantly assailed. Coming through the press, the radio, the movies, and political propaganda, there is enough medical misinformation to keep doctors and patients constantly at daggers' points, if it were not for a native gift of discrimination and tolerance. Among the many evils of this popular mass publicity are the premature and often false claims with reference to new discoveries, new cures, and new drugs. Such publicity sends many unduly excited patients to the doctor, who must spend much time explaining that this claim is not true or that the vaunted new cure is still in the experimental stage, and possibly not without danger, and that the purchase of this or that magic new remedy is a waste of money. Only the old-time doctor who has lived into this new day can fully appreciate what it means to have a wonderful patient who would have trusted him implicitly twenty-five years ago, after receiving complete medical attention and advice, pause at the threshold with this interesting query, "Doctor, don't you think I need some vitamins," or, "Shall I continue to take my vitamins?" The latter no doubt were purchased with her shoes or her swiss chard. If premature babies had the vitality and vigor of premature lay medical publicity, we could throw away our incubators.

Recently there has been a revival of the long-time patient-physician-priest relationship. In other words, the profession and the clergy come together for discussions on the relationship of soul and body and its significance when disease strikes. The one objective of this mutual interest is better service to the patient. At the present time all medical schools are undergoing a thorough self-imposed inspection with the expressed hope of giving the people better medical care through better medical education.

In addition to medicine's routine care of the sick, rich and poor, it has voluntarily become "the guardian of health and life itself." Through the sleepless critical pursuit of scientific research it has thwarted disease, minimized suffering, stayed the hand of death, and doubled longevity. Its phenomenal discoveries, once proven beneficial to humanity, have been made available without thought of commercial gain.

Through scientific advances, medicine has provided the principles for progress in public health and social medicine and has pointed the way for government participation without regimentation. Finally, it may be said that the medical profession in the United States, conscious of the changing socioeconomic picture, is actively encouraging all voluntary insurance programs in an effort to help meet economic emergencies ever arising on account of illness, particularly in the lower income groups. About seventy million of the people in the United States now have Blue Cross hospitalization insurance. Approximately sixty million are protected against surgical emergencies by Blue Shield, and many others are protected by voluntary plans offered by the nation's great insurance industry.

There is reason to believe that these manifestations of medicine's willingness to meet new issues through newly conceived ways and means, including compromise and adjustment, will bring about a renewal of confidence and a spirit of cooperation that will overcome all obstacles to the normal evolution of the most remarkable medical era in the history of man.

CHAPTER XXVII

Abroad and at Home

AFTER living long enough to witness the present state of socioeconomic unrest and the resulting professional insecurity and having developed satisfactory principles of medical practice in the American pattern of life, I was grateful for an invitation early in 1949 which took me abroad. Travel in European countries gave me a look at medicine where certain social and political trends already had taken their inevitable toll and had toppled one-time sound medical structures from the very foundations that gave rise to our own methods of medical care.

In July, I arrived in London to attend the Second Commonwealth and Empire Conference on Health and Tuberculosis and to participate in the commemoration of Sir William Osler's one hundredth birthday on July 12 at the Royal College of Surgeons. The great Commonwealth and Empire Conference was sponsored by the British National Association for the Prevention of Tuberculosis. The Osler anniversary was under the auspices of the London Osler Club.

At the meeting of the Commonwealth and Empire Conference I participated in a symposium under the general subject of social and industrial readaptation of people suffering from chronic disease. I spoke on "The Importance of the Patient-Physician Relationship in the Readaptation of the Ex-Sanatorium Patient." In the light of present medical attitudes, especially in the Commonwealth under the Labor government, this theme was significantly appropriate.

After calling attention to the usual long and intimate relationship between patient and physician in the management of tuberculosis and the great loss to the patient, the physician, and the people at large when this relationship is interrupted, I stressed the importance of a close and continuous partnership between the two, regardless of the course medical service may take in a changing world. Perhaps I should have said that good medicine rests upon a tripod—the patient, the physician, and God—and that, left to their own resources, the patient and the physician usually find this relationship mutually helpful; and when this is not the case, they are free to say what they think. God exacts no accounting except the exercise of conscience and presents no incomprehensible, interminable blanks to be filled out in triplicate.

In the interval between this Commonwealth conference and the Osler Club meeting, I visited Oxford and tried to trace the steps of the one-time Regius Professor, Sir William Osler, and worshiped at the shrine of this, my ideal exponent of culture in the profession of medicine. Later I had the good fortune to meet Dr. and Mrs. F. Holmes Dudden, who were close friends of Sir William and Lady Osler. Dr. Dudden, the master of Pembroke College for fifty years, eagerly recalled Sir William's erudition, marveling at his astounding store of knowledge outside the field of medicine and his facile gift of quoting freely from the world's literature, which added so much to his conversational charm.

Speaking on "Osler the Man" at the Osler Club meeting, I stressed his influence upon American medicine, enumerated his cultural gifts, and emphasized their importance in this new world where medicine is being forced into utilitarian channels with the cold, impersonal relationship inevitable under such circumstances. In order that the reader may know more about the man whose life and letters made him great in three countries and five universities and exercised a chastening influence throughout the world as well as on my own professional life, I am repeating my closing remarks.

"It was he who gave us 'The Leaven of Science,' 'The Master Word,' 'Unity, Peace, and Concord,' 'A Way of Life,' and finally, 'Equanimitas.' It was Osler, the man, who taught us to strive for something above the common level.

"While conveying the art and science of medicine to his pupils, he was giving comfort, health, and life to his patients, and yet he was living in the mystic realm of the shadowland, always on guard for glimpses that might make us less forlorn. He knew that the hopes and fears which make us men are inseparable, and bravely he trod the wine press of doubt that others might not be afraid. The things that created Osler, the man, became the criteria for the young men who came under his power and experienced his love of youth.

"In a recent meeting of the American Association of the History of Medicine at a great dinner session devoted to the theme we now pursue, I heard some of these one-time young men tell of the master's love of youth and its influence upon his pupils. I had the honor of sitting with Mrs. Rachel Abbott, Sir William's niece, the cousin of W. W. Francis who last read to him during his fatal illness and forged the final link between the man and his books and suggested this valedictory, 'He prayeth best who loveth best all things both great and small.' In addition to Mrs. Abbott's gracious response to the president's invitation to speak of her distinguished uncle, I was favored with intimate flashes from her memory of him. One of these is sufficient to explain Osler's intellectual ascendancy. At a gay informal dinner party he whispered in her ear, 'Please excuse me, I have an appointment with Plato.'

"His facility for friendship, his personal charm, his magnetic appeal, his spontaneous mirth, his unmatched erudition, his artless exhibition of rare gifts, and his unbounded generosity captivated all who came. Unlike Atlas, he never stooped to shoulder the world, but always kept his arms around it.

"According to his own record he left Canada rich in the goods 'which neither rust nor moth have been able to corrupt.'

"He left America saying truly:

'I have loved no darkness,
sophisticated no truth,
nursed no delusion,
allowed no fear.'

"He left England with the last verses of 'The Ancient Mariner' in his mind and a simple, affectionate 'nighty-night' on his tongue."

In order to follow the footprints of a few of my favorite medical men who have achieved immortality through their service to humanity, I traveled from London to Edinburgh. Here I recalled the beloved Dr. John Brown (1810–82), who in his day, like Sir William Osler, carried culture to the bedside, where it served as a soothing adjuvant to his medical ministrations. His little sermons on personal and household hygiene and public health entitled "Plain Words on Health" placed him far ahead of his times. It was through his three-volume set of essays, *Horae Subsecivae,* that I first met my ideal country doctor, Francis Adams of Banchory (1796–1861).

Driven by the urge to plant my feet on Deeside where this devoted family physician had practiced day and night on horseback, reared his children, nursed his invalid wife, mastered the classics, and translated Greek medicine into English for medical students and physicians throughout the world, I traveled from Edinburgh to Aberdeen and from there to Banchory. It is unfortunate that those who read medicine brought from ancient tongues into modern English know so little of the critical, sleepless hours devoted to the difficult task of translation. We are indebted to Adams not only for the translation of Hippocrates but for that of the important works of Aretaeus (A.D. 54–81) and the seven books of Paul of Aegina (A.D. 625–690).

When I was traveling the South Deeside to Banchory, my anticipation was sharpened by a long-cherished interest in the accomplishments of this scholarly general practitioner. As we entered the little village, I paused on the Bridge of Feughs to see the salmon leaping just as they no doubt had when Adams and his faithful horse forded the stream on various missions of mercy one hundred years before.

I was not wholly without knowledge of modern Banchory. Through correspondence with Dr. David Lawson, who had located there early enough to attend Dr. Adams' only surviving daughter in her last illness more than forty-five years ago, I was fairly well informed. Through Dr. William Anderson of Aberdeen, I had received photographs of the monument erected in this little village in honor of the famous practitioner. Unfortunately Dr. Lawson, now retired, could not be found, and it was only after some difficulty that I learned that the almost forgotten monument was at the old Adams homestead. After locating the estate, I was glad to learn that one of Banchory's leading physicians now occupies a beautiful home on the site of the old Adams house where Hippocrates and the works of other Greek medical authors laboriously passed from Greek into English. The present occupant's wife, who is the attractive young daughter of an American-born mother now residing in Aberdeen, escorted me to the monument in a silent, secluded spot marked by towering evergreens. Standing in the shadow of these sheltering trees, bareheaded and humbled by the memory of a great personality, I was abundantly compensated for my long quest.

Returning by way of North Deeside, I sat in silent contemplation of the remarkable physician and scholar who declined a chair in the classics at the University of Aberdeen because he preferred to serve his people in what was then a wild outlying region in North Scotland. Arriving in Aberdeen too late in the day to see the Adams bust at the university, where his memory is carefully guarded, I boarded a train for Inverness. As I looked out upon the beautiful countryside, my thoughts were transferred to Sir William Osler and his son Revere, who had whipped the trout streams somewhere in this region shortly before the German artillery forever interrupted their delightful companionship.

After a visit to the University of Glasgow with the hope

of absorbing some of its medical lore and to see the interesting John Hunter Museum, I returned to London through the little town of Stafford, where my old friend William Withering (1741–99) lived and loved (having married one of his patients) and labored with his foxglove (digitalis) which, having yielded its therapeutic secrets to this country doctor's clinical investigations, still flaunts its flaming bells everywhere along the roadside. While thinking of this country doctor and his hard work (including the devotion of two hours daily to charity), I recalled that his famous monograph on digitalis was not published until ten years after his researches had been completed. He had moved to Birmingham and become one of the busiest doctors in England before an attack of tuberculosis put him to bed. This alone made it possible for him to find time to assemble the facts and prepare them for publication. This bit of clinical investigation with belated reporting places cardiologists (heart specialists) and their patients under everlasting obligation to this one-time country doctor.

Knowing that Isaac Walton was born at Stafford and once lived at Shallowford Bridge not far away, I was interested in seeing the cottage where he wrote *The Compleat Angler* and following his favorite trout stream, the meandering Mece, where oft he had placed his fly with eager anticipation. This experience renewed my sense of fellowship with the angler's poet and the doctor's friend—an imaginary fellowship never to be forgotten, not even in London's busy streets. Between these treasured east-shore and west-shore experiences, in memory I shall hold the purple heather of the highlands and thank God for England and Scotland so rich in natural beauty, historic acclaim, and medical lore.

Leaving untouched the haunts of Thomas Sydenham, Edward Jenner, and Sir James Mackenzie, all plain practitioners made famous by their contribution to human weal, I flew from London to Zurich and came down in the land of true democracy, where a free people peacefully follow their pastoral pursuits in pleasant valleys under the shadow of Alpine Mountains radiating the fragrance of flowering gardens and evergreen forests. Here my thoughts turned to the poet-physician Friedrich Schiller (1750–1805), who voluntarily became a refugee from his German dukedom because he refused to practice military medicine at the Duke's behest. Under the spell of this freedom he delineated the principles embodied in our democracy when he wrote the story of William Tell. Apparently Schiller was the first to rebel against modern medical regimentation.

In Paris, I retraced the steps of Laënnec (1781–1826) and Louis (1787–1872) as they brought our knowledge of tuberculosis and our diagnostic skills to a new high mark, laying a solid foundation for the progress of the nineteenth century and the remarkable achievements of the twentieth. Both of these great physicians, as previously mentioned, suffered from tuberculosis. Laënnec exhibited the toxic type with repeated acute febrile bouts, punctuated by periods in bed, only to be followed by a return to his work under the driving urge for accomplishment, as though physical inactivity had speeded the tempo of his intellectual drive. Finally, in a heroic attempt to follow his work and give to the world what he had learned, he was forced to give attention to his own thin, tired body and its shocking lack of energy. Suddenly sensing the meaning of this physical depletion, he realized that he was dying of tuberculosis. One last trip to his beloved Brittany, one last look at the blue sea under friendly skies full of white gulls, and he was ready to go. He, who with incredible skill had learned the signals of death, removed the rings from his fingers to save others the trouble and calmly gave up the fight. But his influence has encircled the world for the everlasting benefit of humanity.

Louis suffered from the less obvious chronic type of tuberculosis, not incompatible with a long, useful life richly exemplified by the full harvest of his lengthening years. Wherever clinical medicine is taught, the spirit of Louis and Laënnec prevails.

Back in London sitting in the golden dusk of the Palace Theatre's chaste foyer, influenced by the soft strains of the orchestra and the subdued echoes of the chorus behind the scenes, awaiting the second act of *Lilac Time,* I imagined my spotted ponies streaking through the stardust—no doubt a baby being born in a prairie dugout. Swiftly, a shift of nearly fifty years carried me back to my plain country people where in humble, bare homes again I heard the strange first note from the newborn babe's unpracticed throat and observed the joyous consciousness of paternity illuminating the rugged features of simple, honest faces.

Returning from this strange fantasy to the beautiful performance of *Lilac Time,* my wayward mind kept toying with the thought that William Shakespeare and Bobby Burns were born in beds just as humble and under ceilings just as low as these babes of mine, and wondering why my prairie bairns were not endowed with their poetic brains. Although I must die without the honor of having brought genius into the world, no one can deny that taming bronchos, tying longhorns, cutting out dogies, stemming stampedes, and singing restless herds to sleep in the dead of night, connote the skillful co-ordination of a calculating brain.

With the popular play *Oklahoma* on the London boards at Drury Lane, lilting the spirit of American freedom before the vanishing British broadcloth, it seemed a good time to turn from the green fields of Britain to my own land of homespun and buckskin. Yet I was in love with England and Scotland, and it was sad to see a great brave people with a proud past on the cross of so-called social security courageously accepting the gall and vinegar and the sharp thrust of the political rapier without a grimace, while holding fast to "hope the charmer."

Before returning to Oklahoma, I decided to visit my favorite American medical shrine. Boarding a plane in New York City, soon I was cruising over Saranac Lake with Trudeau Sanatorium spreading beneficently below, where Borglum's bronze statue of Edward Livingston Trudeau looks serenely out upon the silent mountains, appropriately blending his love of nature with his love of man. The latter is amply attested by the inscription on the monument "To cure sometimes, to relieve often, to comfort always."

Later I sat in the Sanatorium Medical Building with my friends Ned Packard and Bill Steenken while the shades of Trudeau, Brown, Heise, Gardner, and Baldwin crowded the corridors of my consciousness. Still later a visit with my good friends Dr. and Mrs. Woods Price and Mrs. Lawrason Brown sharpened by retrospective vision and accentuated my appreciation of Trudeau's remarkable past. I was reliving my first trip to Saranac forty odd years ago with a letter from Henry Christian to Lawrason Brown, who in turn introduced me to Dr. Trudeau. The story of Trudeau and his illustrious associates needs no retelling. Yet I believe his affectionate description of the site of this shrine is worthy of repetition. After referring to his favorite stand at "the old fox runway on the side of Pisgah Mountain," he said: "Many a beautiful afternoon, for the first four winters after I came to Saranac Lake, I had sat for hours alone while hunting, facing the ever-changing phases of light and shade on the imposing mountain panorama at my feet, and dreamed the dreams of youth; dreamed of life and death and God, and yearned for a closer contact with the Great Spirit who planned it all, and for light on the hidden meaning of our troublous existence. The grandeur and peace of it had ever brought refreshment to my perplexed spirit."

No doubt, before founding his sanatorium on this site, Trudeau realized that fifteen years earlier, the great, good, tuberculous fisherman, Ralph Waldo Emerson, had skirted this sheltered slope of Pisgah and scanned the beautiful valley with the discerning eye of a poet while sweeping the Saranac with his oars.

> *By the bright morn the gay flotilla slid*
> *Through files of flags that gleamed like bayonets,*
> *Through gold-moth-haunted beds of pickerel flower,*
> *Where the deer feeds at night, the teal by day,*
> *On through the Upper Saranac . . . .*

Here at Trudeau Sanatorium in the promising field of tuberculosis control, patients perennially pursue the cure, and unceasingly clinical and animal research here and at other recognized centers attempts to track down the wary tubercle bacillus while the world with an abiding new hope anxiously awaits the light.

Once more in my own home among the things I love, I contemplate the strange new world; and while scanning my remembrance book, I thank God for what has gone before, and knowing that Nature, the mother of us all, will wipe the world's tears away, I am content to say with Virgil, "Fortunate old man, here among familiar rivers and these sacred founts shalt thou take the shadowy coolness."

Index

Aberdeen, Scotland: 236
Abbott, John: 194
Abbott, Mrs. Rachel: 235
Adams, Francis: 236
Adams, John: 162
Africa, South: 160
Alabama: 37
American Medical Association, *Journal* of: 37
American Medical Colleges Association: 208, 216, 219
American Public Health Association: 170
American Red Cross: 201
American Sanatorium Association: 5, 153, 171
American Tobacco Trust: 16
American Trudeau Society: 171–72
Ames, Fisher: 161–62
Amiel Henri Frédéric: 224
Anderson, William: 237
Arcturus: 103
Aretaeus: 143
Aristotle: 4
Arkansas River: 46, 100
Auenbrugger, Leopold: 117, 145 ff.

Baillie, Matthew: 145 ff.
Baird, A. B.: 42
Baker, Bryant: 97
Balzac, Honoré de: 6
Banchory, Scotland: 236

Barbour, Philip F.: 112
Barnes, J. Henry: 34, 38, 49, 52, 54
Bayle, Gaspard-Laurent: 117, 145 ff.
Beaumont, Francis: 6
Beaver Dam, Kentucky: 38–39
Bennet, Christopher: 144
Berlin, Germany: 124, 150, 200
Bessemer, Alabama: 39
Bichat, Marie François: 117, 147
Biggs, Hermann M.: 170
Big Rock, Tennessee: 7, 21–22, 26, 30, 105
Birmingham, Alabama: 37 ff.
Birmingham, England: 159, 238
Bodington, George: 149 ff.
Boerhaave, Hermann: 117
Boone, Daniel: 57
Boston, Massachusetts: 190
Brackenridge County, Kentucky: 53
Bradley, General Omar: 228
Brehmer, Hermann: 152
Bridgeport, Oklahoma: 55
Broch, Hermann: 178
Brown, John: 236
Brown, Lawrason: 241
Budapest, Hungary: 124
Burroughs, John: 115

Caddo Hotel (El Reno): 44
Caesar, Augustus: 33, 178
Caesar, Julius: 81
Calmette, Albert: 152
Canada: 191
Carnegie Foundation for the Advancement of Teaching: 220
Carr, James G.: 211
Caughron, Sherrill: 133
Cherokee Strip: 53
Chesterton, Gilbert K.: 98
Chicago, Illinois: 123
Chickasha, Oklahoma: 52

INDEX

Chisholm Trail: 43, 47
Christian, Henry A.: *xi–xii*, 211, 241
Cicero: 156
Clarksville, Tennessee: 22, 29
Clendening, Logan: 206
Cleveland, President Grover: 206
Clinton, Oklahoma: 134
Cody, William ("Buffalo Bill"): 57
Coldwater, Oklahoma: 60
Commonwealth and Empire Conference on Health and Tuberculosis: 233
Cooper, James Fenimore: 57
Covisart, Lucient: 146 ff.
Cowley, Abraham: 98
Cummins, S. Lile: 150
Cushing, Harvey: 210, 212
Custer, George Armstrong: 73

Danville, Kentucky: 137
Davidson, Jo: 97
Davis, Richard: 40
Delpech, Jacques Mathieu: 145
Democritus: 123
Descartes, René: 6
Dettweiler, Peter: 152
Dudden, F. Holmes: 234
Dudden, Mrs. F. Holmes: 234

Edinburgh, Scotland: 124, 235–36; University of, 145
Ellis, James W.: 118
Ellsworth, Henry L.: 48
El Reno, Oklahoma: 40 ff.; land sale, 1901, 42–46, 51
Emerson, Ralph Waldo: 6, 79, 241
Entragues, Henriette d': 24
Erick, Oklahoma: 134

Fairfax, Lord: 9
Falta, Wilhelm: 120
Ferber, Edna: 66

Finch, Urshel: 95
Flexner, Abraham: 220
Flick, Lawrence F.: 146
Forbes, John: 147
Forlanini, Carlo: 174
Fort Reno, Oklahoma: 47
Fort Sill, Oklahoma: 48
Fort Supply, Oklahoma: 73
Fort Worth, Texas: 43
Fracastorius, Girolamo: 144

Galen: 143, 157–58
Gardner, LeRoy U.: 241
Garland, Hamlin: 63, 115
Garrard, Lewis H.: 66
Gerlach, A. C.: 149
Germany: 191
Ghon, Anton: 120–21
Glasgow, Scotland, University of: 237
Goethe, Johann Wolfgang von: 180, 183
Gray's *Anatomy:* 30
Grayson, David: 115
Gray Street Infirmary (Louisville): 33
Great Britain: 191
Greece: 136
Greeley, Horace: 40
Gross, Samuel W.: 209
Guérin, C.: 152

Haen, Anton de: 117
Hamburger, Professor: 122
Hammurabi, Code of: 143
Harned, Dr.: 53–54
Harum, David: 124
Harvard Medical College: 211
Harvey, William: 69
Hawley, General Paul R.: 228
Heise, Fred: 241
Hesiod: 67, 227

INDEX

Hippocrates: 33, 123, 143, 177 ff., 193, 210, 227, 236
Hitler, Adolph: 201
Holmes, Oliver Wendell: 32, 120
Homer: 5, 67, 79, 156
Horses: Nancy Hanks, 201; Dot, 22, 29, 105; Indian ponies, 54 ff., 65, 68, 105–106; Old Billy, 85, 106 ff.
Hospitals: New York City Polyclinic, 90; St. Anthony's (Oklahoma City), 133; St. George's (London), 145; Allgemeines Krankenhaus (Vienna), 146
Howells, William Dean: 63
Hubbard, Ken: 67
Hunter, John: 159

Indians: Plains, 35; Cheyennes and Arapahoes, 47
Irving, Washington: 41, 48

Jackson, Stonewall: 106
James, Marquis: 64
Janssen, Zacharias: 144
Jay, John: 161
Jenner, Edward: 4, 88, 238
Jet, Warner: 61
Jet, Oklahoma: 54, 60 ff., 86 ff., 95 ff., 221
Johns Hopkins Medical School (Baltimore): 212

Kansas: 85, 95
Kansas City, Missouri: 47, 137
Kant, Immanuel: 6
Keats, John: 6, 121
Kenton, Simon: 57
Kentucky: 7, 10 ff., 24, 29, 42, 94, 107, 136–37; Sunset Lick region, 9
Kerfoot Hotel (El Reno): 47
Kipling, Rudyard: 91
Klebs, Edwin: 149
Koch, Robert: 5, 122, 150 ff., 169
Korns, Horace M.: 147
Krause, Allen K.: 150, 172

Laënnec, René T. H.: 117, 147–48, 207, 239

Landor, Walter Savage: 98
Lang, Andrew: 4
Lawrence, Thomas Edward: 195
Lawson, David: 237
Lawton, Oklahoma: 49
Lee, Robert E.: 106
Lexington, Kentucky: 137
Link, Henry: 183
Littlejohn, Jean: 72
Locke, John: 6
London, England: 92, 124, 159, 233, 235, 239–40
Long Beach, California: 138
Lorenz, Adolph: 122
Louis, Pierre Charles Alexander, 117, 147 ff., 239
Louisville, Kentucky: 13, 35, 39, 40, 112
Louisville Medical School: 30 ff., 35

McCormick, Cyrus Hall: 17
McCrae, Thomas: 210
McDowell, Ephraim: 137
Macedonia: 4
McGill University: 210
Mackenzie, Sir James: 215, 238
McKenzie, Tait: 198
McKinley, President William: 42
McLaurin, C.: 190
MacLure, William: 23, 106
McMurty, Lewis S.: 124
Madison, President James: 160–61
Manget, John Jacob: 144
Mansfield, Katherine: 189
Mayo, William J.: 183
Meakins, Jonathan C.: 212
Medical Education Council: 216
Minco, Oklahoma: 55
Mitchell, S. Weir: 226
Molière (Jean Baptiste Poquelin): 6, 134
Montaigne: 178
Montreal, Neurological Institute of: 191

INDEX

Moorman, Floyd: 138
Morgagni, Giovanni Battista: 144
Morley, Christopher: 4, 98
Morton, Richard: 144–45
Mount Scott (Oklahoma): 49
Muir, John: 115
Murphy, John B.: 124

Nash, Oklahoma: 83
Nashville, Tennessee: 21
Nation, Carry: 85
National Conference of Tuberculosis Secretaries: 171
National Tuberculosis Association: 5, 162, 168 f.
Nebuchadnezzar: 22
New York City: 240
North Canadian River: 44; *see also* Salt Fork River

Oklahoma: 39, 69
Oklahoma City: 41, 42, 43, 86, 113, 114 ff., 123 ff., 153
Oklahoma Medical Association: 208
Oklahoma Medical Research Foundation: 208
Oklahoma, University of, School of Medicine: 75, 190, 207–208
Osler, Grace Revere: 209
Osler, William: 32, 169, 209–10, 227, 233 ff.
Osler Club (London): 233
Oxford, England: 234; University of, 160

Packard, Edward N.: 241
Paracelsus: 144
Paris, France: 239
Parkman, Francis: 115
Pawhuska, Oklahoma: 194
Pericles: 161
Peter, Arthur, Drug Company (Louisville): 40
Peters, Leroy S.: 135
Petit, Marc-Antone: 145
Philadelphia, Pennsylvania: 170
Phoestis: 4
Pickwick Club (Oklahoma City): 115

Pirquet, Professor: 122
Plato: 4, 33, 178, 235
Pliny the Elder: 156
Ponca City, Oklahoma: 67, 97
Pope, Alexander: 92
Portal, Antoine: 145 ff.
Pott, Percival: 145
Price, Woods: 241
Price, Mrs. Woods: 241

Reed, Horace: 124–125, 131
Remington, Frederic: 47, 63, 73
Rhodes, Cecil: 160
Riesman, David: 153
Roentgen, Wilhelm Konrad: 151, 162, 207
Rogers, Will: 67
Rokitansky, Carl: 149
Roosevelt, President Theodore: 63
Rousseau, Jean Jacques: 6
Royal College of Surgeons (London): 233

Salt Fork River (of the Canadian): 64
Saranac Lake, New York: 240
Sayre, Oklahoma: 134
Schauta, Dr.: 124
Schiller, Friedrich: 6, 239
Schlesinger, Professor Hermann: 120
Scott, A. C.: 41–42
Sears, Paul B.: 65
Sedalia, Missouri: 40
Seneca, Lucius Anneus: 156
Shelley, Percy Bysshe: 6
Skinner, Edward: 137
Skoda, Josef: 117, 148, 149
Socrates: 32, 177
Solomon: 43
Southern Medical Association: 39
Spain: 46
Spinoza, Benedict: 6

INDEX

Stark, William: 145 ff.
Steenken, Bill: 241
Steinbeck, John: 66
Stevenson, Robert Louis: 101, 115
Stoerk, Oskar: 120–21
Stoll, Maximilian: 117, 146
Sydenham, Thomas: 144, 238
Sylvius, Franciscus: 144

Taft, President William Howard: 129
Tennessee State Medical Board Examination: 6, 21
Thackeray, William Makepeace: 53
Thayer, William Roscoe: 161
Thompson, Francis: 6, 121
Tobacco: 16
Trudeau, Edward Livingston: 168; statue of, 240–41
Trudeau Sanatorium (Trudeau, New York): 240
Twain, Mark: 184

Van Leeuwenhoek, Anton: 144
Van Swieten, Gerald: 117
Vestal, Stanley: 94
Veterans Administration: 176, 228; Medical Department of, 176
Vienna: 18, 122 ff.; University of, 17, 146 ff.
Villemin, Jean-Antoine: 149
Virchow, Rudolf: 150
Virgil: 33, 178
Virginia, University of: 91, 112
Voltaire (François Marie Arouet): 6, 180
Von Noorden, Carl: 120

Walton, Isaac: 238
Washington, George: 9, 160 ff.
Washita River: 53
Welch, William H.: 169
Westcott, Edward Noyes: 35
Whitman, Walt: 69
Whytt, Robert: 145
Wichita, Kansas: 86

Willis, Thomas: 144
Wister, Owen: 62
Withering, William: 159, 238
World War I: 125
World War II: 125, 191
Wyeth, John A.: 90

Zuckerkandl, Professor: 120

UNIVERSITY OF OKLAHOMA PRESS

NORMAN

www.ingramcontent.com/pod-product-compliance
Lightning Source LLC
Chambersburg PA
CBHW020832160426
43192CB00007B/619